How to Measure Anything in Cybersecurity Risk

How to Measure Anything in Cybersecurity Risk

DOUGLAS W. HUBBARD
RICHARD SEIERSEN

WILEY

Cover images: Cyber security lock © Henrik5000/iStockphoto; Cyber eye © kasahasa/
iStockphoto; Internet Security concept © bluebay2014/iStockphoto; Background
© omergenc/iStockphoto; Abstract business background © Natal'ya Bondarenko/
iStockphoto; Abstract business background © procurator/iStockphoto; Cloud
Computing © derrrek/iStockphoto
Cover design: Wiley

Published by John Wiley & Sons, Inc., Hoboken, New Jersey.
Published simultaneously in Canada.

For general information on our other products and services or for technical support,
please contact our Customer Care Department within the United States at (800)
762–2974, outside the United States at (317) 572–3993 or fax (317) 572–4002.

Wiley publishes in a variety of print and electronic formats and by print-on-demand.
Some material included with standard print versions of this book may not be included
in e-books or in print-on-demand. If this book refers to media such as a CD or DVD
that is not included in the version you purchased, you may download this material at
http://booksupport.wiley.com. For more information about Wiley products, visit www.
wiley.com.

Library of Congress Cataloging-in-Publication Data:
ISBN 978-1-119-08529-4 (Hardcover)
ISBN 978-1-119-22460-0 (ePDF)
ISBN 978-1-119-22461-7 (ePub)

Printed in the United States of America

V10016920_011420

Douglas Hubbard's dedication: To my children, Evan, Madeleine, and Steven, as the continuing sources of inspiration in my life; and to my wife, Janet, for doing all the things that make it possible for me to have time to write a book, and for being the ultimate proofreader.

Richard Seiersen's dedication: To all the ladies in my life: Helena, Kaela, Anika, and Brenna. Thank you for your love and support through the book and life. You make it fun.

Doug and Richard would also like to dedicate this book to the military and law enforcement professionals who specialize in cybersecurity.

Contents

Foreword

Daniel E. Geer, Jr., ScD

Daniel Geer is a security researcher with a quantitative bent. His group at MIT produced Kerberos, and a number of startups later he is still at it—today as chief information security officer at In-Q-Tel. He writes a lot at every length, and sometimes it gets read. He's an electrical engineer, a statistician, and someone who thinks truth is best achieved by adversarial procedures.

It is my pleasure to recommend *How to Measure Anything in Cybersecurity Risk*. The topic is nothing if not pressing, and it is one that I have myself been dancing around for some time.[1] It is a hard problem, which allows me to quote Secretary of State John Foster Dulles: "The measure of success is not whether you have a tough problem to deal with, but whether it is the same problem you had last year." At its simplest, this book promises to help you put some old, hard problems behind you.

The practice of cybersecurity is part engineering and part inference. The central truth of engineering is that design pays if and only if the problem statement is itself well understood. The central truth of statistical inference is that all data has bias—the question being whether you can correct for it. Both engineering and inference depend on measurement. When measurement gets good enough, metrics become possible.

I say "metrics" because metrics are derivatives of measurement. A metric encapsulates measurements for the purpose of ongoing decision support. I and you, dear reader, are not in cybersecurity for reasons of science, though those who are in it for science (or philosophy) will also want measurement of some sort to backstop their theorizing. We need metrics derived from solid measurement because the scale of our task compared to the scale of our tools demands force multiplication. In any case, no game play improves without a way to keep score.

Early in the present author's career, a meeting was held inside a market-maker bank. The CISO, who was an unwilling promotion from Internal

---

We are fortunate to have two forewords from two leading thinkers in cybersecurity risk assessment—Daniel E. Geer, Jr., and Stuart McClure.

Audit, was caustic even by the standards of NYC finance. He began his comments mildly enough:

> Are you security people so stupid that you can't tell me:
> - How secure am I?
> - Am I better off than I was this time last year?
> - Am I spending the right amount of money?
> - How do I compare to my peers?
> - What risk transfer options do I have?

Twenty-five years later, those questions remain germane. Answering them, and others, comes only from measurement; that is the "Why?" of this book.

Yet even if we all agree on "Why?," the real value of this book is not "Why?" but "How?": *how* to measure and then choose among methods, *how* to do that both consistently and repeatedly, and *how* to move up from one method to a better one as your skill improves.

Some will say that cybersecurity is impossible if you face a sufficiently skilled opponent. That's true. It is also irrelevant. Our opponents by and large pick the targets that maximize their return on their investment, which is a polite way of saying that you may not be able to thwart the most singularly determined opponent for whom cost is no object, but you can sure as the world make other targets more attractive than you are. As I said, no game play improves without a way to keep score. That is what this book offers you—a way to improve your game.

This all requires numbers because numbers are the only input to both engineering and inference. Adjectives are not. Color codes are not. If you have any interest in taking care of yourself, of standing on your own two feet, of knowing where you are, then you owe it to yourself to exhaust this book. Its writing is clear, its pedagogy is straightforward, and its downloadable Excel spreadsheets leave no excuse for not trying.

Have I made the case? I hope so.

Note

1. Daniel Geer, Jr., Kevin Soo Hoo, and Andrew Jaquith, "Information Security: Why the Future Belongs to the Quants," *IEEE Security & Privacy* 1, no. 4 (July/August 2003): 32–40, geer.tinho.net/ieee/ieee .sp.geer.0307.pdf.

Foreword

Stuart McClure

Stuart McClure is the CEO of Cylance, former global CTO of McAfee, and founding author of the *Hacking Exposed* series.

My university professors always sputtered the age-old maxim in class: "You can't manage what you cannot measure." And while my perky, barely-out-of-teenage-years ears absorbed the claim aurally, my brain never really could process what it meant. Sure, my numerous computer science classes kept me chasing an infinite pursuit of improving mathematical algorithms in software programs, but little did I know how to really apply these quantitative efforts to the management of anything, much less cyber.

So I bounded forward in my career in IT and software programming, looking for an application of my unique talents. I never found cyber measurement all that compelling until I found cybersecurity. What motivated me to look at a foundational way to measure what I did in cybersecurity was the timeless question that I and many of you get almost daily: "Are we secure from attack?"

The easy answer to such a trite yet completely understandable question is "No. Security is never 100%." But some of you have answered the same way I have done from time to time, being exhausted by the inane query, with "Yes. Yes we are." Why? Because we know a ridiculous question should be given an equally ridiculous answer. For how can we know? Well, you can't—without metrics.

As my cybersecurity career developed with InfoWorld and Ernst & Young, while founding the company Foundstone, taking senior executive roles in its acquiring company, McAfee, and now starting Cylance, I have developed a unique appreciation for the original professorial claim that you really cannot manage what you cannot measure. While an objective metric may be mythical, a subjective and localized measurement of your current risk posture and where you stand relative to your past and your peers is very possible.

Measuring the cyber risk present at an organization is nontrivial, and when you set the requirement of delivering on quantitative measurements rather than subjective and qualitative measurements, it becomes almost beyond daunting.

The real questions for all of us security practitioners are ultimately "Where do we start? How do we go about measuring cybersecurity's effectiveness and return?" The only way to begin to answer those questions is through quantitative metrics. And until now, the art of cybersecurity measurement has been elusive. I remember the first time someone asked me my opinion on a security-risk metrics program, I answered something to the effect of, "It's impossible to measure something you cannot quantify."

What the authors of this book have done is begin to define a framework and a set of algorithms and metrics to do exactly what the industry has long thought impossible, or at least futile: measure security risk. We may not be perfect in our measurement, but we can define a set of standard metrics that are defensible and quantifiable, and then use those same metrics day in and day out to ensure that things are improving. And that is the ultimate value of defining and executing on a set of security metrics. You don't need to be perfect; all you need to do is start somewhere and measure yourself relative to the day before.

Acknowledgments

We thank these people for their help as we wrote this book:

- Jack Jones
- Jack Freund
- Jim Lipkis
- Thomas Lee
- Christopher "Kip" Bohn
- Scott Stransky
- Tomas Girnius
- Jay Jacobs
- Sam Savage
- Tony Cox
- Michael Murray
- Patrick Heim
- Cheng-Ping Li
- Michael Sardaryzadeh
- Stuart McClure
- Rick Rankin
- Anton Mobley
- Vinnie Liu
- SIRA.org Team
- Dan Geer
- Dan Rosenberg

A very special thanks to Bonnie Norman and Steve Abrahamson for providing additional editing.

About the Authors

Douglas Hubbard is the creator of the Applied Information Economics method and the founder of Hubbard Decision Research. He is the author of one of the best-selling business statistics books of all time, *How to Measure Anything: Finding the Value of "Intangibles" in Business*. He is also the author of *The Failure of Risk Management: Why It's Broken and How to Fix It*, and *Pulse: The New Science of Harnessing Internet Buzz to Track Threats and Opportunities*. He has sold more than 100,000 copies of his books in eight different languages, and his books are used in courses at many major universities. His consulting experience in quantitative decision analysis and measurement problems totals over 27 years and spans many industries including pharmaceuticals, insurance, banking, utilities, cybersecurity, interventions in developing economies, mining, federal and state government, entertainment media, military logistics, and manufacturing. He is also published in several periodicals including *Nature, The IBM Journal of R&D, Analytics, OR/MS Today, InformationWeek*, and *CIO Magazine*.

Richard Seiersen is a technology executive with nearly 20 years of experience in information security, risk management, and product development. Currently he is the general manager of cybersecurity and privacy for GE Healthcare. Many years ago, prior to his life in technology, he was a classically trained musician—guitar, specifically. Richard now lives with his family of string players in the San Francisco Bay Area. In his limited spare time he is slowly working through his MS in predictive analytics at Northwestern. He should be done just in time to retire. He thinks that will be the perfect time to take up classical guitar again.

Introduction

Why This Book, Why Now?

This book is the first of a series of spinoffs from Douglas Hubbard's successful first book, *How to Measure Anything: Finding the Value of "Intangibles" in Business*. For future books in this franchise, we were considering titles such as *How to Measure Anything in Project Management* or industry-specific books like *How to Measure Anything in Healthcare*. All we had to do was pick a good idea from a long list of possibilities.

Cybersecurity risk seemed like an ideal first book for this new series. It is extremely topical and filled with measurement challenges that may often seem impossible. We also believe it is an extremely important topic for personal reasons (as we are credit card users and have medical records, client data, intellectual property, and so on) as well as for the economy as a whole.

Another factor in choosing a topic was finding the right co-author. Because Doug Hubbard—a generalist in measurement methods—would not be a specialist in any of the particular potential spinoff topics, he planned to find a co-author who could write authoritatively on the topic. Hubbard was fortunate to find an enthusiastic volunteer in Richard Seiersen—someone with years of experience in the highest levels of cybersecurity management with some of the largest organizations.

So, with a topical but difficult measurement subject, a broad and growing audience, and a good co-author, cybersecurity seemed like an ideal fit.

What Is This Book About?

Even though this book focuses on cybersecurity risk, this book still has a lot in common with the original *How to Measure Anything* book, including:

1. Making better decisions when you are significantly uncertain about the present and future, and
2. Reducing that uncertainty even when data seems unavailable or the targets of measurement seem ambiguous and intangible.

This book in particular offers an alternative to a set of deeply rooted risk assessment methods now widely used in cybersecurity but that have no basis in the mathematics of risk or scientific method. We argue that these methods impede decisions about a subject of growing criticality. We also argue that methods based on real evidence of improving decisions are not only practical but already have been applied to a wide variety of equally difficult problems, including cybersecurity itself. We will show that we can start at a simple level and then evolve to whatever level is required while avoiding problems inherent to "risk matrices" and "risk scores." So there is no reason not to adopt better methods immediately.

What to Expect

You should expect a gentle introduction to measurably better decision making—specifically, improvement in high-stakes decisions that have a lot of uncertainty and where, if you are wrong, your decisions could lead to catastrophe. We think security embodies all of these concerns.

We don't expect our readers to be risk management experts or cyber-security experts. The methods we apply to security can be applied to many other areas. Of course, we do hope it will make those who work in the field of cybersecurity better defenders and strategists. We also hope it will make the larger set of leaders more conscious of security risks in the process of becoming better decision makers.

Is This Book for Me?

If you really want to be sure this book is for you, here are the specific personas we are targeting:

- You are a decision maker looking to improve—that is, *measurably improve*—your high-stakes decision making.
- You are a security professional looking to become more strategic in your fight against the bad guy.
- You are neither of the above. Instead, you have an interest in understanding more about cybersecurity and/or risk management using readily accessible quantitative techniques.

- If you are a hard-core quant, consider skipping the purely quant parts. If you are a hard-core hacker, consider skipping the purely security parts. That said, we will often have a novel perspective, or "epiphanies of the obvious," on topics you already know well. Read as you see fit.

We Need More Than Technology

We need to lose less often in the fight against the bad guys. Or, at least, lose more gracefully and recover quickly. Many feel that this requires better technology. We clamor for more innovation from our vendors in the security space even though breach frequency has not been reduced. To effectively battle security threats, we think there is something equally important as innovative technology, if not more important. We believe that "something" must include a better way to think quantitatively about risk.

New Tools for Decision Makers

We need decision makers who consistently make better choices through better analysis. We also need decision makers who know how to deftly handle uncertainty in the face of looming catastrophe. Parts of this solution are sometimes referred to with current trendy terms like "predictive analytics," but more broadly this includes all of decision science or decision analysis and even properly applied statistics.

Our Path Forward

Part I of this book sets the stage for reasoning about uncertainty in security. We will come to terms on things like security, uncertainty, measurement, and risk management. We also argue against toxic misunderstandings of these terms and why we need a better approach to measuring cybersecurity risk and, for that matter, measuring the performance of cybersecurity risk analysis itself. We will also introduce a very simple quantitative method that could serve as a starting point for anyone, no matter how averse they may be to complexity.

Part II of this book will delve further into evolutionary steps we can take with a very simple quantitative model. We will describe how to add further complexity to a model and how to use even minimal amounts of data to improve those models.

Last, in Part III we will describe what is needed to implement these methods in the organization. We will also talk about the implications of this book for the entire cybersecurity "ecosystem," including standards organizations and vendors.

PART I

Why Cybersecurity Needs Better Measurements for Risk

CHAPTER 1

The One Patch Most Needed in Cybersecurity

There is nothing more deceptive than an obvious fact.

—Sherlock Holmes
The Bascombe Valley Mystery[1]

In the days after September 11, 2001, increased security meant overhauled screening at the airport, no-fly lists, air marshals, and attacking terrorist training camps. But just 12 years later, the FBI was emphasizing the emergence of a very different concern: the "cyber-based threat." In 2013, FBI director James B. Comey, testifying before the Senate Committee on Homeland Security and Governmental Affairs, stated the following:

> . . .we anticipate that in the future, resources devoted to cyber-based threats will equal or even eclipse the resources devoted to non-cyber based terrorist threats.
>
> —FBI director James B. Comey, November 14, 2013[2]

This is a shift in priorities we cannot overstate. How many organizations in 2001, preparing for what they perceived as the key threats at the time, would have even imagined that cyber threats would have not only equaled but exceeded more conventional terrorist threats? Yet as we write this book, it is accepted as our new "new normal."

Admittedly, those outside of the world of cybersecurity may think the FBI is sowing seeds of Fear, Uncertainty, and Doubt (FUD) to some political end. But it would seem that there are plenty of sources of FUD, so why pick cyber threats in particular? Of course, to cybersecurity experts this is a non-epiphany. We are under attack and it will certainly get worse before it gets better.

Yet resources are limited. Therefore, the cybersecurity professional must effectively determine a kind of "return on risk mitigation." Whether or not such a return is explicitly calculated, we must evaluate whether a given defense strategy is a better use of resources than another. In short, we have to measure and monetize risk and risk reduction. What we need is a "how to" book for professionals in charge of allocating limited resources to addressing ever-increasing cyber threats, and leveraging those resources for optimum risk reduction. This includes methods for:

- How to measure risk assessment methods themselves.
- How to measure reduction in risk from a given defense, control, mitigation, or strategy (using some of the better-performing methods as identified in the first bullet).
- How to continuously and measurably improve on the implemented methods, using more advanced methods that the reader may employ as he or she feels ready.

Let's be explicit about what this book isn't. This is not a technical security book—if you're looking for a book on "ethical hacking," then you have certainly come to the wrong place. There will be no discussions about how to execute stack overflows, defeat encryption algorithms, or execute SQL injections. If and when we do discuss such things, it's only in the context of understanding them as parameters in a risk model.

But don't be disappointed if you're a technical person. We will certainly be getting into some analytic nitty-gritty as it applies to security. This is from the perspective of an analyst or leader trying to make better bets in relation to possible future losses. For now, let's review the scale of the challenge we are dealing with and how we deal with it currently, then outline a direction for the improvements laid out in the rest of the book.

The Global Attack Surface

Nation-states, organized crime, hacktivist entities, and insider threats want our secrets, our money, and our intellectual property, and some want our complete demise. Sound dramatic? If we understand the FBI correctly, they expect to spend as much or more on protecting us from cyber threats than from those who would turn airplanes, cars, pressure cookers, and even people into bombs. And if you are reading this book, you probably already accept the gravity of the situation. But we should at least spend some time emphasizing this point if for no other reason than to help those who already agree with this point make the case to others.

The Global Information Security Workforce Study (GISWS)—a survey conducted in 2015 of more than 14,000 security professionals, including 1,800 federal employees—showed we are not just taking a beating, we are backpedaling:

> When we consider the amount of effort dedicated over the past two years to furthering the security readiness of federal systems and the nation's overall security posture, our hope was to see an obvious step forward. The data shows that, in fact, we have taken a step back.
>
> —(ISC)² on the announcement of the GISWS, 2015[3]

Indeed, other sources of data support this dire conclusion. The UK insurance market, Lloyd's of London, estimated that cyberattacks cost businesses $400 billion globally per year.[4] In 2014, one billion records were compromised. This caused *Forbes* magazine to refer to 2014 as "The Year of the Data Breach."[5,6] Unfortunately, identifying 2014 as the year of the data breach may still prove to be premature. It could easily get worse.

In fact, the founder and head of XL Catlin, the largest insurer in Lloyd's of London, said cybersecurity is the "biggest, most systemic risk" he has seen in his 42 years in insurance.[7] Potential weaknesses in widely used software; interdependent network access between companies, vendors, and clients; and the possibility of large coordinated attacks can affect much more than even one big company like Anthem, Target, or Sony. XL Catlin believes it is possible that there could be a simultaneous impact on multiple major organizations affecting the entire economy. They feel that if there are multiple major claims in a short period of time, this is a bigger burden than insurers can realistically cover.

What is causing such a dramatic rise in breach and the anticipation of even more breaches? It is called attack surface. "Attack surface" is usually defined as the kind of total of all exposures of an information system. It exposes value to untrusted sources. You don't need to be a security professional to get this. Your home, your bank account, your family, and your identity all have an attack surface. If you received identity theft protection as a federal employee, or a customer of Home Depot, Target, Anthem, or Neiman Marcus, then you received that courtesy of an attack surface. These companies put the digital you within reach of criminals. Directly or indirectly, the Internet facilitated this. This evolution happened quickly and without the knowledge or direct permission of all interested parties (organizations, employees, customers, or citizens).

Various definitions of the phrase consider the ways into and out of a system, the defenses of that system, and sometimes the value of data in that system.[8,9] Some definitions of attack surface refer to the attack surface of a system and some refer to the attack surface of a network, but either might be too narrow even for a given firm. We might also define an "Enterprise Attack Surface" that not only consists of all systems and networks in that organization but also the exposure of third parties. This includes everyone in the enterprise "ecosystem" including major customers, vendors, and perhaps government agencies. (Recall that in the case of the Target breach, the exploit came from an HVAC vendor.)

Perhaps the total attack surface that concerns all citizens, consumers, and governments is a kind of "global attack surface": the total set of cybersecurity exposures—across all systems, networks, and organizations—we all face just by shopping with a credit card, browsing online, receiving medical benefits, or even just being employed. This global attack surface is a macro-level phenomenon driven by at least four macro-level causes of growth: increasing users worldwide, variety of users worldwide, growth in discovered and exploited vulnerabilities per person per use, and organizations more networked with each other resulting in "cascade failure" risks.

- *The increasing number of persons on the Internet.* Internet users worldwide grew by a factor of 6 from 2001 to 2014 (half a billion to 3 billion). It may not be obvious that the number of users is a dimension in some attack surfaces, but some measures of attack surface also include the value of a target, which would be partly a function of number of users (e.g., gaining access to more personal records)[10] Also, on a global scale, it acts as an important multiplier on the following dimensions.
- *The number of uses per person for online resources.* The varied uses of the Internet, total time spent on the Internet, use of credit cards, and various services that require the storage of personal data-automated transactions are growing. Per person. Worldwide. For example, since 2001 the number of websites alone has grown at a rate five times faster than the number of users—a billion total by 2014. Connected devices constitute another potential way for an individual to use the Internet even without their active involvement. One forecast regarding the "Internet of Things" (IoT) was made by Gartner, Inc: "4.9 billion connected things will be in use in 2015, up 30 percent from 2014, and will reach 25 billion by 2020."[11] A key concern here is the lack of consistent security in designs. The National Security Telecommunications Advisory Committee determined that "there is a small—and rapidly closing—window to ensure that the IoT is adopted in a way that maximizes security and minimizes risk. If the country fails to do so, it will be coping with the consequences for generations."[12]

- *Vulnerabilities increase.* A natural consequence of the previous two factors is the number of ways such uses can be exploited increases. This is due to the increase in systems and devices with potential vulnerabilities, even if vulnerabilities per system or device do not increase. At least the number of *discovered* vulnerabilities will increase partly because the number of people actively seeking and exploiting vulnerabilities increases. And more of those will be from well-organized and well-funded teams of individuals working for national sponsors.
- *The possibility of a major breach "cascade."* More large organizations are finding efficiencies from being more connected. The fact that Target was breached through a vendor raises the possibility of the same attack affecting multiple organizations. Organizations like Target have many vendors, several of which in turn have multiple large corporate and government clients. Mapping this cyber-ecosystem of connections would be almost impossible, since it would certainly require all these organizations to divulge sensitive information. So the kind of publicly available metrics we have for the previous three factors in this list do not exist for this one. But we suspect most large organizations could just be one or two degrees of separation from each other.

It seems reasonable that of these four trends the earlier trends magnify the latter trends. If so, the risk of the major breach "cascade" event could grow faster than the growth rate of the first couple of trends.

Our naïve, and obvious, hypothesis? Attack surface and breach are correlated. If this holds true, then we haven't seen anything yet. We are heading into a historic growth in attack surface, and hence breach, which will eclipse what has been seen to date. Given all this, the FBI director's comments and the statements of Lloyd's of London insurers cannot be dismissed as alarmist. Even with the giant breaches like Target, Anthem, and Sony behind us, we believe we haven't seen "The Big One" yet.

The Cyber Threat Response

It's a bit of a catch-22 in that success in business is highly correlated with exposure. Banking, buying, getting medical attention, and even being employed is predicated on exposure. You need to expose data to transact business, and if you want to do more business, that means more attack surface. When you are exposed, you can be seen and affected in unexpected and malicious ways. In defense, cybersecurity professionals try to "harden" systems—that is, removing all nonessentials, including programs, users, data, privileges, and vulnerabilities. Hardening shrinks, but does not eliminate, attack surface. Yet even this partial reduction in attack surface requires significant resources, and the trends show that the resource requirements will grow.

Generally, executive-level attention on cybersecurity risks has increased, and attention is followed by resources. The boardroom is beginning to ask questions like "Will we be breached?" or "Are we better than Sony?" or "Did we spend enough on the right risks?" Asking these questions eventually brings some to hire a chief information security officer (CISO). The first Fortune 100 CISO role emerged more than 20 years ago, but for most of that time growth in CISOs was slow. *CFO Magazine* acknowledged that hiring a CISO as recently as 2008 would have been considered "superfluous."[13] In fact, large companies are still in the process of hiring their first CISOs, many just after they suffer major breaches. By the time this book was written, Target finally hired their first CISO,[14] and JPMorgan did likewise after their breach.[15]

In addition to merely asking these questions and creating a management-level role for information security, corporations have been showing a willingness, perhaps more slowly than cybersecurity professionals would like, to allocate serious resources to this problem:

- Just after the 9/11 attacks the annual cybersecurity market in the United States was $4.1 billion.[16] By 2015 the information technology budget of the United States Defense Department had grown to $36.7 billion.[17]
- This does not include $1.4 billion in startup investments for new cybersecurity-related firms.[18]
- Cybersecurity budgets have grown at about twice the rate of IT budgets overall.[19]

So what do organizations do with this new executive visibility and inflow of money to cybersecurity? Mostly, they seek out vulnerabilities, detect attacks, and eliminate compromises. Of course, the size of the attack surface and the sheer volume of vulnerabilities, attacks, and compromises means organizations must make tough choices; not everything gets fixed, stopped, recovered, and so forth. There will need to be some form of acceptable (tolerable) losses. What risks are acceptable is often not documented, and when they are, they are stated in soft, unquantified terms that cannot be used clearly in a calculation to determine if a given expenditure is justified or not.

On the vulnerability side of the equation, this has led to what is called "vulnerability management." An extension on the attack side is "security event management," which can generalize to "security management." More recently there is "threat intelligence" and the emerging phrase "threat management."

While all are within the tactical security solution spaces, the management portion attempts to rank-order what to do next. So how do organizations conduct security management? How do they prioritize the allocation of significant, but limited, resources for an expanding list of vulnerabilities? In other words, how do they make cybersecurity decisions to allocate limited resources in a fight against such uncertain and growing risks?

Certainly a lot of expert intuition is involved, as there always is in management. But for more systematic approaches, the vast majority of organizations concerned with cybersecurity will resort to some sort of "scoring" method that ultimately plots risks on a "matrix." This is true for both very tactical level issues and strategic, aggregated risks. For example, an application with multiple vulnerabilities could have all of them aggregated into one score. Using similar methods at another scale, groups of applications can then be aggregated into a portfolio and plotted with other portfolios. The aggregation process is typically some form of invented mathematics unfamiliar to actuaries, statisticians, and mathematicians.

In one widely used approach, "likelihood" and "impact" will be rated subjectively, perhaps on a 1 to 5 scale, and those two values will be used to plot a particular risk on a matrix (variously called a "risk matrix," "heat map," "risk map," etc.). The matrix—similar to the one shown in Figure 1.1—is then often further divided into sections of low, medium, and high risk. Events with high likelihood and high impact would be in the upper-right "high risk" corner, while those with low likelihood and low impact would be in the opposite "low risk" corner. The idea is that the higher the score, the more important something is and the sooner you should address it. You may intuitively think such an approach is reasonable, and if you thought so you would be in good company.

			Impact				
			Negligible	Minor	Moderate	Critical	Catastrophic
			1	2	3	4	5
Likelihood	Frequent	5	Medium	Medium	High	High	High
	Likely	4	Medium	Medium	Medium	High	High
	Occasional	3	Low	Medium	Medium	Medium	High
	Seldom	2	Low	Low	Medium	Medium	Medium
	Improbable	1	Low	Low	Low	Medium	Medium

FIGURE 1.1 The familiar risk matrix (a.k.a. heat map or risk map)

Various versions of scores and risk maps are endorsed and promoted by several major organizations, standards, and frameworks such as the National Institute of Standards and Technology (NIST), the International Standards Organization (ISO), MITRE.org, and the Open Web Application Security Project (OWASP), among others. Most organizations with a cybersecurity function claim at least one of these as part of their framework for assessing risk. In fact, most major software organizations like Oracle, Microsoft, and Adobe rate their vulnerabilities using a NIST-supported scoring system called the "Common Vulnerability Scoring System" (CVSS). Also, many security solutions also include CVSS ratings, be it for vulnerability and/or attack related. While the control recommendations made by many of these frameworks are good, it's how we are guided to prioritize risk management on an enterprise scale that is amplifying risk.

Literally hundreds of security vendors and even standards bodies have come to adopt some form of scoring system. Indeed, scoring approaches and risk matrices are at the core of the security industry's risk management approaches.

In all cases, they are based on the idea that such methods are of some sufficient benefit. That is, they are assumed to be at least an improvement over not using such a method. As one of the standards organizations has put it, rating risk this way is adequate:

> Once the tester has identified a potential risk and wants to figure out how serious it is, the first step is to estimate the *likelihood*. At the highest level, this is a rough measure of how likely this particular vulnerability is to be uncovered and exploited by an attacker. It is not necessary to be over-precise in this estimate. Generally, identifying whether the likelihood is low, medium, or high is sufficient.
>
> —OWASP[20] (emphasis added)

Does this last phrase, stating "low, medium, or high is sufficient," need to be taken on faith? Considering the critical nature of the decisions such methods will guide, we argue that it should not. This is a testable hypothesis and it actually *has been* tested in many different ways. The growing trends of cybersecurity attacks alone indicate it might be high time to try something else.

So let's be clear about our position on current methods: *They are a failure. They do not work.* A thorough investigation of the research on these methods and decision-making methods in general indicates the following (all of this will be discussed in detail in Chapters 4 and 5):

- There is no evidence that the types of scoring and risk matrix methods widely used in cybersecurity improve judgment.
- On the contrary, there is evidence these methods add noise and error to the judgment process. One researcher—Tony Cox—goes as far as to say they can be "worse than random." (Cox's research and many others will be detailed in Chapter 5.)
- Any appearance of "working" is probably a type of "analysis placebo." That is, a method may make you feel better even though the activity provides no measurable improvement in estimating risks (or even adds error).
- There is overwhelming evidence in published research that quantitative, probabilistic methods are effective.
- Fortunately, most cybersecurity experts seem willing and able to adopt better quantitative solutions. But common misconceptions held by some—including misconceptions about basic statistics—create some obstacles for adopting better methods.

How cybersecurity assesses risk, and how it determines how much it reduces risk, are the basis for determining where cybersecurity needs to prioritize the use of resources. And if this method is broken—or even just leaves room for significant improvement—then that is the highest-priority problem for cybersecurity to tackle! Clearly, putting cybersecurity risk-assessment and decision-making methods on a solid foundation will affect everything else cybersecurity does. If risk assessment itself is a weakness, then fixing risk assessment is the most important "patch" a cybersecurity professional can implement.

A Proposal for Cybersecurity Risk Management

In this book, we will propose a different direction for cybersecurity. Every proposed solution will ultimately be guided by the title of this book. That is, we are solving problems by describing how to measure cybersecurity risk—*anything* in cybersecurity risk. These measurements will be a tool in the solutions proposed but also reveal how these solutions were selected in the first place. So let us propose that we adopt a new quantitative approach to cybersecurity, built upon the following principles:

- *It is possible to greatly improve on the existing methods.* Many aspects of existing methods have been measured and found wanting. This is not acceptable for the scale of the problems faced in cybersecurity.

- *Cybersecurity can use the same quantitative language of risk analysis used in other problems.* As we will see, there are plenty of fields with massive risk, minimal data, and profoundly chaotic actors that are regularly modeled using traditional mathematical methods. We don't need to reinvent terminology or methods from other fields that also have challenging risk analysis problems.
- *Methods exist that have already been measured to be an improvement over expert intuition.* This improvement exists even when methods are based, as are the current methods, on only the subjective judgment of cybersecurity experts.
- *These improved methods are entirely feasible.* We know this because it has already been done. One or both of the authors have had direct experience with using every method described in this book in real-world corporate environments. The methods are currently used by cybersecurity analysts with a variety of backgrounds.
- *You can improve further on these models with empirical data.* You have more data available than you think from a variety of existing and newly emerging sources. Even when data is scarce, mathematical methods with limited data can still be an improvement on subjective judgment alone. Even the risk analysis methods themselves can be measured and tracked to make continuous improvements.

The book is separated into three parts that will make each of these points in multiple ways. Part I will introduce a simple quantitative method that requires little more effort than the current scoring methods, but uses techniques that have shown a measurable improvement in judgment. It will then discuss how to measure the measurement methods themselves. In other words, we will try to answer the question "How do we know it works?" regarding different methods for assessing cybersecurity. The last chapter of Part I will address common objections to quantitative methods, detail the research against scoring methods, and discuss misconceptions and misunderstandings that keep some from adopting better methods.

Part II will move from the "why" we use the methods we use and focus on how to add further improvements to the simple model described in Part I. We will talk about how to add useful details to the simple model, how to refine the ability of cybersecurity experts to assess uncertainties, and how to improve a model with empirical data (even when data seems limited).

Part III will take a step back to the bigger picture of how these methods can be rolled out to the enterprise, how new threats may emerge, and how evolving tools and methods can further improve the measurement of cybersecurity risks. We will try to describe a call to action for the cybersecurity industry as a whole.

But first, our next chapter will build a foundation for how we should understand the term "measurement." That may seem simple and obvious, but misunderstandings about that term and the methods required to execute it are behind at least some of the resistance to applying measurement to cybersecurity.

Notes

1. Sir Arthur Conan Doyle, "The Boscombe Valley Mystery," *The Strand Magazine*, 1891.
2. Greg Miller, "FBI Director Warns of Cyberattacks; Other Security Chiefs Say Terrorism Threat Has Altered," *Washington Post,* November 14, 2013, www.washingtonpost.com/world/national-security/fbi-director-warns-of-cyberattacks-other-security-chiefs-say-terrorism-threat-has-altered/2013/11/14/24f1b27a-4d53-11e3-9890-a1e0997fb0c0_story.html.
3. Dan Waddell, Director of Government Affairs, National Capital Regions of (ISC)² in an announcement of the Global Information Security Workforce Study (GISWS), www.isc2.org, May 14, 2015.
4. Stephen Gandel, "Lloyd's CEO: Cyber Attacks Cost Companies $400 Billion Every Year," Fortune.com, January 23, 2015, http://fortune.com/2015/01/23/cyber-attack-insurance-lloyds/.
5. Sue Poremba, "2014 Cyber Security News Was Dominated by the Sony Hack Scandal and Retail Data Breaches," *Forbes Magazine*, December 31, 2014, www.forbes.com/sites/sungardas/2014/12/31/2014-cyber-security-news-was-dominated-by-the-sony-hack-scandal-and-retail-data-breaches/#1c79203e4910.
6. Kevin Haley, "The 2014 Internet Security Threat Report: Year Of The Mega Data Breach," *Forbes Magazine*, July 24, 2014, www.forbes.com/sites/symantec/2014/07/24/the-2014-internet-security-threat-report-year-of-the-mega-data-breach/#724e90a01a98.
7. Matthew Heller, "Lloyd's Insurer Says Cyber Risks Too Big to Cover," CFO.com, February 6, 2015, ww2.cfo.com/risk-management/2015/02/lloyds-insurer-says-cyber-risks-big-cover/.
8. Jim Bird and Jim Manico, "Attack Surface Analysis Cheat Sheet." OWASP.org. July 18, 2015, www.owasp.org/index.php/Attack_Surface_Analysis_Cheat_Sheet.
9. Stephen Northcutt, "The Attack Surface Problem." SANS.edu. January 7, 2011, www.sans.edu/research/security-laboratory/article/did-attack-surface.
10. Pratyusa K. Manadhata and Jeannette M. Wing, "An Attack Surface Metric," *IEEE Transactions on Software Engineering* 37, no. 3 (2010): 371–386.

11. Gartner, "Gartner Says 4.9 Billion Connected 'Things' Will Be in Use in 2015" (press release), November 11, 2014, www.gartner.com/newsroom/id/2905717.

12. The President's National Security Telecommunications Advisory Committee, "NSTAC Report to the President on the Internet of Things," November 19, 2014, www.dhs.gov/sites/default/files/publications/IoT%20Final%20Draft%20Report%2011-2014.pdf.

13. Alissa Ponchione, "CISOs: The CFOs of IT," *CFO*, November 7, 2013, ww2.cfo.com/technology/2013/11/cisos-cfos/.

14. Matthew J. Schwartz, "Target Ignored Data Breach Alarms," *Dark Reading* (blog), *InformationWeek*, March 14, 2014, www.darkreading.com/attacks-and-breaches/target-ignored-data-breach-alarms/d/d-id/1127712.

15. Elizabeth Weise, "Chief Information Security Officers Hard to Find—and Harder to Keep," *USA Today*, December 3, 2014, www.usatoday.com/story/tech/2014/12/02/sony-hack-attack-chief-information-security-officer-philip-reitinger/19776929/.

16. Kelly Kavanagh, "North America Security Market Forecast: 2001–2006," Gartner, October 9, 2002, www.bus.umich.edu/KresgePublic/Journals/Gartner/research/110400/110432/110432.html.

17. Sean Brodrick, "Why 2016 Will Be the Year of Cybersecurity," *Energy & Resources Digest*, December 30, 2015, http://energyandresourcesdigest.com/invest-cybersecurity-2016-hack-cibr/.

18. Deborah Gage, "VCs Pour Money into Cybersecurity Startups," *Wall Street Journal*, April 19, 2015, www.wsj.com/articles/vcs-pour-money-into-cybersecurity-startups-1429499474.

19. PWC, *Managing Cyber Risks in an Interconnected World: Key Findings from the Global State of Information Security Survey 2015*, September 30, 2014, www.pwc.be/en/news-publications/publications/2014/gsiss2015.html.

20. OWASP, "OWASP Risk Rating Methodology," last modified September 3, 2015, www.owasp.org/index.php/OWASP_Risk_Rating_Methodology.

CHAPTER 2

A Measurement Primer
for Cybersecurity

*Success is a function of persistence and doggedness and the willingness
to work hard for twenty-two minutes to make sense of something that
most people would give up on after thirty seconds.*

—Malcom Gladwell, *Outliers*[1]

Before we can discuss how literally anything can be measured in cybersecurity, we need to discuss measurement itself, and we need to address
early the objection that some things in cybersecurity are simply not measurable. The fact is that a series of misunderstandings about the methods of
measurement, the thing being measured, or even the definition of measurement itself will hold back many attempts to measure.

This chapter will be mostly redundant for readers of the original *How
to Measure Anything: Finding the Value of "Intangibles" in Business.* This
chapter has been edited from the original and the examples geared slightly
more in the direction of cybersecurity. However, if you have already read
the original book, then you might prefer to skip this chapter. Otherwise, you
will need to read on to understand these critical basics.

We propose that there are just three reasons why anyone ever thought
something was immeasurable—cybersecurity included—and all three are
rooted in misconceptions of one sort or another. We categorize these three
reasons as concept, object, and method. Various forms of these objections to
measurement will be addressed in more detail later in this book (especially
in Chapter 5). But for now, let's review the basics:

1. *Concept of measurement.* The definition of measurement itself is widely
   misunderstood. If one understands what "measurement" actually means,
   a lot more things become measurable.

2. *Object of measurement.* The thing being measured is not well defined. Sloppy and ambiguous language gets in the way of measurement.
3. *Methods of measurement.* Many procedures of empirical observation are not well known. If people were familiar with some of these basic methods, it would become apparent that many things thought to be immeasurable are not only measurable but may have already been measured.

A good way to remember these three common misconceptions is by using a mnemonic like "howtomeasureanything.com," where the *c*, *o*, and *m* in ".com" stand for concept, object, and method. Once we learn that these three objections are misunderstandings of one sort or another, it becomes apparent that everything really is measurable.

The Concept of Measurement

As far as the propositions of mathematics refer to reality, they are not certain; and as far as they are certain, they do not refer to reality.

—Albert Einstein

Although this may seem a paradox, all exact science is based on the idea of approximation. If a man tells you he knows a thing exactly, then you can be safe in inferring that you are speaking to an inexact man.

—Bertrand Russell (1872–1970), British mathematician and philosopher

For those who believe something to be immeasurable, the concept of measurement—or rather the *mis*conception of it—is probably the most important obstacle to overcome. If we incorrectly think that measurement means meeting some nearly unachievable standard of certainty, then few things will be measurable even in the physical sciences.

If you ask a manager or cybersecurity expert what measurement means, you would usually get answers like "to quantify something," "to compute an exact value," "to reduce to a single number," or "to choose a representative amount," and so on. Implicit or explicit in all of these answers is that measurement is a single, exact number with no room for error. If that was really what the term means, then, indeed, very few things would be measurable.

Perhaps the reader has heard—or said—something like, "We can't measure the true impact of a data breach because some of the consequences can't be known exactly." Or perhaps, "There is no way we can put a probability on being the target of a massive denial-of-service attack because there is too much uncertainty." These statements indicate a presumed definition of measurement that is both unrelated to real decision making and also unscientific. When scientists, actuaries, or statisticians perform a measurement, they are using a different de facto definition.

A Definition of Measurement

For all practical decision-making purposes, we need to treat measurement as *observations that quantitatively reduce uncertainty*. A mere reduction, not necessarily an elimination, of uncertainty will suffice for a measurement. Even if some scientists don't articulate this definition exactly, the methods they use make it clear that, to them, measurement is only a probabilistic exercise. Certainty about real-world quantities is usually beyond their reach. The fact that some amount of error is unavoidable but can still be an improvement on prior knowledge is central to how experiments, surveys, and other scientific measurements are performed.

Definition of Measurement

Measurement: A quantitatively expressed reduction of uncertainty based on one or more observations.

The practical differences between this definition and the most popular definitions of measurement are enormous. Not only does a true measurement not need to be infinitely precise to be considered a measurement, but the lack of reported error—implying the number is exact—can be an indication that empirical methods, such as sampling and experiments, were not used (i.e., it's not really a measurement at all). Measurements that would pass basic standards of scientific validity would report results with some specified degree of uncertainty, such as, "There is a 90% chance that an attack on this system would cause it to be down somewhere between 1 and 8 hours."

This conception of measurement might be new to many readers, but there are strong mathematical foundations—as well as practical reasons—for looking at measurement this way. A measurement is, ultimately, just information, and there is a rigorous theoretical construct for information. A field called "information theory" was developed in the 1940s by Claude Shannon, an American electrical engineer and mathematician. In 1948, he published a paper titled "A Mathematical Theory of Communication,"[2] which laid the foundation for information theory and, ultimately, much of the world of information technology that cybersecurity professionals work in.

Shannon proposed a mathematical definition of "information" as the amount of uncertainty reduction in a signal, which he discussed in terms of the "entropy" removed by a signal. To Shannon, the receiver of information could be described as having some prior state of uncertainty. That is, the receiver already knew something, and the new information merely removed some, not necessarily all, of the receiver's uncertainty. The receiver's prior state of knowledge or uncertainty can be used to compute such things as the limits to how much information can be transmitted in a signal, the minimal amount of signal to correct for noise, and the maximum data compression possible.

This "uncertainty reduction" point of view is what is critical to business. Major decisions made under a state of uncertainty—such as whether to approve large information technology (IT) projects or new security controls—can be made better, even if just slightly, by reducing uncertainty. Sometimes even small uncertainty reductions can be worth millions of dollars.

A Taxonomy of Measurement Scales

Okay, so measuring cybersecurity is like any other measurement in the sense that it does not require certainty. Various types of measurement scales can push our understanding of measurement even further. Usually, we think of measurements as involving a specific, well-defined unit of measure such as dollars per year in the cybersecurity budget or minutes of duration of system downtime.

But could a scale like "high," "medium," or "low" constitute a proper measurement? Cybersecurity professionals will recognize scales like this as common in many standards and practices in all areas of risk assessment. It is common to see quantities like "impact" or "likelihood" assessed subjectively on a scale of 1 to 5 and then for those scales to be combined further to assess risk as high, medium, or low. These are deceptively simple methods that introduce a series of issues that will be discussed in further detail later in this book. For now, let's talk about where it might make sense to use scales other than conventional units of measure.

Note that the definition I offer for measurement says a measurement is "quantitatively expressed." The uncertainty, at least, has to be quantified, but the subject of observation might not be a quantity itself—it could be entirely qualitative, such as a membership in a set. For example, we could "measure" something where the answer is yes or no—like whether a data breach will occur this year or whether a cyberinsurance claim will be made—while still satisfying our precise definition of measurement. But our uncertainty about those observations must still be expressed quantitatively (e.g., there is a 15% chance of a data breach this year, there is a 20% chance of making a cyberinsurance claim, etc.).

The view that measurement applies to questions with a yes/no answer or other qualitative distinctions is consistent with another accepted school of thought on measurement. In 1946, the psychologist Stanley Smith Stevens wrote an article called "On the Theory of Scales and Measurement."[3] In it he describes four different scales of measurement: nominal, ordinal, interval, and ratio scales. If the reader is thinking of Celsius or dollars as a measurement, they are thinking of an interval and ratio scale, respectively. These scales both have a well-defined "unit" of a regular size. In both cases we can say a 6 is 2 more than a 4 (6 degrees Celsius or $6). An interval scale, however, doesn't really allow us to say that a 6 is "50% more" than a 4 or "twice as much" as a 3. For example, 6 degrees Celsius is not "twice as hot" as 3 degrees Celsius (since the "zero" position on the Celsius scale is set arbitrarily at the freezing point of water). But $6 million is twice as much as $3 million. So, there are some mathematical operations we cannot do with interval scales, like multiplication or division.

Nominal and ordinal scales are even more limited. A nominal scale has no implied order or magnitude—like gender or location or whether a system has a given feature. A nominal scale expresses a state without saying that one state is twice as much as the other or even, for that matter, more or less than the other—each state scale is just a *different* state, not a higher or lower state. Ordinal scales, on the other hand, denote an order but not by how much. We can say, for example, that someone with admin rights has more privilege than a regular user. But we don't say it is five times the privilege of a normal user and twice as much as another user. So most mathematical operations—other than basic logic or set operations—are not applicable to nominal or ordinal scales.

Still, it is possible for nominal and ordinal scales to be informative even though they vary from more conventional measurement scales like kilograms and seconds. To a geologist, it is useful to know that one rock is harder than another, without necessarily having to know by how much. The method they use for comparing hardness of minerals—called the Mohs hardness scale—is an ordinal scale.

So the use of ordinal scales like those often found in cybersecurity are not strictly a violation of measurement concepts, but how it is done, what it is applied to, and what is done with these values afterward actually does violate basic principles and can cause a lot of problems. Geologists don't multiply Mohs hardness scale values times the rock's color. And while the Mohs scale is a well-defined measurement, the uses of ordinal scales in cybersecurity often are not.

We will show later that measures based on well-defined quantities—like the annual probability of an event and a probability distribution of potential losses—are preferable to the types of ordinal scales typically used in cybersecurity. In fact, nothing in science and engineering really relies on an ordinal scale. Even the Mohs hardness scale has been replaced in many uses. (Outside of geology, the Vickers scale, a proper ratio scale, is considered more suitable for materials in science and engineering problems.)

These are all important distinctions about the concept of measurement that contain many lessons for managers in general as well as cybersecurity specialists. The commonplace notion that presumes measurements are exact quantities ignores the usefulness of simply reducing uncertainty, if eliminating uncertainty is not possible or economical. And not all measurements even need to be about a conventional quantity. Measurement applies to discrete, nominal points of interest like "Will we experience a major data breach?" as well as continuous quantities like "How much will it cost if we do have a data breach?" In business, decision makers make decisions under uncertainty. When that uncertainty is about big, risky decisions, then uncertainty reduction has a lot of value—and that is why we will use this definition of measurement.

Bayesian Measurement: A Pragmatic Concept for Decisions

Therefore the true logic for this world is the calculus of Probabilities, which takes account of the magnitude of the probability which is, or ought to be, in a reasonable man's mind.

—James Clerk Maxwell, 1850

When we talk about measurement as "uncertainty reduction," we imply that there is some prior state of uncertainty to be reduced. And since this uncertainty can change as a result of observations, we treat uncertainty as a feature of the observer, not necessarily the thing being observed.[4] When we conduct a penetration test on a system, we are not changing the state of the application with this inspection; rather, we are changing our uncertainty about the state of the application.

We quantify this initial uncertainty and the change in uncertainty from observations by using probabilities. This means that we are using the term "probability" to refer to the state of uncertainty of an observer or what some have called a "degree of belief." If you are almost certain that a given system will be breached, you can say there is a 99% probability. If you are unsure, you may say there is a 50% probability (as we will see in Chapter 7, assigning these probabilities subjectively is actually a skill you can learn). Likewise, if you are very uncertain about the duration of an outage from a denial of service attack, you may say there is a 90% probability that the true value falls between 10 minutes and 2 hours. If you had more information, you might give a much narrower range and still assign a 90% probability that the true value falls within that range.

This view of probabilities is called the "subjectivist" or sometimes the "Bayesian" interpretation. The original inspiration for the Bayesian interpretation, Thomas Bayes, was an eighteenth-century British mathematician and Presbyterian minister whose most famous contribution to statistics would not be published until after he died. His simple formula, known as Bayes's theorem, describes how new information can update prior probabilities. "Prior" could refer to a state of uncertainty informed mostly by previously recorded data, but it can also refer to a point before any objective and recorded observations. At least for the latter case, the prior probability often needs to be subjective.

For decision making, this is the most relevant use of the word "probability." It is not just something that must be computed based on other data. A person represents uncertainty by stating a probability. Being able to express a prior state of uncertainty is an important starting point in all practical decisions. In fact, you usually already have a prior uncertainty—even though you might not explicitly state probabilities. Stating priors even allows us to compute the value of additional information since, of course, the value of additional information is at least partly dependent on your current state of uncertainty before you gather the information. The Bayesian approach does this while also greatly simplifying some problems and allowing us to get more use out of limited information.

This is a distinction that cybersecurity professionals need to understand. Those who think of probabilities as *only* being the result of calculations on data—and not also a reflection of personal uncertainty—are, whether they know it or not, effectively presuming a particular interpretation of probability. They are choosing the "frequentist" interpretation, and while they might think of this as "objective" and scientific, many great statisticians, mathematicians, and scientists would beg to differ. (The original *How to Measure Anything* book has an in-depth exposition of the differences.)

So, there is a fundamental irony when someone in cybersecurity says they lack the data to assign probabilities. We use probability *because* we lack perfect information, not *in spite* of it. This position was stated best by the widely recognized father of the field of decision analysis, Professor Ron Howard of Stanford University. During a podcast for an interview with *Harvard Business Review*, the interviewer asked Howard how to deal with the challenge of analysis "when you don't know the probabilities." Howard responded:

> Well, see, but the whole idea of probability is to be able to describe by numbers your ignorance or equivalently your knowledge. So no matter how knowledgeable or ignorant you are, that's going to determine what probabilities are consistent with that.

> —Ron Howard, *Harvard Business Review* podcast,
> interviewed by Justin Fox, November 20, 2014

There are cases where "probability" is a computed value but, as great minds like Howard and James Clerk Maxwell (from the earlier quote) state, probability is also used to represent our current state of uncertainty about something, no matter how much that uncertainty is. But keep in mind that, while subjective, the probability we refer to is not just irrational and capricious. We need subjective uncertainties to at least be mathematically coherent as well as consistent with repeated, subsequent observations. A rational person can't simply say, for instance, that there is a 25% chance of their organization being hit by a particular type of cyberattack *and* a 90% chance that it won't be (of course, these two possibilities should have a total probability of 100%). Also, if someone keeps saying they are 100% certain of their predictions and they are consistently wrong, then we can reject their subjective uncertainties on objective grounds just as we would with the readings of a broken digital scale or ammeter. In Chapter 7, you will see how probabilities can be subjective and yet rational.

Finally, we need to remember that there is another edge to the "uncertainty reduction" sword. Total elimination of uncertainty is not necessary for a measurement, but there *must be some* uncertainty reduction. If a decision maker or analyst engages in what they believe to be measurement activities, but their estimates and decisions actually get worse or don't at least improve, then they are not actually reducing their error and are not conducting a measurement according to the stated definition.

And so, to determine whether these ordinal scales so commonly used in cybersecurity are proper measurements, we at least need to ask whether such scales really constitute a reduction in uncertainty. (These finer points will be developed further in Chapter 5.)

The Object of Measurement

A problem well stated is a problem half solved.

—Charles Kettering (1876–1958), American inventor, holder of over 100 patents, including electrical ignition for automobiles

There is no greater impediment to the advancement of knowledge than the ambiguity of words.

—Thomas Reid (1710–1796), Scottish philosopher

Even when the more useful concept of measurement (as uncertainty-reducing observations) is adopted, some things seem immeasurable because we simply don't know what we mean when we first pose the question. In this case, we haven't unambiguously defined the *object* of measurement. If someone asks how to measure "damage to reputation" or "threat" or "business disruption," we simply ask, "What do you mean, exactly?" It is interesting how often people further refine their use of the term in a way that almost answers the measurement question by itself.

Once managers figure out what they mean and why it matters, the issue in question starts to look a lot more measurable. This is usually the first level of analysis when one of the authors, Hubbard, conducts what he calls "clarification workshops." It's simply a matter of clients stating a particular, but initially ambiguous, item they want to measure. Just ask questions like "What do you mean by [fill in the blank]?" and "Why do you care?"

This applies to a wide variety of measurement problems, and cybersecurity is no exception. In 2000, when the Department of Veterans Affairs asked Hubbard to help define performance metrics for what they referred to as "IT security," Hubbard asked: "What do you mean by 'IT security'?" and over the course of two or three workshops, the department staff defined it for him. They eventually revealed that what they meant by IT security were things like a reduction in intrusions and virus infections. They proceeded to explain that these things impact the organization through fraud, lost productivity, or even potential legal liabilities (which they may have narrowly averted when they recovered a stolen notebook computer in 2006 that contained the Social Security numbers of 26.5 million veterans). All of the identified impacts were, in almost every case, obviously measurable. "Security" was a vague concept until they decomposed it into what they actually expected to observe.

What we call a "clarification chain" is just a short series of connections that should bring us from thinking of something as an intangible to thinking of it as a tangible. First, we recognize that if X is something that we care about, then X, by definition, must be detectable in some way. How could we care about things like "quality," "risk," "security," or "public image" if these things were totally undetectable, in any way, directly or indirectly? If we have reason to care about some unknown quantity, it is because we think it corresponds to desirable or undesirable results in some way. Second, if this thing is detectable, then it must be detectable in some amount. If you can observe a thing at all, you can observe more of it or less of it. Once we accept that much, the final step is perhaps the easiest. If we can observe it in some amount, then it must be measurable.

Clarification Chain

1. If it matters at all, it is detectable/observable.
2. If it is detectable, it can be detected as an amount (or range of possible amounts).
3. If it can be detected as a range of possible amounts, it can be measured.

If the clarification chain doesn't work, I might try what scientists would call a "thought experiment." Imagine you are an alien scientist who can clone not just sheep or even people but entire organizations. You create a pair of the same organization, calling one the "test" group and one the "control" group. Now imagine that you give the test group a little bit more "damage to reputation" while holding the amount in the control group constant. What do you imagine you would actually observe—in any way, directly or indirectly—that would change for the first organization? Does it mean sales go down in the near term or long term? Does it mean it becomes harder to recruit applicants who want to work at prestigious firms? Does it mean that you have to engage in expensive PR campaigns to offset these consequences? If you can identify even a single observation that would be different between the two cloned organizations, then you are well on the way to identifying how you would measure it.

It also helps to state *why* we want to measure something in order to understand *what* is really being measured. The purpose of the measurement is often the key to defining what the measurement is really supposed to be. Measurements should always support some kind of decision, whether that decision is a one-off or a frequent, recurring decision. In the case of measuring cybersecurity risks, we are presumably conducting measurements to better allocate resources to reduce risks. The purpose of the measurement gives us clues about what the measure really means and how to measure it. In addition, we find several other potential items that may need to be measured to support the relevant decision.

Identifying the object of measurement really is the beginning of almost any scientific inquiry, including the truly revolutionary ones. Cybersecurity experts and executives need to realize that some things seemed intangible only because they have been poorly defined. Avoidably vague terms like "threat capability" or "damage to reputation" or "customer confidence" seem immeasurable at first, perhaps, only because what they mean is not well understood. These terms may actually represent a list of distinct and observable phenomena that need to be identified in order to be understood. Later in this book (especially Chapter 6) we will offer ways of decomposing them into lists of more specific things.

We should start clarifying the objective of measurement by defining some of the other terms we've used many times up to now. To measure cybersecurity, we would need to ask such questions as "What do we mean by 'cybersecurity'?" and "What decisions depend on my measurement of cybersecurity?"

To most people, an increase in security should ultimately mean more than just, for example, who has attended security training or how many desktop computers have new security software installed. If security is better, then some risks should decrease. If that is the case, then we also need to know what we mean by risk. Clarifying this problem requires that we jointly clarify uncertainty and risk. Not only are they measurable; they are key to understanding measurement in general. So let's define these terms and what it means to measure them.

Definitions for *Uncertainty* and *Risk*, and Their Measurements

Uncertainty: The lack of complete certainty, that is, the existence of more than one possibility. The "true" outcome/state/ result/value is not known.

Measurement of Uncertainty: A set of probabilities assigned to a set of possibilities. For example: "There is a 20% chance we will have a data breach sometime in the next five years."

Risk: A state of uncertainty where some of the possibilities involve a loss, catastrophe, or other undesirable outcome.

Measurement of Risk: A set of possibilities, each with quantified probabilities and quantified losses. For example: "We believe there is a 10% chance that a data breach will result in a legal liability exceeding $10 million."

We will explain how we assign these probabilities (initially by using skills you will learn in Chapter 7), but at least we have defined what we mean—which is always a prerequisite to measurement. We chose these definitions because they are the most relevant to how we measure the example we are using here: security and the value of security. But, as we will see, these definitions also are the most useful when discussing *any* other type of measurement problem we have.

Now that we have defined "uncertainty" and "risk," we have a better tool box for defining terms like "security" (or "safety," "reliability," and "quality," but more on that later). When we say that security has improved, we generally mean that particular risks have decreased. If I apply the definition of risk given earlier, a reduction in risk must mean that the probability and/or severity (loss) decreases for a particular list of events. That is the approach mentioned earlier to help measure some very large IT security investments—including the $100 million overhaul of IT security for the Department of Veterans Affairs.

In short, figure out what you mean and you are halfway to measuring it. Chapter 6 will dive deeper into approaches for defining the observable consequences of cybersecurity, how to break down the effects of a cybersecurity event, and how to clarify the necessary decision. (There you will find that we will again refer to Ron Howard's work in decision analysis.)

The Methods of Measurement

It's not what you don't know that will hurt you, it's what you know that ain't so.

—Mark Twain[5]

When thinking about measurement methods, someone may imagine a fairly direct case of measurement. If you measure the downtime of a system or the number of people who attended security training, there is no larger "unseen" population you are trying to assess. You have direct access to the entire object of measurement. If this is the limit of what one understands about measurement methods, then, no doubt, many things will seem immeasurable. Statistics and science in general would be much easier if we could directly see everything we ever measured. Most "hard" measurements, however, involve indirect deductions and inferences. This definitely applies to cybersecurity, where we often need to infer something unseen from something seen. Studying populations too large or dynamic to see all at once is what statistics is really all about.

Cybersecurity is not some exceptional area outside the domain of statistics but rather exactly the kind of problem statistics was made for. (Cybersecurity experts who are convinced otherwise should consider Mark Twain's quote above.) They may believe they correctly recall and understand enough about statistics and probability so that they can make confident declarations about what inferences can be made from some data without attempting any math. Unfortunately, their mental math is often not at all close to correct. There are misconceptions about the methods of measurement that get in the way of assessing risk in many fields, including cybersecurity.

Statistical Significance: What's the Significance?

You may often hear someone claim that a set of sample data is not large enough to be "statistically significant." If you hear someone say that, you know one thing for sure: They misunderstand the concept of statistical significance. A recent survey of 171 cybersecurity professions conducted by the authors demonstrates that these misconceptions are just as prevalent in this industry as in any other (more about the findings from this survey will be covered in Chapter 5). You may notice that the beliefs some hold about statistics will contradict the following facts:

- There is no single, universal sample size required to be "statistically significant."
- To compute it correctly, statistical significance is a function of not only sample size, but also the variance within a sample and the hypothesis being tested. These would be used to compute something called a "P-value." This result is then compared to a stated "significance level." Lacking those steps, the declaration of what is statistically significant cannot be trusted.
- Once you know not only how to compute statistical significance but also how to understand what it means, then you will find out that it isn't even what you wanted to know in the first place. Statistical significance does not mean you learned something and the lack of statistical significance does not mean you learned nothing.

This issue is explored in further detail at a mathematical level in the original *How to Measure Anything: Finding the Value of "Intangibles" in Business*. For now, it is probably better if you drop the phrase "statistically significant" from your vocabulary. What you want to know is whether you have less uncertainty after considering some source of data and whether that reduction in uncertainty warrants some change in actions. Statisticians know that is not the question statistical significance answers and they find themselves constantly correcting those who believe otherwise. There is math for questions like how much uncertainty was reduced, but they can be answered without reference to statistical significance or what the cybersecurity analyst believes they recall about it.

Cybersecurity experts, like many in virtually all fields of management, need to unlearn some misconceptions about statistics as much as they need to learn new concepts about statistics. Later, we will discuss how several proven measurement methods can be used for a variety of issues to help measure something you may have at first considered immeasurable. Here are a few examples involving inferences about something unseen from something seen:

- *Measuring with very small random samples of a very large population:* You can learn something from a small sample of data breaches and other events—especially when there is currently a great deal of uncertainty.
- *Measuring when many other, even unknown, variables are involved:* We can estimate how much a new security control reduced risk even

when there are many other factors affecting whether or not losses due
to cyberattacks occurred.

- *Measuring the risk of rare events:* The chance of a launch failure of
  a rocket that has never flown before, or the chance of another major
  financial crisis, can be informed in valuable ways through observation
  and reason. These problems are at least as difficult as the risk of the
  rare major breach in cybersecurity, yet measurements can and have
  been applied.
- *Measuring subjective preferences and values:* We can measure the value
  of art, free time, or reducing risk to your life by assessing how much
  people actually pay for these things. Again, the lessons from other
  fields apply equally well to cybersecurity.

Most of these approaches to measurements are just variations on basic
methods involving different types of sampling and experimental controls
and, sometimes, choosing to focus on different types of questions that
are indirect indicators of what we are trying to measure. Basic methods
of observation like these are often absent from certain decision-making
processes in business, perhaps because such quantitative procedures are
considered to be some elaborate, overly formalized process. Such methods
are not usually considered to be something you might do, if necessary, on
a moment's notice with little cost or preparation. But we will show some
methods that—to use a popular concept in systems engineering—can even
be considered "agile."

Small Samples Tell You More Than You Think

When someone in cybersecurity or any other field says something like, "We
don't have enough data to measure this," they probably do not understand
that they are making a very specific mathematical claim—for which they
provided no actual math to support. Did they actually compute the uncertainty reduction from a given amount of data? Did they actually compute the
economic value of that uncertainty reduction? Probably not.

Our intuition is one problem when it comes to making probabilistic
inferences about data. But perhaps a bigger problem is what we think we
learned (but learned incorrectly) about statistics. Statistics actually helps us
make some informative inferences from surprisingly small samples.

Consider a random sample of just five of anything. It could be time
spent by employees on websites, a survey of firms in some industry reporting cybersecurity budgets, and so on. What is the chance that the median of
the entire population (the point at which half the population is below and
half above) is between the largest and smallest of that sample of five? The

answer is 93.75%. In *How to Measure Anything*, Hubbard refers to this as the "Rule of Five." With a sample this small, the range might be very wide, but if it is any narrower than your previous range, then it counts as a measurement according to our previous definition. The Rule of Five is simple, it works, and it can be proven to be statistically valid for a surprisingly wide range of problems. If your intuition—or your recollection of statistics—disagrees with this, it's not the math that is wrong.

Rule of Five

There is a 93.75% chance that the median of a population is between the smallest and largest values in any random sample of five from that population.

It might seem impossible to be 93.75% certain about anything based on a random sample of just five, but it's not. If we randomly picked five values that were all above the median or all below it, then the median would be outside our range. But what is the chance of that, really? Remember, the chance of randomly picking a value above the median is, by definition, 50%—the same as a coin flip resulting in "heads." The chance of randomly selecting five values that happen to be all above the median is like flipping a coin and getting heads five times in a row. The chance of getting heads five times in a row in a random coin flip is 1 in 32, or 3.125%; the same is true with getting five tails in a row. The chance of *not* getting all heads or all tails is then 100% − (3.125% × 2), or 93.75%. Therefore, the chance of at least one out of a sample of five being above the median *and* at least one being below is 93.75% (round it down to 93% or even 90% if you want to be conservative). Some readers might remember a statistics class that discussed statistics for very small samples. Those methods were more complicated than the Rule of Five, but the answer is really not much better. (Both methods make some simplifying assumptions that work very well in practice.)

We can improve on a rule of thumb like this by getting more samples and by using simple methods to account for certain types of bias we will discuss later. Still, even with acknowledged shortcomings, the Rule of Five is something that the person who wants to develop an intuition for measurement keeps handy.

Let's make some deliberate and productive assumptions instead of ill-considered presumptions. We propose a contrarian set of assumptions that—because they are assumptions—may not always be true in every single case but in practice turn out to be much more effective. We will cover these points in more detail later but for now we will just point them out:

1. No matter how complex or "unique" your measurement problem seems, assume it has been measured before.
2. If you are resourceful, you can probably find more sources of data than you first thought.
3. You probably need less data than your intuition tells you—this is actually even more the case when you have a lot of uncertainty now.

There might be the rare case where, only for lack of the most sophisticated measurement methods, something seems immeasurable. But for those things labeled "intangible," more advanced, sophisticated methods are almost never what are lacking. Things that are thought to be intangible tend to be so uncertain that even the most basic measurement methods are likely to reduce some uncertainty. Cybersecurity is now such a critical endeavor that even small reductions in uncertainty can be extremely valuable.

In the next chapter, we will show how these concepts can be just partially applied through a very simple yet quantitative method for evaluating cybersecurity risks, which will take barely any more time than the common risk matrix.

Notes

1. Malcolm Gladwell, *Outliers: The Story of Success* (London: Hachette UK, 2008).
2. C. Shannon, "A Mathematical Theory of Communication," *The Bell System Technical Journal* 27 (July/October, 1948): 379–423, 623–656.
3. S. S. Stevens, "On the Theory of Scales and Measurement," *Science* 103 (1946): 677–80.
4. Leonard J. Savage, *The Foundations of Statistics* (New York: John Wiley & Sons, 1954).
5. This statement is often incorrectly attributed to Mark Twain, although he surely helped to popularize it. Twain got it from either one of two nineteenth-century British politicians, Benjamin Disraeli or Henry Labouchere.

CHAPTER 3

Model Now!

An Introduction to Practical Quantitative Methods for Cybersecurity

Build a little. Test a little. Learn a lot.

—Rear Admiral Wayne Meyer,
Aegis Weapon System Program Manager

In this chapter we will propose a simple starting point for developing a quantitative risk assessment. Later, we will explore more detailed models (starting in Chapter 6) and more advanced methods (starting in Chapter 8). But for now we will start with a model that merely replaces the common risk matrix. It will simply be a way to capture subjective estimates of likelihood and impact, but do so probabilistically.

To make it work, we need to introduce a few methods. First, we need to introduce the idea of subjectively assessing probabilities, but we will defer the exercises to train you to do that until Chapter 7 (for now, hang in there). We will also introduce a very basic simulation method, and the work of actually building the simulation is mostly done for you. The example will be demonstrated with an Excel spreadsheet you can download from www.howtomeasureanything.com/cybersecurity.

When you are done with this chapter, you will have the foundation to build on for the rest of the book. Later, we will incrementally add further improvements. You will learn how to test your subjective assessments of probability and improve on them. You will learn how even a few observations can be used in mathematically sound ways to improve your estimates further. And you will learn how to improve your models with additional detail and complexity. For now, we will just stick to the simplest possible substitution methods commonly used in cybersecurity today.

A Simple One-for-One Substitution

We can start down a path for better risk assessment simply by replacing elements of the method most cybersecurity experts are already familiar with—the risk matrix. Like the risk matrix, we will only depend on the judgment of subject matter experts in cybersecurity. They continue to make a subjective, expert judgment about likelihood and impact, just as analysts now do with the risk matrix. No data is required other than the information that cybersecurity analysts may already use to inform their judgments with a risk matrix. As before, experts can use as much data as they like to inform what ultimately comes down to a subjective judgment.

We only propose that instead of using the scales like "high, medium, low" or 1 to 5, experts learn how to subjectively assess the actual quantities behind those scales—that is, probability and dollar impact. In Table 3.1, we summarize how we propose to replace each element of the common risk matrix with a method that uses explicit probabilities.

The method proposed is, like the risk matrix, really just another expression of your current state of uncertainty. It does not yet reflect a proper

TABLE 3.1 Simple Substitution of Quantitative vs. the Risk Matrix

Instead of:	We Substitute:
Rating likelihood on a scale of 1 to 5 or "low" to "high." Example: "Likelihood of X is a 2" or "Likelihood of X is medium"	Estimating the probability of the event occurring in a given period of time (e.g., 1 year). Example: "Event X has a 10% chance of occurring in the next 12 months."
Rating impact on a scale of 1 to 5 or "low" to "high." Example: "Impact of X is a 2" or "Impact of X is medium"	Estimating a 90% confidence interval for a monetized loss. Example: "If event X occurs, there is a 90% chance the loss will be between $1 million and $8 million."
Plotting likelihood and impact scores on a risk matrix	Using the quantitative likelihood and impact to generate a "loss exceedance curve"—a quantitative approach to expressing risk—using a simple Monte Carlo simulation done in a spreadsheet
Further dividing the risk matrix into risk categories like "low/medium/high" or "green/yellow/red" and guessing whether you should do something and what you should do	Comparing the loss exceedance curve to a risk tolerance curve and prioritizing actions based on return on mitigation

"measurement" in the sense that we have further reduced uncertainty based on additional observations. We are merely stating our prior uncertainty. But now we have expressed this level of uncertainty in a way that allows us to unambiguously communicate risk and update this uncertainty with new information.

Let's put together the pieces of this approach, starting with how the cybersecurity expert comes up with subjective estimates of probability.

The Expert as the Instrument

In the spirit of the one-for-one substitution we will start with, we will use the same source for an estimate as the current risk matrix—the cybersecurity expert. Just as experts already assess likelihood and impact on the conventional risk matrix, they can simply assess these values using meaningful quantities. We will deal with how to incorporate additional external information in a later step. But simply capturing your current state of uncertainty is an important starting point in any measurement problem. We just need to set up a basic structure with the following steps.

1. Define a list of risks. There are different options for categorizing risks, but for now let's just say that it is the same list that would have been plotted on the conventional risk matrix.
2. Define a specific period of time over which that risk event could materialize (e.g., "A data breach will occur for application X in the next 12 months, a loss of availability for system X long enough to incur a productivity loss will occur in the next 5 years, etc.").
3. For each risk, subjectively assign a probability (0% to 100%) that the stated event will occur in the specified time (e.g., "There is a 10% chance a data breach of system X will occur in the next 12 months.").
4. For each risk, subjectively assign a range for a monetary loss if such an event occurs as a "90% confidence interval" (CI). This is a range wide enough that you are 90% certain that the actual loss will be within the stated range (e.g., if there is a data breach of application X, then it is 90% likely that there will be a loss equal to somewhere between $1 million and $10 million).
5. Get the estimates from multiple experts if possible, but don't have a joint meeting and attempt to reach consensus. Simply provide the list of defined events and let individuals answer separately. If some individuals give very different answers than others, then investigate whether they are simply interpreting the problem differently. For example, if one person says something is 5% likely to happen in a year, and another says it is 100% likely to happen every day, then they

probably interpreted the question differently (the authors have personally seen this very result). But as long as they at least interpret the question similarly, simply average their responses. That is, average all event probabilities to get one probability, and average the lower bounds to produce one lower bound and upper bounds to produce one upper bound.

Some may object to the idea of subjectively assessing probabilities. Some analysts who had no problem saying likelihood was a "4" on a scale of 1 to 5 or a "medium" on a verbal scale will argue that there are requirements for quantitative probabilities that make quantification infeasible. Somehow, the problems that were not an issue using more ambiguous methods are major roadblocks when attempting to state meaningful probabilities.

This is a common misunderstanding. As we first introduced in Chapter 2, it is a mathematically valid position to use a subjective probability to represent the prior state of uncertainty of a subject matter expert. In fact, there are problems in statistics that can *only* be solved by using a probabilistically expressed prior state of uncertainty. And these are actually the very situations most relevant to decision making in any field, including cybersecurity. Later, we will discuss the sources supporting this approach, including some very large empirical studies demonstrating its validity. Additionally, we have a chapter dedicated to helping readers measure and improve their own skill at assessing probabilities using a short series of exercises that can help them continue to improve it over time. We call this "calibrated probability assessment," and we will show that there is quite a bit of research backing up the validity of this approach.

For now, just recognize that most experts can be trained to subjectively assess probabilities and that this skill is *objectively* measurable (as ironic as that sounds). *Remember, if the primary concern about using probabilistic methods is the lack of data, then you also lack the data to use nonquantitative methods.* As we've stated, both methods are based on the same source of data so far—that is, the expert opinion of cybersecurity specialists. And we cannot assume that whatever errors you may be introducing to the decision by using quantitative probabilities without being trained are being avoided by using qualitative methods.

The expert can also be improved by using methods that account for two other sources of error in judgment: the high degree of expert inconsistency, and a tendency to make common inference errors when it comes to thinking probabilistically. These improvements will also be addressed in upcoming chapters. (Of course, these sources of error are not dealt with in the typical risk matrix at all.)

Doing "Uncertainty Math"

Using ranges to represent your uncertainty instead of unrealistically precise point values clearly has advantages. When you allow yourself to use ranges and probabilities, you don't really have to assume anything you don't know for a fact. But precise values have the advantage of being simple to add, subtract, multiply, and divide in a spreadsheet. If you knew each type of loss exactly it would be easy to compute the total loss. Since we only have ranges for each of these, we have to use probabilistic modeling methods to "do the math."

So how do we add, subtract, multiply, and divide in a spreadsheet when we have no exact values, only ranges? Fortunately, there is a practical, proven solution, and it can be performed on any modern personal computer—the "Monte Carlo" simulation method. A Monte Carlo simulation uses a computer to generate a large number of scenarios based on probabilities for inputs. For each scenario, a specific value would be randomly generated for each of the unknown variables. Then these specific values would go into a formula to compute an output for that single scenario. This process usually goes on for thousands of scenarios.

In the 1940s, some mathematicians and scientists started using such simulations of thousands of random trials to help solve certain very hard mathematical problems. Stanislaw Ulam, John von Neumann, and Nicholas Metropolis had developed a way to use this method on the rudimentary computers available at the time to help solve math problems related to the development of the first atomic bomb. They found that randomly running thousands of trials was a way to work out the probabilities of various outcomes when a model has a number of highly uncertain inputs. At the suggestion of Metropolis, Ulam named this computer-based method of generating random scenarios after Monte Carlo, a famous gambling hotspot, in honor of Ulam's uncle, a gambler.[1] Now, with the advantage of greater computing power (easily billions of times greater than what was available on the Manhattan Project, by almost any measure), Monte Carlo simulations have been used to simulate risk models on power plants, supply chains, insurance, project risks, financial risks, and, yes, cybersecurity.

If you have no experience with Monte Carlo simulations, they're probably easier than you think. The authors and many of their staff routinely apply Monte Carlo simulations on a variety of practical business problems. We have seen that many people who initially were uncomfortable with the idea of using Monte Carlo simulations eventually became avid supporters after tinkering with the tools themselves.

Let's start with a very simple problem and provide some tools for solving it. Suppose you have a set of possible events that could occur in a given one-year period. Each event has an assigned probability and, if it occurs, a range of possible losses. Let's suppose that some events have a probability of 1% and perhaps some have a probability of more than 10%. In any given year it is possible that no significant loss event occurs, and it is also possible that several events occur. It is even possible that the same event could happen multiple times in the same year. There is a solution to that, but for now we will keep it simple and just model an event as an either/or outcome that happens no more than once per year. The risk matrix doesn't make this distinction anyway (and it misses quite a few other issues we will introduce later), so this will help keep the example closer to a one-for-one substitution.

We will have an opportunity to get into much further detail for this kind of modeling later in the book. But to help get you started, we have provided some easy examples in an Excel spreadsheet that can be downloaded from www.howtomeasureanything.com/cybersecurity. Armed with this information and some of the more detailed content of upcoming chapters, you should be able to model your uncertainty and answer questions like "What is the chance we will lose more than X next year due to a cyberattack?"

To do this we will simulate thousands of scenarios for every risk. We just need to determine in each scenario whether an event occurs for each type of risk and, if it occurs, what its impact will be.

An Introduction to Generating Random Events and Impacts in Excel

Let's start with whether the event occurred for a single risk in a single scenario. To simulate whether a particular event occurs, we can randomly generate a "1" if it occurs and a "0" if it does not occur, where the probability of a "1" is equal to the stated probability of the event. In Excel, we can write this as

$$= if(rand() < event\_probability, 1, 0)$$

For example, if the event probability is .15, then this equation would produce a "1" (meaning the event occurred) 15% of the time. In Excel, every time you recalculate this (press F9), you will see a different result. If you did this a thousand times, you would see the event occur about 150 times. Note that this would be for each individual risk you are listing in your simulation. So if you have 100 risks each with different probabilities and you run 1,000 scenarios, this little formula would have been executed 100,000 times.

For the impact, we need to generate not just a "0" or "1," but a continuum of values. We can do this using one of Excel's "inverse probability functions." Some probability functions in Excel will tell you the probability of a given result in a particular probability distribution. For example, normdist(x,mean,stddev,1) will tell you the probability that a normal distribution with a given mean and standard deviation will produce a value of x or less. The inverse probability function, on the other hand, tells you the value of x given a probability. In Excel, the inverse probability function for a normal distribution is

$$= \text{norminv}(\text{probability}, \text{mean}, \text{standard deviation})$$

(Note: Recent versions of Excel also use "norm.inv()" but "norminv()" will still work.) If you use the Excel rand() function in place of the probability term, this will produce a normally distributed random value with the stated mean and standard deviation. The standard deviation is a sort of measure of the width of a probability distribution, but it is not really a very intuitive quantity for an expert to estimate. It will be better if we just ask the expert for a 90% confidence interval as described earlier. This can be used to compute the required parameters like a mean and standard deviation based on an upper bound (UB) and lower bound (LB) of describing a range of potential losses provided by the expert.

We are going to turn that range into a probability distribution of a particular type that we will use often: the "lognormal" distribution. The lognormal distribution is a variation of the more familiar, bell-shaped "normal" distribution. It is just a normal distribution on the log of a value we want to simulate and it is a distribution that is usually a much better representation of reality.

Figure 3.1 illustrates an example of this distribution compared to the normal distribution. Notice how the lognormal distribution is lopsided or "skewed," unlike the normal distribution. The lognormal distribution can't generate a zero or negative amount, but it has a tail to the right that allows for the possibility of extremely large outcomes. This is why it is often a realistic representation of the probability of various amounts of loss. A normal

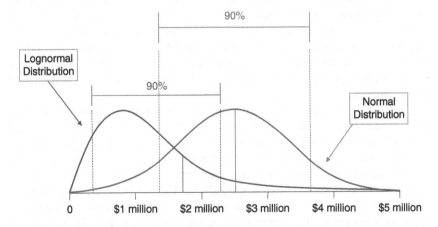

FIGURE 3.1 The Lognormal versus Normal Distribution

distribution wide enough to capture some extreme events could also produce illogical negative results on the other end of the scale (you can't have a negative number of records breached or a negative downtime for a system). This is why the lognormal is also used to model a variety of quantities that can't be negative but could possibly (but rarely) be very large.

To generate a lognormal distribution, the tool provided on the book's website uses the following formula in Excel:

= lognorm.inv(rand(), Mean of (ln(X)), standard deviation of (ln(X))

where:

Standard deviation of ln(X) = (ln(UB) − ln(LB))/3.29)

Mean of ln(X) = (ln(UB)+ln(LB))/2)

So if we had a 90% CI for an impact of $100,000 to $8 million, then the mean and standard deviation we need to use for lognorm.inv (which is the mean and standard deviation of the *log* of the original distribution) would be:

Mean of ln(x) = (ln(8000000) + ln(100000))/2 = 13.7

Standard deviation of ln(x) = (ln(8000000) − ln(100000))/3.29 = 1.33

To generate the loss for an event with a 5% chance of occurrence and an impact of $1 million to $9 million, we would write

= if(rand() < .05, lognorm.inv(rand(), (ln(9000000) + ln(1000000))/2,

(ln(9000000) − ln(1000000))/3.29), 0)

Most of the time (95%), this function would produce a zero. And just 5% of the time it would generate a value with a 90% chance of falling between $1 million and $9 million. Note that since this is a 90% CI, there is a 5% chance of being below the lower bound (but above zero, since the log normal distribution can only produce positive values) and a 5% chance of being above the upper bound and sometimes well above. If the event occurs in the example above, there is a 1% chance the loss could exceed $14.2 million.

Here is one note of caution in using lognormal distributions. The extreme losses for a given 90% CI may be unrealistic when the upper bound is many times the lower bound. This can happen when the expert estimating the value makes the mistake of believing the upper bound represents a worst case extreme, which it is not. The upper bound of a 90% confidence interval allows for a 5% chance the value is higher. Extreme outcomes are also sensitive to the lower bound. If the 90% CI is $10,000 to $1 million, then the upper bound is 100 times as much as the lower bound. In this case there is a 1% chance the loss will exceed 2.6 times the stated upper bound ($2.6 million). If the 90% CI was $1,000 to $10 million, then there is a 1% chance the loss could be more than 6.7 times the upper bound ($67 million). If that seems like too much, then reconsider the width of the range or simply truncate the generated value to some maximum. If we wanted to say that $10 million was the maximum loss, then we could use the Excel function =min(Loss,$10000000) to take the lesser of the loss or $10 million.

Appendix A has more distributions that will be more appropriate for certain kinds of problems. It provides the Excel formulas for them, along with a description of when different distributions are appropriate. Later, we will review some considerations for choosing distributions.

Adding Up the Risks

For a large number of events and impacts, we could make a table like Table 3.2 to simulate all of the losses for all of the events (an example is provided for download at www.howtomeasureanything.com/cybersecurity.)

The value of interest in this particular trial is the total losses: $23,345,193. All you have to do now is run a few thousand more trials to see what the distribution of losses will be. Every time you recalculate this table you would see a different value come up in the total. (If you are an MS Office user on a PC, "recalculate" should be your F9 key.) If you could somehow record every result in a few thousand trials, then you have the output of a Monte Carlo simulation.

TABLE 3.2 Excel Example of Cyber Incidents

Event	Probability of the event occurring in a year	Lower Bound of the 90% CI	Upper Bound of the 90% CI	Random Result (zero when the event did not occur)
AA	.1	$50,000	$500,000	0
AB	.05	$100,000	$10,000,000	$8,456,193
AC	.01	$200,000	$25,000,000	0
AD	.03	$100,000	$15,000,000	0
AE	.05	$250,000	$30,000,000	0
AF	.1	$200,000	$2,000,000	0
AG	.07	$1,000,000	$10,000,000	$2,110,284
AH	.02	$100,000	$15,000,000	0
⇩	⇩	⇩	⇩	⇩
ZM	.05	$250,000	$30,000,000	0
ZN	.01	$1,500,000	$40,000,000	0
Total:				$23,345,193

The easiest way to do this in Excel is with a "data table" in the "What-If Analysis" tools. You can run as many trials as you like and show each individual result without you having to copy Table 3.2 thousands of times. The data table lets the Excel user see what a series of answers would look like in a formula if you could change one input at a time. For example, you might have a very big spreadsheet for computing retirement income that includes current savings rates, market growth, and several other factors. You might want to see how the estimate of project duration changes if you modified your monthly savings from $100 to $5,000 in $100 increments. A data table would automatically show all of the results as if you manually changed that one input each time yourself and recorded the result. The spreadsheet you can download at www.howtomeasureanything.com/cybersecurity uses this method.

If you want to find out more about data tables in general, the help pages for Excel can take you through the basics, but we do make one modification in the example spreadsheet. Usually, you will need to enter either a "column input cell" or "row input cell" (we would just use "column input cell" in our example) to identify which value the data table will be repeatedly changing to produce different results. In this case, we don't really need to identify an input to change because we already have the

TABLE 3.3 The Excel Data Table Showing 10,000 Scenarios of Cybersecurity Losses

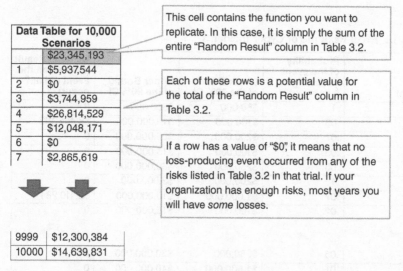

Data Table for 10,000 Scenarios	
	$23,345,193
1	$5,937,544
2	$0
3	$3,744,959
4	$26,814,529
5	$12,048,171
6	$0
7	$2,865,619

This cell contains the function you want to replicate. In this case, it is simply the sum of the entire "Random Result" column in Table 3.2.

Each of these rows is a potential value for the total of the "Random Result" column in Table 3.2.

If a row has a value of "$0", it means that no loss-producing event occurred from any of the risks listed in Table 3.2 in that trial. If your organization has enough risks, most years you will have *some* losses.

9999	$12,300,384
10000	$14,639,831

(From the example provided in www.howtomeasureanything.com/cybersecurity.)

rand() function that changes every time we recalculate. So our "input" values are just arbitrary numbers counting from 1 to the number of scenarios we want to run.

There is an important consideration for the number of trials when simulating cybersecurity events. We are often concerned with rare but high-impact events. If an event likelihood is only 1% each year, then 10,000 trials will produce about 100 of these events most of the time, but this varies a bit. Out of this number of trials, it can vary randomly from an exact value of 100 (just as flipping a coin 100 times doesn't necessarily produce exactly 50 heads). In this case the result will be between 84 and 116 about 90% of the time.

Now, for each of these times the event occurs, we have to generate a loss. If that loss has a long tail, there may be a significant variation each time the Monte Carlo is run. By "long tail," what I mean is that it is not infeasible for the loss to be much more than the average loss. We could have, for example, a distribution for a loss where the most likely outcome is a $100,000 loss, but there is a 1% chance of a major loss ($50 million or more). The one-percentile worst-case scenario in a risk that has only a 1% chance per year of occurrence in the first place is a situation that would happen with a probability of 1/100 x 1/100 or 1 in 10,000 per year. Since 10,000 is our number of trials, we could run a simulation where this worst-case event occurred one or more times in 10,000 trials, and we could run another 10,000 trials where it never occurred at all. This means that every time you ran a Monte Carlo simulation, you would see the average total loss jump around a bit.

The simplest solution to this problem for the Monte Carlo modeler who doesn't want to work too hard is to throw more trials at it. This simulation-to-simulation variation would shrink if we ran 100,000 trials or a million. You might be surprised at how little time this takes in Excel on a decently fast machine. We've run 100,000 trials in a few seconds using Excel, which doesn't sound like a major constraint. We have even run a *million* scenarios—in plain ol' native Excel—of models with several large calculations in 15 minutes or less. As events get rarer and bigger, however, there are more efficient methods available than just greatly increasing the number of trials. But for now we will keep it simple and just throw cheap computing power at the problem.

Now we have a method of generating thousands of outcomes in a Monte Carlo simulation using native Excel—no add-ins or Visual Basic code to run. Given that Excel is so widely used, it is almost certain any cybersecurity analyst has the tools to use this. We can then use this data for another important element of risk analysis—visualizing the risk quantitatively.

Visualizing Risk

The risk matrix familiar to anyone in cybersecurity is widely used because it appears to serve as a simple illustration of likelihood and impact on one chart. In our proposed simple solution, we have simply replaced the likelihood scale with an explicit probability, and the impact with a 90% CI representing a range of potential losses.

In our proposed solution, the vertical axis can still be represented by a single point—a probability as opposed to a score. But now the impact is represented by more than a single point. If we say that an event has a 5% chance of occurrence, we can't just say the impact will be exactly $10 million. There is really a 5% chance of losing *something*, while perhaps there is a 2% chance of losing more than $5 million, a 1% chance of losing more than $15 million, and so on.

This amount of information cannot be plotted with a simple point on a two-dimensional chart. Instead, we can represent this with a chart called a "loss exceedance curve" or LEC. In the spirit of not reinventing the wheel (as risk managers in many industries have done many times), this is a concept also used in financial portfolio risk assessment, actuarial science, and what is known as "probabilistic risk assessment" in nuclear power and other areas of engineering. In these other fields, it is also variously referred to as a "probability of exceedance" or even "complementary cumulative probability function." Figure 3.2 shows an example of an LEC.

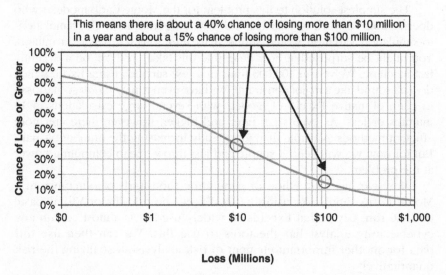

FIGURE 3.2 Example of a Loss Exceedance Curve

Explaining the Elements of the Loss Exceedance Curve

Figure 3.2 shows the chance that a given amount would be lost in a given period of time (e.g., a year) due to a particular category of risks. This curve can be constructed entirely from the data generated in the previous data table example (Table 3.3). A risk curve could be constructed for a particular vulnerability, system, business unit, or enterprise. An LEC can show how a range of losses is possible (not just a point value) and that larger losses are less likely than smaller ones. In the example shown in Figure 3.2 (which, given the scale, would probably be enterprise-level cybersecurity risks for a large organization), there is a 40% chance per year of losing $10 million *or more*. There is also about a 15% chance of losing $100 million or more. A logarithmic scale is used on the horizontal axis to better show a wider range of losses (but that is just a matter of preference—a linear scale can be used, too).

We can also create another variation of this chart by adding a couple more curves. Figure 3.3 shows three curves: inherent risk, residual risk, and risk tolerance. Inherent versus residual risk is a common distinction made in cybersecurity to represent risks before the application of proposed controls (i.e., methods of mitigating risks) and risks after the application of controls, respectively. Inherent risk, however, doesn't have to mean a complete lack of controls, since this is not a realistically viable alternative. Inherent risk might be defined instead as including only minimal required controls. Those are controls where it would be considered negligent to exclude them so there really is no dilemma about whether to include them. The differences between inherent and residual risks are only truly discretionary controls—the sorts of controls where it would be considered a reasonable option to exclude them. Examples of minimal controls may be password protection, firewalls, some required frequency of updating patches, limiting

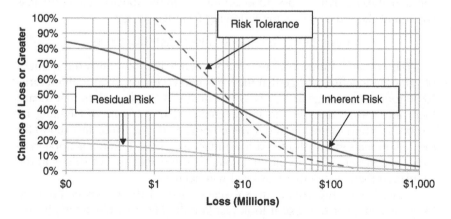

FIGURE 3.3 Inherent Risk, Residual Risk, and Risk Tolerance

certain types of access to administrators, and so on. The organization can make its own list of minimal controls. If a control is considered a required minimum, then there is no dilemma, and where there is no dilemma, there is no value to decision analysis. So it is helpful to focus our attention on controls where having them or not are both reasonable alternatives.

The LEC provides a simple and useful visual method for comparing a risk to a risk tolerance, which can also be unambiguously and quantitatively expressed as an LEC. As Figure 3.3 shows, part of the inherent risk curve (shown in the thicker curve) is above the risk tolerance curve (shown as the dashed curve). The part of the inherent risk curve that is over the risk tolerance curve is said to "violate" or "break" the risk tolerance. The residual risk curve, on the other hand, is on or underneath the risk tolerance curve at all points. If this is the case, we say that the risk tolerance curve "stochastically dominates" the residual risk curve. This simply means that the residual risks are acceptable. We will talk about a simple process for defining a risk tolerance curve shortly, but first we will describe how to generate the other curves from the Monte Carlo simulation we just ran.

Generating the Inherent and Residual Loss Exceedance Curves

Remember, as with the other methods used in this chapter, the downloadable spreadsheet at the previously mentioned website shows all the technical details. As Table 3.4 shows, the histogram has two columns, one showing a series of loss levels. These would be the values shown on the horizontal axis of an LEC. The second column shows the percentage of Monte Carlo results that generated something equal to or higher than the value in the first column. The simplest method involves using a "countif()" function in Excel. If we use "Monte Carlo Results" to stand for the second column of values in Table 3.3 and "Loss" to mean the cell in the spreadsheet in the loss column of the same row as the following formula, we get:

$$= \text{Countif(Monte Carlo Results, ">"\&Loss)}/10000$$

The countif() function does what it sounds like. It counts the number of values in a defined range that meet a stated condition. If countif() returns 8,840 for a given range and if "Loss" is equal to $2 million, then that means there are 8,840 values in the range greater than $2 million. Dividing by 10,000 is to turn the result into a value between 0 and 1 (0% and 100%) for the 10,000 trials in the Monte Carlo simulation. As this formula is applied to larger and larger values in the loss column, the percentage of values in the simulation that exceed that loss level will decrease.

Now, we simply create an XY scatterplot on these two columns in Excel. If you want to make it look just like the LEC that has been shown, you will want to use the version of the scatterplot that interpolates points with curves and without markers for the point. This is the version set up

TABLE 3.4 Histogram for a Loss Exceedance Curve

Histogram for Loss Exceedance Curve	
Loss	Probability per Year of Loss or Greater
$ –	99.9%
$500,000	98.8%
$1,000,000	95.8%
$1,500,000	92.6%
$2,000,000	88.4%
$2,500,000	83.4%
$3,000,000	77.5%

$24,000,000	3.0%
$24,500,000	2.7%

in the spreadsheet. More curves can be added simply by adding more columns of data. The residual risk curve, for example, is just the same procedure but based on your estimated probabilities and impacts (which would presumably be smaller) after your proposed additional controls are implemented.

One disadvantage of the LEC chart is that if multiple LECs are shown, it can get very busy looking. While in the typical risk matrix, each risk is shown as a single point (although an extremely unrealistic and ambiguous point), an LEC is a curve. This is why one organization that produced a chart with a large number of LECs called it a "spaghetti chart." However, this complexity was easily managed just by having separate charts for different categories. Also, since the LECs can always be combined in a mathematically proper way, we can have aggregate LEC charts where each curve on that chart could be decomposed into multiple curves shown on a separate, detailed chart for that curve. This is another key advantage of using a tool like an LEC for communicating risks. We provide a spreadsheet on the book's website to show how this is done.

Now, compare this to popular approaches in cybersecurity risk assessment. The typical low/medium/high approach lacks the specificity to say that "seven lows and two mediums are riskier than one high" or "nine lows add up to one medium," but this can be done with LECs. Again, we need to point out that the high ambiguity of the low/medium/high method in no way saves the analyst from having to think about these things. With the risk matrix, the analyst is just forced to think about risks in a much more ambiguous way.

What we need to do is to create another table like Table 3.3 that is then rolled up into another Table 3.4, but where each value in the table is the total of several simulated categories of risks. Again, we have a downloadable spreadsheet for this at www.howtomeasureanything.com/cybersecurity. We can run another 10,000 trials on all the risks we want to add up, and we follow the LEC procedure for the total. You might think that we could just take separately generated tables like Table 3.3 and add up the number of values that fall within each bin to get an aggregated curve, but that would produce an incorrect answer unless risks are perfectly correlated (I'll skip over the details of why this is the case, but a little experimentation would prove it to you if you wanted to see the difference between the two procedures). Following this method we can see the risks of a system from several vulnerabilities, the risks of a business unit from several systems, and the risks across the enterprise for all business units.

Where Does the Risk Tolerance Curve Come from?

Ideally, the risk tolerance curve is gathered in a meeting with a level of management that is in a position to state, as a matter of policy, how much risk the organization is willing to accept. Hubbard has gathered risk tolerance curves of several types (LEC is one type of risk tolerance quantification) from many organizations, including risk tolerance for multiple cybersecurity applications. The required meeting is usually done in about 90 minutes. It involves simply explaining the concept to management and then asking them to establish a few points on the curve. We also need to identify which risk tolerance curve we are capturing (e.g., the per-year risk for an individual system, the per-decade risk for the entire enterprise, etc.). But once we have laid the groundwork, we could simply start with one arbitrary point and ask the following:

Analyst: Would you accept a 10% chance, per year, of losing more than $5 million due to a cybersecurity risk?

Executive: I prefer not to accept any risk.

Analyst: Me too, but you accept risk right now in many areas. You could always spend more to reduce risks, but obviously there is a limit.

Executive:	True. I suppose I would be willing to accept a 10% chance per year of a $5 million loss or greater.
Analyst:	How about a 20% chance of losing more than $5 million in a year?
Executive:	That feels like pushing it. Let's stick with 10%.
Analyst:	Great, 10%, then. Now, how much of a chance would you be willing to accept for a much larger loss, like $50 million or more? Would you say even 1%?
Executive:	I think I'm more risk averse than that. I might accept a 1% chance per year of accepting a loss of $25 million or more. . .

And so on. After plotting three or four points, we can interpolate the rest and give it to the executive for final approval. It is not a technically difficult process, but it is important to know how to respond to some potential questions or objections. Some executives may point out that this exercise feels a little abstract. In that case, give them some real-life examples from their firm or other firms of given losses and how often those happen.

Also, some may prefer to consider such a curve only for a given cybersecurity budget—as in, "That risk is acceptable depending on what it costs to avoid it." This is also a reasonable concern. You could, if the executive was willing to spend more time, state more risk tolerance at different expenditure levels for risk avoidance. There are ways to capture "risk/return" tradeoffs (see Hubbard's original book, *How to Measure Anything* for details on this method). But most seem willing to consider the idea that there is still a maximum acceptable risk, and this is what we are attempting to capture.

It is also worth noting that the authors have had many opportunities to gather risk tolerance curves from upper management in organizations for problems in cybersecurity as well as other areas. If your concern is that upper management won't understand this, we can say we have not observed this—even when we've been told that management wouldn't understand it. In fact, upper management seems to understand having to determine which risks are acceptable at least as well as anyone in cybersecurity. (We will bring this up again in Chapter 5 when we discuss this and other illusory obstacles to adopting quantitative methods.)

Supporting the Decision: A Return on Mitigation

Ultimately, the point of risk analysis—even with the risk matrix we are replacing—is to support decisions. But the difficulty we had before was making specific resource-allocation choices for specific controls. What is it worth, after all, to move one "high" risk to a "medium"? Is it $5,000 or $5 million? Or what if we have a budget of $8 million for cybersecurity and 80 lows, 30 mediums, and 15 highs? And what if we can mitigate more lows for the same money as one medium? If you have observed (as the authors have) someone asking a question like, "If we spent another million dollars, can we move this risk from a red to a yellow?" then you may have felt the dissatisfaction from this approach. Clearly the traditional risk matrix offers little guidance once the CISO actually has to make choices about allocating resources. You might think that you may as well do without these methods altogether. But, as we will show later, the CISO should definitely not assume they handle these decisions well using their expert intuition alone.

What the CISO needs is a "Return on Control" calculation. That is the monetized value of the reduction in expected losses divided by the cost of the control. If we look only at the benefits in a single year (and ignore other "time value" considerations), we can show this as:

$$\text{Return on Control} = \frac{\text{Reduction in Expected Losses}}{\text{Cost of Control}} - 1$$

The term "expected" in the context of design analysis generally refers to the probability-weighted average of some amount. So "expected loss" is the average of the Monte Carlo simulation losses due to some cause. If we applied a control to reduce risks and then we simulated a new set of losses, the average of those losses would be less (by either reducing the chance of any loss, reducing the impact if the loss event occurred, or both). The difference in the loss before and after the control is the "Reduction in Expected Losses" in the simple formula above. If the Reduction in Expected Losses was exactly as much as the cost, then this formula would say the Return on Control was 0%. This would be the convention for other forms of investment.

You would also have to identify over what period of time this expected reduction in losses would occur. If the control was just an ongoing expense that could be started and stopped at any time, then this simple formula could just be applied to a year's worth of benefits (loss reduction) and a year's worth of costs. If the control is a one-time investment that could provide benefits over a longer period of time, then follow the financial conventions in your firm for capital investments. You will probably be required then to compute the benefits as a "present value" of a stream of investments at a given discount rate. Or you may be asked to produce an "internal rate of return." We won't spend time on those methods here, but there are fairly simple financial calculations that can, again, be done entirely with simple functions in Excel.

A note of caution is needed if you plan on decomposing our simple range for impact further into more variables that go into computing impact. In the example we have shown so far, computing the expected losses is a very simple calculation. We can just multiply the computed mean of the distribution for the impact times the probability of the event occurring (the spreadsheet we provide on the website does this for you). But if we decompose impact into multiple components that need to be multiplied together (e.g., records breached times cost per record, duration of outage times number of people affected times cost per person per hour, etc.), then working with the averages no longer becomes a reasonable estimation. We effectively have to run a separate simulation on each row. But in our simplest model we can ignore that for now. As we make the model more advanced, we can add more detail. Later chapters will describe how you can evolve the model by adding elements that incrementally improve realism.

Where to Go from Here

There are many models cybersecurity analysts could use to represent their current state of uncertainty. You could simply estimate likelihood and impact directly without further decomposition. You could develop a modeling method that determines how likelihood and impact are modified by specifying types of threat, the capabilities of threats, vulnerabilities, or the characteristics of systems. You can list applications and evaluate risk by application, or you can list controls and assess the risks that individual controls would address.

Ultimately, this book will be agnostic regarding which modeling strategy you use, but we will discuss how various modeling strategies should be evaluated. When enough information is available to justify the industry adopting a single, uniform modeling method, then it should do so. Until then, we should let different organizations adopt different modeling techniques while taking care to measure the relative performance of these methods.

To get started, there are some ready-made solutions to decompose risks. In addition to the methods Hubbard uses, solutions include the methodology and tools used by the FAIR method, developed by Jack Jones and Jack Freund.[2] In the authors' opinion, FAIR, as another Monte Carlo–based solution with its own variation on how to decompose risks into further components, could be a step in the right direction for your firm. We can also build quite a lot on the simple tools we've already provided (and with more to come in later chapters). For readers who have had even basic programming, math, or finance courses, they may be able to add more detail without much trouble. So, most readers will be able to extrapolate from this as much as they see fit. The website will also add a few more tools for parts of this, like R and Python for those who are interested. But, since everything we are doing in this book can be handled entirely within Excel, any of these tools would be optional.

So far, this method is still only a very basic solution based on expert judgment—updating this initial model with data using statistical methods comes later. Still, even at this stage there are advantages of a method like this when compared to the risk matrix. It can capture more details about the knowledge of the cybersecurity expert, and it gives us access to much more powerful analytical tools. If we wanted, we could do any or all of the following:

- As we just mentioned, we could decompose impacts into separate estimates of different types of costs—legal, remediation, system outages, public relations costs, and so on. Each of those could be a function of known constraints such as the number of employees or business process affected by a system outage or number of records on a system that could be compromised in a breach. This leverages knowledge the organization has about the details of its systems.
- We could make relationships among events. For example, the cybersecurity analyst may know that if Event X happens, Event Y becomes far more likely. Again, this leverages knowledge that would otherwise not be directly used in a less quantitative method.
- Where possible, some of these likelihoods and impacts can be inferred from known data using proper statistical methods. We know ways we can update the state of uncertainty described in this method with new data using mathematically sound methods.
- These results can be properly "added up" to create aggregate risks for whole sets of systems, business units, or companies.

We will introduce more about each of these improvements later in the book, but we have demonstrated what a simple one-for-one substitution would look like. Now we can turn our attention to evaluating alternative methods for assessing risk. Of all the methods we could have started with in this simple model and for all the methods we could add to it, how do we select the best for our purposes? Or, for that matter, how do we know it works at all?

Notes

1. Stanislaw Ulam, *Adventures of a Mathematician* (Berkeley: University of California Press, 1991).
2. Jack Freund and Jack Jones, *Measuring and Managing Information Risk: A FAIR Approach* (Waltham, MA: Butterworth-Heinemann, 2014).

CHAPTER 4

The Single Most Important Measurement in Cybersecurity

We hope Chapter 2 cleared up how the term "measurement" is used in decision science as well as the empirical sciences in general. We contend that this is the most relevant understanding of measurement for cybersecurity. Chapter 3 gave you an introduction to the most basic level of quantitative risk analysis. There will be a lot more to cover regarding the details of the methods of measurement, but for now we propose that our first target should be a measurement of risk analysis itself.

The authors have observed experts throughout the field with passionately held positions on the relative merits of different cybersecurity risk-assessment methods. One easy observation we could make is that both sides of polar-opposite positions were often argued by highly qualified cybersecurity experts, all with decades of experience. One knowledgeable expert will argue, for example, that a particular framework based on qualitative scores improves decisions, builds consensus, and avoids the problems of more quantitative methods. Another equally qualified expert will argue this is an illusion and that such methods simply "do the math wrong." Since we know at least one (if not both) must be wrong, then we know qualifications and expertise in cybersecurity alone are not sufficient to determine if a given opinion on this topic is correct.

This leaves us with several hard questions. How do we decide which methods work better? Is it possible that the risk analysis methods cybersecurity experts have used for decades—methods in which many cybersecurity experts have a high degree of confidence—could actually not work? Is it possible that the perceived benefits of widely used tools could be an illusion? What do we even mean by whether a method "works" and how would that be measured? We propose that the single most important measurement in cybersecurity risk assessment, or any other risk assessment, is to measure how well the risk assessment methods themselves work.

More fundamentally, does it even matter whether risk analysis works? And by "works," do we really just mean whether it succeeds in putting on a show for compliance, or should we mean it actually improves the identification and management of risks? We will take what we believe to be an obvious position that shouldn't really be controversial:

- *We believe it matters whether risk analysis actually works.*
- What we mean by whether it "works" is whether it *measurably reduces risks* relative to alternative methods with the same resources. That is, we believe that risk analysis in any field, including cybersecurity, is not just a matter of putting on a show for the appearance of compliance.
- Regulators and standards organizations must make measured performance of methods the key feature of what "compliance" means. If complying with standards and regulations does not actually improve risk management, then those standards and regulations must change.
- We also think it is entirely reasonable to say that in order to settle an issue with many contradictory opinions from experts at all levels, we will have to actually begin to measure how well risk analysis methods work.
- We assert that if firms are using cybersecurity risk-analysis methods that cannot show a measurable improvement or, even worse, if they make risk assessment worse, then that is the single biggest risk in cybersecurity, and improving risk assessment will be the single most important risk management priority.

Measuring the methods themselves will be the basis of every recommendation in this book. Either we will propose risk analysis methods based on measurements that have already been done and published, or, if no such measurement has been done, we will propose a measurement that will help identify a valid method. And while we describe how to measure the relative effectiveness of methods, we also need to explain how not to measure them.

By the end of this chapter we will see what published research has already measured about key pieces of the quantitative methods we proposed in Chapter 3. In the next chapter, we will also consider research showing that components of current popular risk-assessment methods may do more harm than good. Now, let's look at why we need to base our methods on research in the first place as opposed to our expert opinion.

The Analysis Placebo: Why We Can't Trust Opinion Alone

The first principle is that you must not fool yourself, and you are the easiest person to fool.

—Richard P. Feynman, Nobel Prize–Winning Physicist

We often hear that a given method is "proven" and is a "best practice." It may be touted as a "rigorous" and "formal" method—implying that this is adequate reason to believe that it improves estimates and decisions. Eventually it gets the title of "accepted standard." Some satisfied users will even provide testimonials to the method's effectiveness.

But how often are these claims ever based on actual measurements of the method's performance? It is not as if large clinical trials were run with test groups and control groups. Estimates are rarely compared to actual outcomes, and costly cybersecurity breaches are almost never tracked over a large number of samples to see if risk really changed as a function of which risk assessment and decision-making methods are used. Unfortunately, the label of "best practice" does not mean it was measured and scientifically proven to be the best performer among a set of practices. Yet, as Feynman's quote states, we are easy to fool. Perceived improvements may actually be a mirage. Even if a method does more harm than good, users may still honestly feel they see a benefit.

How is this possible? Blame an "analysis placebo"—the feeling that some analytical method has improved decisions and estimates even when it has not. The analogy to a placebo as it is used in medical research is actually a bit generous. In that case, there can actually be a positive physiological effect from a mere placebo beyond the mere perception of benefit. But when we use the term in this context we mean there literally is no benefit other than the perception of benefit. Several studies in fields outside of cybersecurity have been done that show how spending effort on analysis improved confidence even when the actual performance was not improved at all. Here are a few examples that have also been mentioned in other books by Hubbard:

- *Sports Picks*: A 2008 study at the University of Chicago tracked probabilities of outcomes of sporting events as assigned by participants given varying amounts of information about the teams without being told the names of teams or players. As the fans were given more information about the teams in a given game, they would increase their confidence that they were picking a winner, even though the actual chance of picking the winner was nearly flat no matter how much information they were given.[1]

- *Psychological Diagnosis*: Another study showed how practicing clinical psychologists became more confident in their diagnosis and their prognosis for various risky behaviors by gathering more information about patients, and yet, again, the agreement with observed outcomes of behaviors did not actually improve.[2]

- *Investments:* A psychology researcher at MIT, Paul Andreassen, did several experiments in the 1980s showing that gathering more information about stocks in investment portfolios improved confidence but without any improvement in portfolio returns. In one study he showed how people tend to overreact to news and assume that the additional information is informative even though, on average, returns are not improved by these actions.[3]

- *Collaboration on Sports Picks*: In another study, sports fans were asked to collaborate with others to improve predictions. Again, confidence went up after collaboration but actual performance did not. Indeed, the participants rarely even changed their views from before the discussions. The net effect of collaboration was to seek confirmation of what participants had already decided.[4]

- *Collaboration on Trivia Estimates:* Another study investigating the benefits of collaboration asked subjects for estimates of trivia from an almanac. It considered multiple forms of interaction including the Delphi technique, free-form discussion, and other methods of collaboration. Although interaction did not improve estimates over simple averaging of individual estimates, the subjects did feel more satisfied with the results.[5]

- *Lie Detection:* A 1999 study measured the ability of subjects to detect lies in controlled tests involving videotaped mock interrogations of "suspects." The suspects were actors who were incentivized to conceal certain facts in staged crimes to create real nervousness about being discovered. Some of the subjects reviewing the videos received training in lie detection and some did not. The trained subjects were more confident in judgments about detecting lies even though they were *worse* than untrained subjects at detecting lies.[6]

And these are just a few of many similar studies showing that we can engage in training, information gathering, and collaboration that improves confidence but not actual performance. Of course, these examples are from completely different types of problems. But what is the basis for assuming that these same problems don't appear in cybersecurity? In the pharmaceutical industry, a new drug is effectively assumed to be a placebo until it is proven that it is not. The fact that a placebo exists in some areas means it could exist in other areas unless the data shows otherwise. With examples in problems as diverse as investments, horse racing, football games, and diagnosis of psychology patients, it would seem that the burden of proof is on the person claiming that some other area, like cybersecurity, avoids these problems. So let's start by assuming that cybersecurity is not particularly immune to problems observed in so many other areas where humans have to make judgments.

What we will *not* do to measure the performance of various methods is rely on the proclamations of any expert regardless of his or her claimed level of knowledge or level of vociferousness. So even though the authors can fairly claim plenty of experience—cybersecurity in the case of Seiersen and quantitative risk analysis in general in the case of Hubbard—we will not rely on any appeals to our authority regarding what works and what does not. (We see this as a shortcoming in many books on risk management and information security.) Our arguments will be based on the published research from large experiments. Any mention of anecdotes or quotes from "thought leaders" will only be used to illustrate a point, never to prove it.

We don't think it is controversial to insist that reason and evidence are the way to reach reliable conclusions about reality. For "reason," we include using math and logic to derive new statements from previously confirmed statements. For "evidence," we don't include anecdotal or testimonial arguments. (Any method, including astrology and pet psychics, can produce those types of "evidence.") The best source of evidence is large, random samples; clinical trials; unbiased historical data; and so on. The data should then be assessed with proper mathematical methods to make inferences.

How You Have More Data Than You Think

What we need to do is define a scientifically sound way to evaluate methods and then look at how different methods compare based on that evaluation. But a common concern is that cybersecurity simply lacks sufficient data for proper, statistically valid measurements. Ironically, this claim is almost always made without actually doing any proper math.

Recall from Chapter 2 that if we can expand our horizons about what data could be informative, we actually have more data than we think. So here are some ways that we actually have more data than we think about the performance of cybersecurity risk assessment methods.

- *We don't have to be limited by looking just at ourselves.* Sure, each organization is unique but that doesn't mean that we can't learn from different examples (indeed, experience would mean nothing if we couldn't generalize from experiences that aren't exactly identical). Using information from larger populations is how insurance companies estimate your health risk even though you never made a claim, or how a doctor believes a drug you never tried will work with you because he knows of a large experiment involving many other people.
- *We can measure components as well as whole systems.* We can measure the overall performance of an entire system, or we can measure individual components of the system. When an engineer predicts the behavior of a new system that has not yet been built, the engineer is using knowledge of the behavior of components and how they interact. It's easier to measure several components of risk assessment than it is to wait for rare events to happen. For example, tracking how well cybersecurity analysts estimate more frequent, small events is a measure of the "expert estimation component" in the risk management system.
- *We can use published research.* If we are willing to consider component level studies of larger populations outside of our own experience, then a lot more data becomes available. When you don't have existing data or outside research of any kind, it might be time to start gathering the data as part of a defined measurement process.

Now, in a perfect world, your firm would have so much of its own data that it doesn't need to make inferences from larger populations of other firms. It can measure the overall performance of a risk assessment system by actually measuring outcomes observed within your own firm. If it were large enough and willing to wait long enough, it could observe variations in major data breaches in different business units using different risk assessment methods. Better yet, industry-wide experiments could include many organizations and would produce a lot of data even about events that would be rare for a single firm.

Of course, large, industry-wide experiments would not be practical for several reasons, including the time it would have to take. (Which organizations would want to be in the "placebo" group using a fake method?) Not surprisingly, no such study has been published in peer-reviewed literature by the date of this writing. So what can be done to compare different risk assessment methods in a scientifically rational way? The other measurement strategy dimensions we just mentioned give us some choices—some of which can give us immediate answers.

A more feasible answer for an initial measurement would be to experiment with larger populations but with existing research at the component level. Component testing is an approach many professionals in information technology are already familiar with. Components we could consider are the individual steps in risk assessment, the tools used, and the methods of collaboration. Even the act of simply putting a probability on a cybersecurity attack is a component of the process we could test. In fact, a lot of research has already been done on this at a component level—including some studies that were very large, conducted over many decades by many separate researchers, and published in leading, peer-reviewed scientific journals.

If the individual components of a method are shown to be an improvement, then a method based entirely on these elements is much more likely to be effective than a method for which the components have no such evidence or, worse yet, have been shown to be flawed. This is no different than a designer of an oil refinery or rocket using established physical principles to evaluate components of a system and then calculating how those components would behave in the aggregate. There are many potential components to evaluate, so let's divide them into two broad categories that are or could be used in cybersecurity risk assessment:

- What is the relative performance of purely historical models in estimating uncertain outcomes as compared to experts?
- Where we use experts, what is the performance of the tools experts use to assist in making estimates of outcomes?

When Algorithms Beat Experts

The key "component" we should consider in cybersecurity risk analysis is the performance of how information is synthesized to make estimates. Specifically, is it better to rely on experts to make a judgment or a statistical model? One particular area where research is plentiful is in the comparison of statistical models to human experts in the task of estimating uncertain outcomes of future events. This research generated one of the most consistently replicated and impactful findings of psychology: that even relatively naïve statistical models seem to outperform human experts in a surprising variety of estimation and forecasting problems.

We aren't saying that we can entirely replace humans in risk assessment. We are simply looking at a few situations where objective, quantitative models were made and compared to expert intuition. We want to investigate the following question: If we could build a purely quantitative model on historical data, would that even be desirable?

As you read about this research, you may also want to know whether any of the research in other areas could even apply to cybersecurity. If you bear with us, we think you will agree that it does. In fact, like the placebo effect mentioned earlier, the studies are so numerous and varied it seems the burden of proof would be on the one arguing that cybersecurity somehow avoids these fundamental issues.

Some Research Comparing Experts and Algorithms

Some of this research started in a very different field and during a time before the concept of cybersecurity had even been imagined. As early as the 1950s, the American psychologist Paul Meehl proposed an idea that shook up the field of clinical psychology. He claimed that expert-based clinical judgments about psychiatric patients might not be as good as simple statistical models. Meehl collected a large set of studies showing that statistical models based on medical records produced diagnoses and prognoses that at least matched but usually beat the judgment of trained clinicians. Meehl was able to show, for example, that personality tests were better than experts at predicting several behaviors regarding neurological disorders, juvenile delinquency, and addictive behaviors.

In 1954, he wrote the seminal book on the subject, *Clinical versus Statistical Prediction*. At the time of this initial research, he could already cite over 90 studies that challenged the assumed authority of experts.[7] Researchers like Robyn Dawes (1936–2010) of the University of Michigan were inspired to build on this body of research, and every new study that was generated only confirmed Meehl's findings, even as they expanded the scope to include experts outside of clinical diagnosis.[8,9,10] The library of studies they compiled included findings predicting the GPAs of college freshmen and medical students, criminal recidivism, sporting events, and medical prognoses. After the studies had grown significantly in number, Meehl felt forced to conclude:

> There is no controversy in social science which shows such a large body of qualitatively diverse studies coming out so uniformly in the same direction as this one. When you're pushing 90 investigations [now closer to 150], predicting everything from the outcome of football games to the diagnosis of liver disease and when you can hardly come up with a half dozen studies showing even a weak tendency in favor of the [human expert], it is time to draw a practical conclusion.[11]

The methods used in this research were fairly straightforward. Ask experts to predict some objectively verifiable outcomes—like whether a new business will fail or the effectiveness of chemotherapy for a cancer patient—then predict the same thing using an algorithm based only on historical data, then lastly track both over a large number of predictions, and see which method performs better.

Such conclusive findings as those of Meehl and his colleagues inevitably draw the interest of other researchers looking for similar phenomena in other fields. In one of the more recent examples, a study of oil exploration firms shows a strong relationship between the use of quantitative methods (including Monte Carlo simulations) to assess risks and a firm's financial performance.[12,13] NASA has been applying Monte Carlo simulations based on historical data along with softer methods (based on subjective scales) to assess the risks of cost and schedule overruns and mission failures. The cost and schedule estimates from the quantitative methods had, on average, less than half the error of scientists and engineers using nonquantitative methods.[14]

In perhaps the most ambitious study of this kind, Philip Tetlock conducted an experiment over a 20-year period and published it in his book *Expert Political Judgment: How Good Is It?* The title indicates a particular focus but he interpreted it broadly to include economics, military affairs, technology, and more. He tracked the probabilities of world events assigned by a total of 284 experts in their respective fields. By the conclusion of the study he had collected over 82,000 individual forecasts.[15] (This puts Tetlock's data equal to or in excess of the largest phase III clinical drug trials published in scientific journals.) Based on this data, Tetlock was willing to make even stronger statements than Meehl and his colleagues:

It is impossible to find any domain in which humans clearly outperformed crude extrapolation algorithms, less still sophisticated statistical ones.

Why Does This Happen?

Robyn Dawes, Meehl's colleague who we mentioned earlier, makes the case that poor performance by humans in forecasting and estimation tasks is partly due to inaccurate interpretations of probabilistic feedback.[16] These researchers came to view the expert as a kind of imperfect mediator of input and output. Very few experts actually measure their performance over time, and they tend to summarize their memories with selected anecdotes. The expert then makes rough inferences from this selective memory, and according to the research published by Dawes, this can lead to an "illusion of learning." That is, experts can interpret experience as evidence of performance. They assume that years of experience *should* result in improved performance so they assume that it *does*. But it turns out that we cannot take learning for granted no matter how many years of experience are gained.

Tetlock proposed in his book that "human performance suffers because we are, deep down, deterministic thinkers with an aversion to probabilistic strategies that accept the inevitability of error." The math of dealing with error and uncertainty is the math of probabilities. If we can't get that math right in our heads, then we would have a lot of difficulty with probabilistic forecasting problems. For example, if someone was not good at simple arithmetic, we wouldn't be surprised if that person was not very good at estimating, say, the costs and duration of a large, complex engineering project with many interrelated elements. Surely a person skilled at those estimates would know how to multiply the number of people involved in a task, their cost of labor, and the duration of the task in order to estimate the task's labor costs. He or she would also know how to total the costs of the separate tasks along with other project costs (e.g., materials, licenses, equipment rental, etc.).

So when an expert says that, based on some experience and data, one threat is a bigger risk than another, they are doing a kind of "mental math" whether intentional or not. We aren't saying they are literally trying to add numbers in their heads; rather, they are following an instinct for something that in many cases really could be computed. How well our intuition matches mathematical facts has also been measured by an impressive array of research including that of Daniel Kahneman, winner of the 2002 Nobel Prize in Economic Sciences, and his colleague Amos Tversky. They showed how even statistically sophisticated researchers will tend to greatly misestimate the odds that new data will confirm or contradict a previous experiment of a given sample size,[17] and will incorrectly estimate expected variations in observations based on sample size.[18]

By "statistically sophisticated," we mean that the subjects of this research were actual scientists published in respected, peer-reviewed journals. As Kahneman and Tversky noted in this research, "It's not just that they should know the math, they *did* know the math." So even those who know the math default to their intuition and their intuition is wrong. Even for trained scientists, various recurring—but avoidable—mathematical errors are just one of the challenges of trying to do math in our heads.

So What? Does This Apply to Cybersecurity?

Even though all of this research is borrowed from fields outside of cybersecurity, the breadth of these findings in so many areas seems to demonstrate that they are fundamental and apply to any area of human judgment, including cybersecurity. But if the variety of findings in so many areas doesn't convince us that these same issues apply to cybersecurity, consider another argument made by Kahneman and another researcher in decision psychology, Gary Klein.

They point out three necessary conditions for experience to result in learning. First, there must be consistent feedback. The person must be given the information about past performance regularly, not rarely. Second, the feedback must be relatively immediate. If a person makes several forecasts for events that may happen years from now (which is often the case in a cost–benefit analysis for some new investment in, say, technology, infrastructure, or new products), the delay in the feedback will make learning more difficult. Third, the feedback should be unambiguous. If the person simply says a cybersecurity project will be a "success" or that risk will be reduced, that may be open to interpretation. And when our past performance is left to interpretation, we are likely to interpret data in a way that would be flattering to ourselves. Unless we get regular, immediate, and unambiguous feedback, we are likely to have selective memory and interpret our experiences in the most flattering way.

So the uncomfortable question cybersecurity risk analysts must ask themselves is this: Does the experience of the cybersecurity expert actually meet those requirements? Do cybersecurity experts actually *record* all their estimates of probability and impact, then compare them to observation? Even assuming they did that, how long would they typically have to wait before they learned if their estimate was correct? Even if estimates are recorded and we wait long enough for the event to occur, was it clear whether the original estimate was correct or the discrete event occurred or not? For example, if we say we lost reputation from a breach, how do we know that, and how did we actually validate—even approximately—the magnitude of the event as originally estimated? In cybersecurity, like many other fields, we cannot assume learning happens without deliberate processes to make sure that is the case. These findings are obvious to researchers like Meehl:

> The human brain is a relatively inefficient device for noticing, selecting, categorizing, recording, retaining, retrieving, and manipulating information for inferential purposes. Why should we be surprised at this?[19]

This does not mean that experts know very little about their fields. They have a lot of detailed technical knowledge. The performance of experts in the research mentioned so far relates only to the estimation of quantities based on subjective inferences of recalled experience. The problem is that experts often seem to conflate the knowledge of a vast set of details in their field with their skill at forecasting uncertain future events. A cybersecurity expert can become well versed in technical details such as conducting penetration tests, using encryption tools, setting up firewalls, and much more—and still be unable to realistically assess their own skills at forecasting future events.

Tools for Improving the Human Component

The research reviewed up to this point might make it look like there is little room for the expert in assessing risks. But we are not making that case at all. When we can make sound mathematical models based on objective observations and historical data, we should do that. But we acknowledge that there are several tasks still left to the expert. The expert is a component of risk analysis we cannot remove but we can improve.

The expert must help define the problem in the first place. He or she must assess situations where the data is ambiguous or where conditions do not fit neatly into existing statistical data. The expert also must propose the solutions that must be tested.

Our goal is actually to elevate the expert. We want to treat the cybersecurity expert as part of the risk assessment system. Like a race car or athlete, they need to be monitored and fine-tuned for maximum performance. The expert is really a type of measurement instrument that can be "calibrated" to improve its output.

It is also worth noting that none of the challenges we are about to list are unique to the cybersecurity profession, but that profession does have some characteristics that put it among a set of professions susceptible to "uncalibrated" judgment. Cybersecurity can borrow from other, very technical engineering fields reliant on expert judgment that have specific methods in place to track and calibrate the judgments of experts. The Nuclear Regulatory Commission (NRC), for example, recognizes the need for expert input during several steps in the risk assessment process. An NRC report on the use and elicitation of expert judgment stated the following:

> Expert judgments are both valid in their own right and comparable to other data. All data are imperfect representations of reality. The validity of expert judgment data, like any data, can vary based on the procedures used to collect it. So-called "hard" data, such as data taken from instruments, cannot be considered to be perfect because of problems such as random noise, equipment malfunction, operator interference, data selection, or data interpretation. The validity of all data varies. The validity of expert judgment depends heavily on the quality of the expert's cognitive representation of the domain and ability to express knowledge. The elicitation of expert judgment is a form of data collection that can be scrutinized; the use of the judgments can, and should, also be scrutinized.[20]

We agree. We must scrutinize the expert as we would any other measurement instrument. We consider the cybersecurity expert to be an essential and ultimately irreplaceable component of any risk analysis. Even as new data sources emerge that will allow even more quantitative analysis of risks, cybersecurity will continue to rely on cybersecurity experts for the foreseeable future. It is because of the key role trained experts will have that we need to take special notice of their performance at various critical tasks. And just as we would not rely on only a measurement instrument to measure its own accuracy, we cannot rely on the experts themselves to evaluate their own performance.

As we did earlier, we will begin by looking at existing research on the topic. We want to consider the tools that experts use and whether they actually help or harm the value of their judgment.

The Subjective Probability Component

A critical component of risk analysis is cybersecurity experts' assessment of the likelihoods of events, like cybersecurity breaches, and the potential costs if those events occur. Whether they are using explicit probabilities or nonquantitative verbal scales, they need to judge whether one kind of threat is more likely than another. Since we will probably have to rely on the expert at some level for this task, we need to consider how the experts' skill at this task can be measured and what those measurements show.

This is a well-documented field of research, occurring with experts and nonexperts in many different fields. Every study takes a similar approach. Large numbers of estimates are collected from individuals and then compared to observed outcomes. The findings are conclusive and repeated by every study that looks at this issue:

- Without training or other controls, almost all of us would assign probabilities that deviate significantly from observed outcomes (e.g., of all the times we say we are 90% confident, the predicted outcome happens much less frequently than 90%).
- There are methods, including training, that greatly improve the ability of experts to estimate subjective probabilities (e.g., when they say they are 90% confident, they turn out to be right about 90% of the time).

One example related to research in a different profession, that of corporate chief financial officer (CFO), illustrates the typical findings of these studies. Researchers in a 2010 study at the National Bureau of Economic Research asked CFOs to provide estimates of the annual returns on the S&P 500.[21] These estimates were in the form of ranges—given as a lower bound and an upper bound—of values that were wide enough that the CFO believed they had an 80% chance that the range would contain the correct answer. We can refer to these as 80% confidence intervals.[22] By simply waiting, it was easy to confirm what the actual return was over a given period of time. Although the CFOs were extremely experienced and well educated for their positions, their 80% CIs actually contained the true answers only 33% of the time. They believed that they provided ranges that would not contain the correct answer only 20% of the time, but in fact the answers were outside of their bounds 67% of the time. This is a rate of "surprise" much higher than they expected.

This is a measure of overconfidence. The confidence of experts, in this case expressed in the width of an 80% CI, contained the correct answer much less often than the experts expected. In other words, they did not have the 80% chance they thought they had of the stated interval containing the eventually observed value. Unfortunately, this phenomenon is not limited to CFOs. Several studies over the last several decades confirm that overconfidence is a pervasive characteristic of nearly all of us. Calibrated probability assessments have been an area of investigation since the 1970s by a large body of published research, led at first by Daniel Kahneman and Amos Tversky.[23] Their research showed that almost all people in many different professions are about as overconfident as the previously mentioned CFOs, regardless of their specific profession.

This research is not purely academic. It affects real-world judgments and affects actions taken to solve real problems. One of the authors (Hubbard) has had the opportunity over the last 20 years to collect one of the largest data sets regarding this phenomenon. Hubbard has tested and trained over 1,000 individuals from several different industries, professions, and levels of management. At least 54 of the subjects in these studies were specifically in the field of cybersecurity.

To measure how well experts assigned subjective probabilities, Hubbard gave them a series of tests similar to those in most other studies. In an initial benchmark test (conducted prior to any training meant to improve estimation skills), Hubbard would ask the participants their 90% CIs for estimates of general trivia knowledge (when was Isaac Newton born, how many meters tall is the world's tallest building, etc.). Most individuals provided ranges that only contained about 40% to 50% of the correct answers, similar to what the previously mentioned researchers had observed.[24]

Overconfidence is also observed when applying probabilities to discrete events—such as whether a cyberattack will result in a major data breach this year. Of course, the outcome of a single event is generally not a good indicator of how realistic a previously stated probability happens to be. If we say that an event is 25% likely to occur by the end of next year, whether it happens or not is not proof the probability was unrealistic. But if we track a number of experts making many probability assessments, then we can compare expectations to observations in a more valid manner.

Suppose, for example, a group of experts gives 1,000 estimates of probabilities of specifically defined events. These could be data breaches of a certain minimum size occurring during a defined period, the probability of loss greater than $10 million, and so on. Suppose for 100 of those estimates they said they were 90% certain of the outcome. Then the stated outcome should have happened about 90 out of 100 times. We would expect some variation just due to random luck, but we can compute (as we will show later) how much random error is acceptable. On the other hand, if they are right only 65 out of 100 times they said they were 90% confident, that result is a lot worse than what we would expect by just bad luck (if only bad luck were at play, there is only a 1 in 68.9 *billion* chance that they would be wrong that often). So the much more likely explanation would be that the experts are simply applying far too high a probability to events they should be less certain about.

Fortunately, other researchers have run experiments[25] showing that experts can be trained to be better at estimating probabilities by applying a battery of estimation tests, giving the experts a lot of quick, repetitive, clear feedback along with training in techniques for improving subjective probabilities. In short, researchers discovered that *assessing uncertainty is a general skill that can be taught with a measurable improvement.* That is, when calibrated cybersecurity experts say they are 85% confident that a major data breach will occur in their industry in the next 12 months, there really is an 85% chance it will occur.

Again, the breadth of different people that have been measured on this "component" includes not just CFOs but also physicians, students, scientists, project managers, and many more. So it is reasonable to say that these observations probably apply to everyone. Remember, just in case someone were to try to make the case that cybersecurity experts were different from all the other fields that have been measured, Hubbard's data does include 54 cybersecurity experts from many industries. They do about as poorly as any other profession in the first test. We also observe that they improve dramatically during the training, just like those in every other field Hubbard has tested, and about the same share succeed in becoming calibrated by the end of the training (85% to 90% of experts become calibrated).

In Chapter 7, we will describe this training and its effects in more detail. We will explain how you can calibrate yourself with some practice and how you can measure your performance over time. This skill will be a starting point for developing more advanced quantitative models.

The Expert Consistency Component

Ultimately, testing subjective probabilities for calibration relative to overconfidence means waiting for observed outcomes to materialize. But another type of calibration can be observed very quickly and easily without necessarily waiting for the predicted outcomes to happen or not: We can measure the consistency of the expert. That is, independent of whether the judgment was accurate, we should also expect the expert to give the same answer consistently when given the exact same situation. Of course, consistent answers do not mean the answers are any good, but we know that two contradictory answers cannot both be correct. The amount of inconsistency must be at least a lower bound for estimation error. In one extreme, if "experts" give wildly different answers every time they look at the exact same issue, then this would be indistinguishable from someone who ignores the information they are given and randomly picks estimates from slips of paper in a bowl. We don't have to wait for predicted events to occur in order to evaluate the consistency of that expert.

Likewise, even if researchers are perfectly consistent with their own previous judgments, but give very different answers than other experts, again, we at least know they can't all be right (of course they could all be wrong). Fortunately, these components of expert performance have also been measured at length. Researchers have given names to both of these measures of consistency:[26]

- Stability: an expert's agreement with their own previous judgment of the identical situation (same expert, same data, different time)
- Consensus: an expert's agreement with other experts (same data, different experts)

In every field tested so far, it has been observed that experts are highly inconsistent—both in stability and consensus—in virtually every area of judgment. This inconsistency applies whether it relates to project managers estimating costs, physicians diagnosing patients, or cybersecurity experts evaluating risks.

In an early twentieth century example of this expert consistency measurement, researchers gave several radiologists a stack of 96 X-rays of stomach ulcers.[27] Each radiologist was asked to judge whether the ulcer was a malignant tumor. A week later the same radiologists were given another set of 96 X-rays to assess. Unbeknownst to the radiologists, they were actually the same X-rays as before but in a different order. Researchers found that radiologists changed their answers 23% of the time.

If we ask an expert in such a situation whether the arbitrary order of the list should have any bearing on their judgments, they would all agree that it should not. And yet the research tells us that the arbitrary order of lists like this actually does affect their judgments.

A particular source of inconsistency appears in another common type of judgment. When estimating numbers, the expert can be influenced by an effect known as "anchoring." Simply thinking of one number affects the value of a subsequent estimate *even on a completely unrelated issue*. Researchers showed how using arbitrary values, such as one's Social Security number or a randomly generated number, affects subsequent estimates of, for instance, the number of doctors in an area or the price of things on eBay.[28,29]

Why shouldn't random, irrelevant factors like anchoring also affect the judgment of cybersecurity experts? We've had a lot of opportunity to gather information on that point, and a summary of this data follows:

- In multiple separate projects over the last five years, Hubbard and his staff asked 54 cybersecurity experts for the probabilities of various types of cybersecurity events. The projects were for clients from four different industries: oil and gas, banking, higher education, and healthcare. Each of these experts had previously completed calibrated probability-assessment training.
- Each expert was given some descriptive data for 80 to 200 different systems or threat scenarios in the organization. The types of scenarios and the data provided varied among the clients, but it could include information about the type of data at risk, the operating systems involved, types of existing controls, the types and numbers of users, and so on.
- For each of these systems or scenarios, each expert was asked to assess the probabilities of up to six different types of events including confidentiality breaches, unauthorized editing of data, unauthorized transfer of funds, theft of intellectual property, availability outages, and so on.
- In total, for the 54 experts assessing up to 6 probabilities for each of 80 to 200 situations—typically about 300 to 1,000 estimates per expert—we have more than 30,000 individual assessments of probabilities.

What the experts were not told at the time they were providing these estimates is that the list they were given included some duplicate pairs of scenarios. In other words, the data provided for the system in the ninth row of the list might be identical to the data provided in the ninety-fifth row, the eleventh might be the same as the eighty-first, and so on. Each expert had several duplicates in the list, totaling 2,428 duplicate pairs.

To measure inconsistency, we simply needed to compare the first estimate the expert provided with their second estimate for the identical scenario. Figure 4.1 shows how the first and second estimates of identical scenarios compare. To better display the concentration of a large number of points in the same locations of this chart, we added a bit of random noise around each point so that they don't all plot directly on top of one another. But the noise added is very small compared to the overall effect, and the noise is only for the display of this chart (it is not used in the statistical analysis of the results).

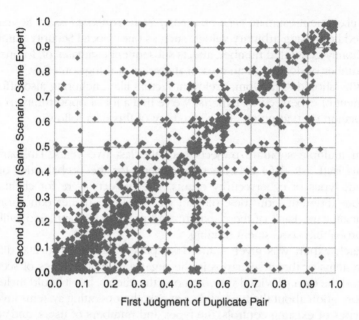

FIGURE 4.1 Duplicate Scenario Consistency: Comparison of First and Second Probability Estimates of Same Scenario by Same Judge

What we observe is that 26% of the time, there was a difference greater than 10 percentage points between the first and second estimate—for example, the first estimate was 15% and the second was 26%. Some differences were much more extreme. There were even 2.7% where the difference was greater than *50 percentage points.* See Figure 4.2 for a summary of these response inconsistencies.

As inconsistent as this may seem, it's actually worse than it looks. We have to compare this inconsistency to the "discrimination" of the expert. That is, how much do the experts' responses vary for a given type of event? The probabilities estimated varied substantially by the type of risk being assessed. For example, availability risk (a system going down) was generally given probabilities that were higher than an integrity risk where someone could actually steal funds with unauthorized transactions. If all of the responses of the expert only varied between, say, 2% and 15% for a given type of risk (say, the chance of a major data breach), then a 5 or 10 percentage point inconsistency would make up a large part of how much the judge varied their answers.

Consistency is partly a measure of how diligently the expert is considering each scenario. For some of the experts, the inconsistency accounted for most of the discrimination. Note that if inconsistency equaled discrimination, this

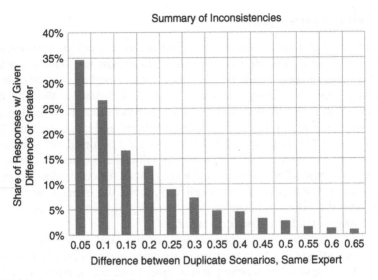

FIGURE 4.2 Summary of Distribution of Inconsistencies

would be what we would observe if an expert were just picking probabilities at random regardless of the information provided. In our surveys, most judges appeared to at least try to carefully consider the responses with the information provided. Still, *we see that inconsistency accounts for at least 21% of discrimination.* That is a significant portion of the expert's judgment reflecting nothing more than personal inconsistency.

We should note that a small percentage of the duplicates were discovered by the participants. Some would send an e-mail saying, "I think there is an error in your survey. These two rows are identical data." But nobody who found a duplicate found more than two, and most people discovered none. More importantly, the discovery of some duplicates by the estimators would only serve to reduce the observed inconsistency. The fact that they happened to notice some duplicates means that their consistency was measured to be higher than it otherwise would have been. In other words, inconsistency is *at least* as high as we show, not lower.

Fortunately, we can also show that this inconsistency can be reduced and this will result in improved estimates. We can statistically "smooth" the inconsistencies of experts using mathematical methods that reduce estimation error of experts. The authors have had the opportunity to apply these methods specifically in cybersecurity (the inconsistency data shown in Figure 4.1 were from real-world projects where we applied these methods). We will describe these methods in more detail later in the book.

The Collaboration Component

We just saw that there is a lot of data about aspects of subjective expert judgment, but there is also interesting research about how to *combine* the judgments of many experts. Perhaps the most common method of combining expert judgments is sometimes referred to in the U.S. military as the "BOGSAT" method—that is, the "Bunch of Guys Sitting Around Talking" method (excuse the gender specificity). The experts meet in a room and talk about how likely an event would be, or what its impact would be if it occurred, until they reach a consensus (or at least until remaining objections have quieted down).

We can apply different mathematical methods for combining judgments and different ways to allow for interaction among the experts. So, as we've done with the other component tests, we ask whether some methods are shown to measurably outperform others.

Some research, for example, shows that the random stability inconsistencies of individuals can be reduced *by simply averaging several individuals together.*[30] Instead of meeting in the same room and attempting to reach consensus as a group, each expert produces their own estimate independently, and their estimates are averaged together.

This approach and some of the research behind it were explained in the book *The Wisdom of Crowds* by James Surowiecki.[31] Surowiecki also described several other collaboration methods, such as "prediction markets,"[32] which show a measurable improvement over the estimates of individual experts.

The same data that allowed Hubbard Decision Research to measure expert stability was also able to measure consensus. If judges were simply personally inconsistent—that is, they had low stability—we would expect disagreements between judges solely due to random personal inconsistency. However, the actual total disagreement between experts was more than could be accounted for by stability alone. In addition to being personally inconsistent, experts in the same organization also had systemic disagreements with each other about the importance of various factors and the overall risk of cybersecurity attacks.

It is interesting to note, however, that cybersecurity experts at a particular organization provided responses that were well correlated with their peers at the same organization. One expert may have estimated the probability of an event to be consistently higher than their peers, but the same information that caused them to increase or decrease a probability also had the same effect on other experts. At least they were more or less in agreement "directionally." So we do not observe that different experts behave as if they were just randomly picking answers. They agree with each other to some degree and, as the previous research shows, they can predict outcomes better if we can average several experts together.

The Decomposition Component

We have already seen that experts don't perform as well as statistical models based on objective, historical data. But what about quantitative models that are still based on subjective estimates? Is it possible for experts to build models, using only their current knowledge, that outperform how they would have done without the quantitative models? The research says yes.

From the 1970s to the 1990s, decision science researchers Donald G. MacGregor and J. Scott Armstrong, both separately and together, conducted experiments about how much estimates can be improved by decomposition.[33] For their various experiments, they recruited hundreds of subjects to evaluate the difficulty of estimates like the circumference of a given coin or the number of pairs of men's pants made in the United States per year. Some of the subjects were asked to directly estimate these quantities, while a second group was instead asked to estimate decomposed variables, which were then used to estimate the original quantity. For example, for the question about pants, the second group would estimate the U.S. population of men, the number of pairs of pants men buy per year, the percentage of pants made overseas, and so on. Then the first group's estimate (made without the benefit of decomposition) was compared to that of the second group.

Armstrong and MacGregor found that decomposition didn't help much if the estimates of the first group already had relatively little error—like estimating the circumference of a U.S. 50-cent coin in inches. But where the error of the first group was high—as they were with estimates for men's pants manufactured in the United States, or the total number of auto accidents per year—then decomposition was a huge benefit. They found that for the most uncertain variables, a simple decomposition—none of which was more than five variables—*reduced error by a factor of as much as 10 or even 100*. Imagine if this were a real-world decision with big uncertainties. Decomposition itself is certainly worth the time.

Doing the math explicitly, even if the inputs themselves were subjective estimates, removes a source of error. If we want to estimate the monetary impact of a denial of service attack on a given system, we can estimate the duration, the number of people affected, and the cost per unit of time per person affected. Once we have these estimates, however, we shouldn't then just *estimate* the product of these values—we should *compute* the product. Since, as we have shown earlier, we tend to make several errors of intuition around such calculations, we would be better off just doing the math in plain sight. It seemed obvious to many of the researchers that we are better off doing whatever math we would have done in our heads explicitly. As Meehl mentioned in one of his papers:

> Surely we all know that the human brain is poor at weighting and computing. When you check out at a supermarket, you don't eyeball the heap of purchases and say to the clerk, "Well it looks to me as if it's about $17.00 worth; what do you think?" The clerk adds it up.[34]

But not all decompositions are as informative. It is possible to "over-decompose" a problem.[35] The reason we decompose is that we have less uncertainty about some things than we do others, but we can compute the latter based on the former. If, however, we do not have less uncertainty about the variables we decompose the problem into, then we may not be gaining ground. In fact, a bad decomposition could make things worse. In Chapter 6, we will discuss what we call "uninformative decompositions" in more detail.

Even assuming your decompositions are useful to you, there are several decomposition strategies to choose from, and we will start with no particular position about which of these decompositions are more informative. The best decomposition method may vary from one organization to the next as the information they have varies. But, as we will see in Chapter 6, there are some hard mathematical rules about whether a decomposition actually reduces uncertainty. We should use these rules as well as empirically measured performance to determine the best method of decomposition for a given organization.

Summary and Next Steps

"In my experience . . ." is generally the start of a sentence that should be considered with caution, especially when applied to evaluating the expert themselves. There are reasons why our experiences, even when they add up to many decades, may not be a trustworthy source of information on some topics. Because of the analysis placebo, we cannot evaluate ourselves in estimation tasks simply by whether we feel better about it. Evaluating experts and the methods they use will require that we look at the scientific research behind them. And the research clearly points to the following conclusions:

1. Wherever possible, explicit, quantitative models based on objective historical data are preferred. The role of experts primarily would be to design and set up these models instead of being responsible for individual estimates.

2. Where we need to estimate probabilities and other quantities, experts can be trained to provide subjective probabilities that can be compared to observed reality.
3. The inconsistency of experts can be moderated with mathematical and collaborative methods to get an improvement in estimates. When using multiple experts, even simple averages of experts appear to be an improvement over individual experts.
4. Decomposition improves estimates, especially when faced with very high uncertainty. Models that force calculations to be explicit instead of "in the head" of the expert avoid many of the inference errors that experts tend to make.

In this chapter, our measurements of different risk assessment methods have focused on previously published scientific research into individual components of risk assessment processes, including alternative tools for estimating probabilities (using experts or algorithms), how to control for inconsistencies, how to collaborate, and the effects of decomposition. We have focused entirely on components where we have research showing how alternative methods measurably improve results.

Every component of the methods we introduced in Chapter 3, and everything we introduce from this point forward, will be guided by this research. We are adopting no method component that doesn't have some research supporting it; just as importantly, we are adopting no methods that have been shown to add error. The importance of cybersecurity risk assessment means that we must continue to seek improvements in our methods. We must persist in the kind of skepticism that forces us to ask, "How do I know this works?"

Later, we will describe how to go beyond existing research to track your own data in a statistically sound manner that can further reduce uncertainty and allow you to continuously improve your risk assessment methods. In the next chapter we will continue with a component-level analysis based on existing research, but we will focus on those methods that either show no improvement—or even make things worse. We need to do this because these components are actually part of the most widely used methods and standards in cybersecurity. So it is time we addressed these issues head on, along with responding to common objections to using the quantitative methods we just recommended.

Notes

1. C. Tsai, J. Klayman, and R. Hastie, "Effects of Amount of Information on Judgment Accuracy and Confidence," *Organizational Behavior and Human Decision Processes* 107, no. 2 (2008): 97–105.

2. Stuart Oskamp, "Overconfidence in Case-Study Judgments," *Journal of Consulting Psychology* 29, no. 3 (1965): 261–265, doi:10.1037/h0022125. Reprinted in *Judgment under Uncertainty: Heuristics and Biases*, ed. Daniel Kahneman, Paul Slovic, and Amos Tversky (Cambridge, UK: Cambridge University Press, 1982).

3. P. Andreassen, "Judgmental Extrapolation and Market Overreaction: On the Use and Disuse of News," *Journal of Behavioral Decision Making* 3, no. 3 (July–September 1990): 153–174.

4. C. Heath and R. Gonzalez, "Interaction with Others Increases Decision Confidence but Not Decision Quality: Evidence against Information Collection Views of Interactive Decision Making," *Organizational Behavior and Human Decision Processes* 61, no. 3 (1995): 305–326.

5. D. A. Seaver, "Assessing Probability with Multiple Individuals: Group Interaction versus Mathematical Aggregation," Report No. 78–3 (Los Angeles: Social Science Research Institute, University of Southern California, 1978).

6. S. Kassin and C. Fong, "I'm Innocent!: Effects of Training on Judgments of Truth and Deception in the Interrogation Room," *Law and Human Behavior* 23 (1999): 499–516.

7. Paul E. Meehl, *Clinical versus Statistical Prediction; A Theoretical Analysis and a Review of the Evidence* (Minneapolis: University of Minnesota Press, 1954).

8. R. M. Dawes, D. Faust, and P. E. Meehl, "Clinical versus Actuarial Judgment," *Science* (1989), doi:10.1126/science.2648573.

9. William M. Grove and Paul E. Meehl, "Comparative Efficiency of Informal (Subjective, Impressionistic) and Formal (Mechanical, Algorithmic) Prediction Procedures: The Clinical-Statistical Controversy," *Psychology, Public Policy, and Law* 2 (1996): 293–323.

10. William M. Grove et al., "Clinical versus Mechanical Prediction: A Meta-Analysis," *Psychological Assessment* 12, no. 1 (2000): 19–30.

11. Paul Meehl, "Causes and Effects of My Disturbing Little Book," *Journal of Personality Assessment* 50 (1986): 370–375.

12. William Bailey et al., "Taking Calculated Risks," *Oilfield Review* 12, no. 3 (Autumn 2000): 20–35.

13. G. S. Simpson et al., "The Application of Probabilistic and Qualitative Methods to Asset Management Decision Making," presented at SPE Asia Pacific Conference on Integrated Modelling for Asset Management, April, 25–26, 2000, Yokohama, Japan.

14. C. W. Freaner et al., "An Assessment of the Inherent Optimism in Early Conceptual Designs and Its Effect on Cost and Schedule Growth." Paper presented at the Space Systems Cost Analysis Group/Cost Analysis and Forecasting/European Aerospace Cost Engineering Working Group 2008 Joint International Conference, European Space Research

and Technology Centre, Noordwijk, The Netherlands, May 15–16, 2008, European Space Agency, Paris, France.

15. Philip E. Tetlock, *Expert Political Judgment: How Good Is It? How Can We Know?* (Princeton, NJ: Princeton University Press, 2005; Kindle edition, location 869).

16. Robyn Dawes, *House of Cards: Psychology and Psychotherapy Built on Myth* (New York: Simon & Schuster, 1996).

17. Amos Tversky and Daniel Kahneman, "Belief in the Law of Small Numbers," *Psychological Bulletin* 76, no. 2 (1971): 105–110.

18. Daniel Kahneman and Amos Tversky, "Subjective Probability: A Judgment of Representativeness," *Cognitive Psychology* 3 (1972): 430–454.

19. William M. Grove and Paul E. Meehl, "Comparative Efficiency of Informal (Subjective, Impressionistic) and Formal (Mechanical, Algorithmic) Prediction Procedures: The Clinical–Statistical Controversy," *Psychology, Public Policy, and Law* 2 (1996), 293–323; #167.

20. Herren DeWispelare and Clemen Bonano, "Background Report on the Use and Elicitation of Expert Judgement," prepared for Center for Nuclear Waste Regulatory Analyses under Contract NRC-02–93–005, September 1994.

21. I. Ben-David, J. R. Graham, and C. R. Harvey, *Managerial Miscalibration* (No. w16215) (Washington, DC: National Bureau of Economic Research, 2010).

22. Some authors would prefer that we distinguish a confidence interval computed from data from a subjectively estimated interval. They may use the terms "subjective confidence interval" or "a credible interval" for finer distinctions. We, however, will use the term "confidence interval" as an expression of uncertainty, whether that uncertainty is derived from expert opinion or from analysis of objective data.

23. D. Kahneman and A. Tversky, "Subjective Probability: A Judgment of Representativeness," *Cognitive Psychology* 4 (1972): 430–454; D. Kahneman and A. Tversky, "On the Psychology of Prediction," *Psychological Review* 80 (1973): 237–251.

24. This benchmark is based on only a sample size of 10 per person. Ten may sound like a small test to begin with, but if a person were well calibrated—such that there was actually a 90% chance that the correct value would fall within the stated ranges—there is only a 1 in 611 chance of getting 5 or fewer out of 10 questions with the answers in the stated range. In other words, the sample size is more than sufficient to detect the level of overconfidence that most professionals have.

25. Sarah Lichtenstein, Baruch Fischhoff, and Lawrence D. Phillips, "Calibration of Probabilities: The State of the Art to 1980," in *Judgement under Uncertainty: Heuristics and Biases*, ed. Daniel Kahneman, Paul Slovic, and Amos Tversky (Cambridge, UK: Cambridge University Press, 1982).

26. L. Goldberg, "Simple Models or Simple Processes?: Some Research on Clinical Judgments," *American Psychologist* 23, no. 7 (July 1968).

27. Paul J. Hoffman, Paul Slovic, and Leonard G. Rorer, "An Analysis-of-Variance Model for the Assessment of Configural Cue Utilization in Clinical Judgment," *Psychological Bulletin* 69, no. 5 (1968): 338.

28. Amos Tversky and Daniel Kahneman, "Judgment under Uncertainty: Heuristics and Biases," *Science* 185, no. 4157 (1974): 1124–1131.

29. D. Ariely et al., "Coherent Arbitrariness: Stable Demand Curves without Stable Preferences," *The Quarterly Journal of Economics* 118, no. 1 (2003): 73–106.

30. R. Clemen and R. Winkler, "Combining Probability Distributions from Experts in Risk Analysis," *Risk Analysis* 19 (1999): 187–203.

31. James Surowiecki, *The Wisdom of Crowds* (New York: Anchor, 2005).

32. In prediction markets, a large number of people can bid on a kind of coupon that pays off if a particular defined event occurs. The market price of the coupon reflects a kind of estimate of the event coming true, whether it is who will be the next U.S. President or who wins the Oscars or World Cup. If the coupon pays one dollar if and when the event comes true and the current market price is 25 cents, then the market is behaving as if it believes the event has approximately a 25% chance of coming true. There are practical constraints on using something like this in cybersecurity (someone may be able to rig the market by bidding on coupons for an event they later cause themselves). But it shows how some forms of collaboration may outperform others.

33. Donald G. MacGregor and J. Scott Armstrong, "Judgmental Decomposition: When Does It Work?" *International Journal of Forecasting* 10, no. 4 (1994): 495–506.

34. Paul Meehl, "Causes and Effects of My Disturbing Little Book," *Journal of Personality Assessment* 50 (1986): 370–375.

35. Michael Burns and Judea Pearl, "Causal and Diagnostic Inferences: A Comparison of Validity," *Organizational Behavior and Human Performance* 28, no. 3 (1981): 379–394.

CHAPTER 5

Risk Matrices, Lie Factors, Misconceptions, and Other Obstacles to Measuring Risk

We are ultimately trying to move cybersecurity in the direction of more quantitative risk assessment methods. The previous chapters showed that there are several methods that are both practical (the authors have used these methods in actual cybersecurity environments) and have evidence of measurably improving risk assessments. We offered an extremely simple method based on a one-for-one substitution of the components of a risk matrix. Anyone who has the technical skills to work in cybersecurity certainly has the skills to implement that solution. Once an analyst becomes familiar with the basics, he or she can build on the foundation we've provided with our methods in later chapters.

But regardless of the evidence shown so far, we expect to see resistance to many of the concepts shown. There will be sacred cows, red herrings, black swans, and a few other zoologically-themed metaphors related to arguments against the use of quantitative methods. In this chapter we will address each of these issues. We have to warn you in advance: This case will be tedious. This chapter is long and it will often feel like we are belaboring a point beyond what it deserves. But we need to systematically address each of these arguments and thoroughly make our case in a manner as airtight as the evidence allows.

Scanning the Landscape: A Survey of Cybersecurity Professionals

In preparation for making this comprehensive case, we wanted to understand something about the backgrounds and opinions that the cybersecurity industry had about many of the points we are making. We wanted to know the level of acceptance of current methods and perceptions about quantitative methods. So, we asked 171 cybersecurity specialists from a variety of backgrounds and industries to answer some questions about statistics and the use of quantitative methods in cybersecurity. Survey participants were recruited from multiple information security related groups including the Society for Information Risk Assessment (SIRA), ISACA, and three of the largest discussion groups on LinkedIn. There were a total of 63 questions covering topics such as personal background, their organizations, and breaches experienced. The survey also included questions related to the use of quantitative methods in cybersecurity and a quiz containing basic statistics-literacy questions.

Part of the survey contained a set of 18 questions we referred to as Attitudes Toward Quantitative Methods (ATQM). These helped us assess the opinions of cybersecurity experts as being more supportive of the use of quantitative methods or more skeptical. Within the ATQM, we had two subsets. Some of the questions (7 to be exact) had responses that were clearly more "anti-quantitative," such as, "Information security is too complex to model with quantitative methods." These questions made much sharper distinctions between supporters and opponents of quantitative methods. Other questions were about attitudes that were not directly anti-quantitative but indicated an acceptance of the value of nonquantitative methods—for example, "Ordinal scales help develop consensus for action." Table 5.1 shows a few examples from each group of ATQM questions.

TABLE 5.1 Selected Examples of Survey Questions About Attitudes Toward Quantitative Methods

Statement from Survey	Percent Agreeing (Positive Responses/Number Responding)
Ordinal scales must be used because probabilistic methods are not possible in cybersecurity.	18% (28/154)
Probabilistic methods are impractical because probabilities need exact data to be computed and we don't have exact data.	23% (37/158)
Quantitative methods don't apply in situations where there are human agents who act unpredictably.	12% (19/158)
Commonly used ordinal scales help us develop consensus for action.	64% (99/154)

We found it encouraging that most who work in cybersecurity (86%) are generally accepting of more quantitative methods based on probabilistic models; that is, they answered more of the "opinions about quantitative methods" in a way that supported quantitative methods. For example, most (75%) agreed with the statement "Cybersecurity should eventually adopt a more sophisticated probabilistic approach based on actuarial methods where it has not already done so."

However, only 32% were always supportive of quantitative methods (i.e., 68% disagreed with some of the statements preferring quantitative methods to softer methods). Even those who support more quantitative methods see value in the continued use of softer methods. For example, 64% agreed with the statement "Commonly used ordinal scales help us develop consensus for action" and 61% stated that they use risk matrices. There is even a small but significant minority (8.3%) who tended to be more anti-quantitative than pro-quantitative. This is a concern because vocal minorities can at least slow an adoption of quantitative methods (the authors have seen some cases of this). And even the majority who are generally accepting of quantitative may be slow to adopt better methods only because it seems a bit too challenging to change or because current methods are perceived as adequate even if flawed.

Of course, any survey that relies on voluntary responses could have a selection bias but it would not be clear whether such a selection bias would be more "pro-" or "anti-" quantitative. Still, the level of acceptance of quantitative methods was on the high end of what we expected. Some readers may already question the methods, sample size, and so on but the statistical significance—and the academic research credentials of the Hubbard Decision Research staff who analyzed the results—will be discussed shortly.

If you personally have reservations about moving cybersecurity risk assessment in the direction of quantitative methods, see if your specific reservation is discussed in this chapter and consider the counterargument. If you are a fan of quantitative methods and we are preaching to the choir, then familiarize yourself with this chapter so that you might be better able to respond to these objections when you hear them.

At first glance, the arguments against the use of quantitative methods seem to be many and varied, but we make the case that these points all boil down to a few basic types of fallacies. We will start by investigating a collection of methods that are currently the most popular in cybersecurity risk assessments: the ordinal scales on a risk matrix. Once we can shine a light on the problems with these techniques and objections, we hope we can move past this to implement mathematically sound risk assessment in a field that needs it badly.

What Color Is Your Risk? The Ubiquitous—and Risky—Risk Matrix

Any cybersecurity expert will recognize and likely embrace the common risk matrix, which is based on ordinal scales. In fact, based on our experience, most executives will laud the risk matrix as "best practice." As mentioned in Chapter 1, these scales represent both likelihood and impact, not in probabilistic or monetary terms, but in ordinal scales. The scales might be represented with labels such as low, medium, or high, or they might be represented as numbers on a scale of, say, 1 to 5. For example, a likelihood and impact might be represented as a 3 and a 4, respectively, and the resulting risk might be categorized as "medium." These scales are then usually plotted onto a two-dimensional matrix where the regions of the matrix are further categorized into "low" to "high" risk or perhaps given colors ("green" is low risk, while "red" is high). In some cases ordinal scales are used without a risk matrix. Perhaps several ordinal scales are added together in an overall risk score, as is the case with OWASP's risk rating methodology.[1] (Note: OWASP, like many frameworks, has great controls recommendations, but a controls checklist does not equate to a risk management methodology). The scales focus on attributes that might indicate risk (such as "ease of discovery" or "regulatory impact"). Then these scores are categorized still further into high, medium, and low risk just like a risk matrix.

As mentioned in Chapter 2, ordinal scales are not in themselves necessarily a violation of measurement theory or statistics. They do have legitimate applications. But are they substitutions for ratio scales of probability and impact? Meaning, are they some form of vague stand-in for probabilities, as have already been used in insurance, decision science, statistics, and many other areas? Should substituting ordinal scales like "high" or "medium" for more quantitative measures strike us as just as odd as an engineer saying the mass of a component on an airplane is "medium," or an accountant reporting that revenue was "high" or a "4" on a scale of 5?

These are important questions because risk matrices using ordinal scales to represent likelihood and impact are common in cybersecurity. In the survey we found that 61% of organizations use some form of the risk matrix, and 79% use ordinal scales to assess and communicate risks. Even partial use of some of the statistical methods, for which we provided so much evidence of their effectiveness in Chapter 4, are much less common. For example, only 13% of respondents say they use Monte Carlo simulations, and 14% say they use some form of Bayesian methods (although both of these are actually much more common responses than the authors expected).

Some form of these ordinal scales are promoted by just about every standards organization, consulting group, and security technology vendor that covers cybersecurity. Dozens if not hundreds of firms help organizations implement methods or software tools that utilize some form of scores and risk matrices. The International Organization for Standardization (ISO) standard 31010, states that the risk map (what Table A.1 of the standard refers to as a "consequency/probability matrix"), is "strongly applicable" for risk identification.[2]

Clearly, these methods are deeply intertwined in the ecosystem of cybersecurity. However, as widely used as these scales are in cybersecurity, *there is not a single study indicating that the use of such methods actually helps reduce risk.* Nor is there even a study that merely shows that individual judgment is improved in any way over expert intuition alone. Granted, there are a lot of advocates of such methods. But advocates, no matter how vocal, should be considered cautiously given the research about the possibility of analysis placebo effects mentioned in Chapter 4.

On the other hand, several studies show that the types of scales used in these risk matrices can make the judgment of an expert worse by introducing sources of error that did not exist in the experts' intuition alone. In fact, we believe that these methods are like throwing rocket fuel on a fire. We have enough uncertainty in battling hard-to-detect threats; why make it worse by abstracting away data through questionable scales?

In the book *The Failure of Risk Management*, Hubbard spends an entire chapter reviewing the research about the problems with scores. Subsequent editions of his book *How to Measure Anything* added more sources as new studies finding problems with these scales were identified. To help make this issue clear we will use the same approach used in Chapter 4. That is, we will look at research regarding three key components of the issue:

- *The Psychology of Scales*: The psychological research behind how we use verbal scales such as "unlikely" to "likely" to evaluate the likelihood of an event, and how arbitrary features of verbal or numeric (e.g., 1–5) ordinal scales affect our choices.
- *Math and the Risk Matrix*: The mathematical problems associated with attempting to do math with ordinal scales or presenting them on a risk matrix.
- *How These Issues Combine*: Each of the two issues above is bad enough but we will show some research that shows what happens when we consider these effects together.

The Psychology of Scales and the Illusion of Communication

Ordinal scales are widely used because of their simplicity, but the psychology of how they are actually used is not quite so simple. The human expert using a scale has to be thought of as a kind of instrument. The instrument can have surprising behaviors and the conditions that elicit these behaviors should be investigated. As we did in earlier component analysis, we resort to research in other fields when research in cybersecurity specifically is lacking.

One component of risk scales that has been researched is how we use words to describe likelihoods. Researchers like the psychologist David Budescu published findings about how differently people will interpret terms that are meant to convey likelihood such as "unlikely" or "extremely likely." This ambiguity obviously would allow for at least some different interpretations, but Budescu wondered how varied those interpretations might be. He had subjects in his experiment read phrases from the Intergovernmental Policy on Climate Change (IPCC) report. Budescu would give his survey subjects a phrase from the IPCC report, which included one of seven probability categories (e.g., "It is very likely that hot extremes, heat waves, and heavy precipitation events will continue to become more frequent"). Budescu found that individuals varied greatly by how much they interpreted the probability implied by the phrase. For example, Budescu finds that "Very Likely" could mean anything from 43% to 99%, and "Unlikely" could mean as low as 8% or as high as 66% depending on who you ask.[3]

The subjects in Budescu's study were 223 students and faculty of the University of Illinois, not professionals charged with interpreting that kind of research. So we might wonder if these findings would not apply to an audience that is more skilled in the topic areas. Fortunately, there is also supporting research in the field of intelligence analysis—a field cybersecurity analysts might appreciate as being more relevant to their profession. In *Psychology of Intelligence Analysis,* a declassified 1999 CIA paper, veteran CIA analyst Richards J. Heuer, Jr. asked 23 NATO officers to evaluate similar probability statements.[4] Similar to what Budescu found for "Very Likely," Heuer found that the phrase "Highly Likely" evoked interpretations ranging from 50% to nearly 100%. Likewise, Heuer's findings for "Unlikely" were not inconsistent with Budescu's, since the responses varied from 5% to 35%. Figure 5.1 shows the range of responses in Heuer's study.

In our survey, 28% of cybersecurity professionals reported that they use verbal or ordinal scales where the probability they are meant to represent is not even defined. However, some scale users attempt to manage this ambiguity by offering specific definitions for each phase. For example, "Very Unlikely" can be defined as a probability of less than 10%. (In fact, this is what NIST 800–30 does).[5] In our survey, 63% of respondents who use ordinal scales indicated that they use verbal or numbered ordinal scales where the probabilities are defined in this way. However, Budescu finds that offering these definitions doesn't help, either.

Even in situations where each of the verbal scales was assigned specific probability ranges (e.g., "Very Likely" was defined as "Greater than 90%"

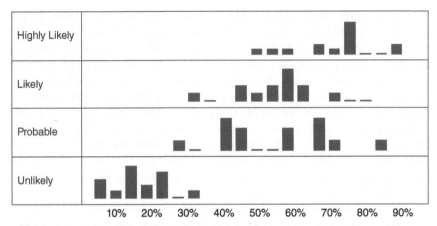

FIGURE 5.1 Variations of NATO Officers' Interpretations of Probability Phrases
Source: Heuer, *Psychology of Intelligence Analysis,* 1999.

and "Very Unlikely" was defined as "Less than 10%"), these rules were violated over half the time. In other words, even when participants were told exactly what the terms meant, they interpreted the terms in the context of the statement they were presented in. In that way, the phrase "Very Likely" meant something different to the subjects when it was in the context of temperature extremes, glaciers melting, or sea level rise.

Table 5.2 shows how widely the subjects in Budescu's study interpreted these verbal scales even when they were given specific directions regarding what they meant. It appears that about half of respondents ignored the guidelines (perhaps the term "guideline" itself invited too much interpretation).

TABLE 5.2 Variance in Understanding Selected Common Terms Used to Express Uncertainty in the IPCC Report

Examples of Some Likelihood Terms Used in the Report	IPCC Guidelines for Meaning	Minimum of All Responses	Maximum of All Responses	Percentage of Responses That Violated Guidelines
Very Likely	More than 90%	43%	99%	58%
Likely	Between 66% to 90%	45%	84%	46%
Unlikely	Between 10% and 33%	8%	66%	43%
Very Unlikely	Less than 10%	3%	75%	67%

Source: David V. Budescu, Stephen Broomell, and Han-Hui Por, University of Illinois at Urbana-Champaign.

Some of the more extreme results beg for further explanation. In the case of "very unlikely" we see a remarkable range of 3% to 75%. The 75% isn't just a single outlier, either, since two-thirds of the respondents violated the guideline (meaning they interpreted it to mean something greater than 10%). How could this be? Budescu found very little relationship between the subjects' probability interpretations and their predisposition on climate research (i.e., they did not simply put higher probabilities on events if they indicated more concern about climate research). But he did point out that the ambiguity of some of the statements might have had some bearing on responses. If the statement was about the likelihood of "heat extremes," the user may have included uncertainty about the meaning of "heat extremes" when they assessed a probability.

Hubbard has another potential explanation. Anecdotally, he has observed conversations about risks with clients where something was judged "highly likely" in part because of the impact it would have. Of course, impact and likelihood are supposed to be judged separately, but managers and analysts have been heard making statements like "A 10% chance per year is far too high for such a big event, so I think of 10% as highly likely." This is purely anecdotal, of course, and we don't rely on these sorts of observations—the data from Budescu and Heuer is sufficient to detect the problem. But in terms of potential explanations, the fact that such statements have been observed at least introduces a possibility: Some users of these terms are attempting to combine likelihood, impact, and their own aversion to risk in highly ad hoc ways. These users require methods that unpack these distinct concepts.

Furthermore, to adequately define a probability of an event, we can't exclude the time period it is meant to cover. If, for example, we say that an event is 10% likely, do we mean there is a 10% chance of it happening sometime next year or sometime in the next decade? Obviously, these would be very different estimates. How is it that management or analysts could come to agree on these points when they haven't even specified such a basic unit of measure in risk?

All these factors together combine to create what Budescu refers to as the "illusion of communication." Individuals may believe they are communicating risks when they have very different understandings of what is being said. They may believe they have come to an agreement when they all say that some risk is "medium" and another is "high." And even when specific numbers are presented for probabilities, the listener or the presenter may conflate their own risk tolerance with the assessment of probability, or they may be assuming that the probability is for an event over a longer time period than someone else is assuming it to be.

So far we have only discussed the psychology of how people interpret ambiguous terminology in regard to risk, but that is not the end of it.

Separate from the use of nonquantitative labels for probabilities or the consequences of other ambiguities, there are some curious human behaviors that arise in their responses to subjective ordinal scales in general. Relatively arbitrary features of the scale have a much larger effect on judgment than the users would expect.

For example, Professor Craig Fox of UCLA conducted studies showing that arbitrary features of how scales are partitioned have unexpected effects on responses, regardless of how precisely individual values are defined.[6] On a scale of 1 to 5, the value of "1" will be chosen more often than if it were a scale of 1 to 10, even if "1" is defined identically in both (e.g., "1" could mean an outage duration of less than 10 minutes or a breach resulting in less than $100,000 in losses). In addition, there is plenty of research showing how other arbitrary features of scales affect response behavior in ways that are unexpected and larger than you might think. These include whether ordinal numbers are provided in addition to verbal scales or instead of them,[7] or how the direction of the scale (5 is high or 5 is low) affects responses.[8]

Issues like these are fairly standard considerations in the field of psychometrics and survey design. Surveys are designed with various sorts of controls and item testing so that the effects of some biases can be estimated. These are referred to as "artifacts" of the survey and can then be ignored when drawing conclusions from it. But we see no evidence that any of these considerations are ever entertained in the development of risk scales. We need to consider the psychology of how we assess risks and how we use these tools. It cannot be taken for granted.

> *Intelligence analysts should be self-conscious about their reasoning process. They should think about how they make judgments and reach conclusions, not just about the judgments and conclusions themselves.*
>
> —Richards J. Heuer Jr., *Psychology of Intelligence Analysis*

How the Risk Matrix Doesn't Add Up

At first glance, the math behind a risk score or risk matrix could hardly be simpler. But, as with the psychology of scales, further investigation reveals new concerns. This may seem like a bit of esoterica, but, just as with every other component of risk analysis, the scale of the problem means we shouldn't leave such a widely used tool unexamined.

Perhaps nobody has spent more time on this topic than Tony Cox, PhD, an MIT-trained risk expert. He has written extensively about the problems that ordinal scales introduce in risk assessment and how those scales are then converted into a risk matrix (which is then often converted into regions of "low" to "high" risk). He investigates all the less-than-obvious consequences of various forms of ordinal scales and risk matrices and how they can lead to decision-making error.[9]

One such error is what he refers to as "range compression." Range compression is a sort of extreme rounding error introduced by how continuous values like probability and impact are reduced to a single ordinal value. No matter how the buckets of continuous quantities are partitioned into ordinal values, choices have to be made that undermine the value of the exercise. For example, the upper end of impact may be defined as "losses of $10 million or more" so that $10 million and $100 million are in the same bucket. To adjust for this, either the $10 million must be increased—which means the ranges in the lower categories also must be widened—or the number of categories must be increased.

Range compression is further exacerbated when two ordinal scales are combined onto a matrix. Cox shows how this can result in two very different risks being plotted in the same cell (i.e., the position at a given row and column in a matrix) and how a higher-risk cell can contain a risk that is lower than a risk in a low-risk cell. To see this, consider the risk matrix shown in Table 5.3. It is drawn from an actual risk matrix example promoted by a major consulting organization.

First, let's look at how two very different risks can end up in the same cell. We'll plot two risks in the "Seldom" likelihood category, which ranges from "greater than 1% and up to 25%" to the maximum loss category, "$10 million or more." The two risks are:

- Risk A: likelihood is 2%, impact is $10 million
- Risk B: likelihood is 20%, impact is $100 million

TABLE 5.3 Risk Matrix Example to Illustrate Range Compression Problems

			Impact				
			Negligible	Minor	Moderate	Critical	Catastrophic
			<$10K	$10K to <$100K	$100K to <$1 Million	$1 Million to <$10 Million	≥$10 Million
Likelihood	Frequent	99%+	Medium	Medium	High	High	High
	Likely	>50%–99%	Medium	Medium	Medium	High	High
	Occasional	>25%–50%	Low	Medium	Medium	Medium	High
	Seldom	>1%–25%	Low	Low	Medium	Medium	Medium
	Improbable	≤1%	Low	Low	Low	Medium	Medium

With this information Cox computes the "expected loss" (probability weighted loss), just as an actuary would do for many types of risks. He compares the products of the likelihoods and impacts of the risks: $200,000 for Risk A (2% × $10 million) and $20 million for Risk B (20% × $100 million). In other words, to an actuary, Risk B would be considered to have *100 times* the risk of Risk A. Yet these two very different risks would actually be plotted in the same cell (that is, same row, same column) on a risk matrix!

Next, let's look at how Cox shows that two very different risks can be plotted in cells that are the opposite order by expected loss. Again, this relies on the fact that in order to map continuous values with wide ranges to discrete bins, some "bins" on the likelihood and impact axes have to contain wide ranges of values. Here are another two risks:

- Risk A: Likelihood is 50%, impact is $9 million
- Risk B: Likelihood is 60%, impact is $2 million

In this case, Risk A has an expected loss of $4.5 million and Risk B has an expected loss of $1.2 million. Yet, if we followed the rules of this matrix, Risk B is considered a "High" risk and Risk A is only "Medium." Cox says that these properties combine to make a risk matrix literally "worse than useless." As remarkable as this sounds, he argues (and demonstrates) it could even be worse than *randomly* prioritized risks.

Some might argue that this is a straw man argument because we don't usually have the specific probabilities and impacts used in these examples. We only have vague ideas of the ranges, they might argue. But the ambiguity hides problems instead of facilitating the lack of information. Cox also points out that risk matrices ignore factors such as correlations between events. He stated in an interview with this book's authors that "it is traditional to completely ignore correlations between vulnerability, consequence, and threat. Yet, the correlations can completely change the implications for risk management."

Cox sees the potential for conflation of computed risks and risk tolerance: "The risk attitude used in assessing uncertain consequences is never revealed in conjunction with the risk matrix. But without knowing that, there is no way to decipher what the ratings are intended to mean, or how they might change if someone with a different risk attitude were to do the ratings. The assessments shown in the matrix reflect an unknown mixture of factual and subjective components." He asks what seems like a basic question: "The problem arises when you ask 'What did I just see?' when looking at a score or matrix."

The reader could make the case that this is just a feature of this particular risk matrix, and a different matrix with different categories wouldn't have this problem. Actually, there will still be examples of inconsistencies like this regardless of how the ranges are defined for impact and likelihood. Cox himself even worked on how some of these issues can be avoided—but only some. Cox's "risk matrix theorem" shows how certain rules and arrangements of categories can at least lead to a weakly consistent matrix. He defines "weakly consistent" in a very specific way and never concedes that a matrix could be entirely consistent. In short, matrices are ambiguity amplifiers. Cox summarizes his position for us by saying, "Simply on theoretical grounds there is no unambiguous way of coming up with such ratings in a risk matrix when the underlying severities are uncertain."

Other scoring methods don't necessarily rely on risk matrices. As mentioned earlier, methods such as OWASP simply add up multiple ordinal scales to get to an overall risk score. We also noted that this method and others like it in security find precedence in various scoring systems like the Common Vulnerability Scoring System (CVSS), the Common Weakness Scoring System (CWSS), the Common Configuration Scoring System (CCSS), and so forth. All of these scoring systems do improper math on nonmathematical objects for the purpose of aggregating some concept of risk. These wouldn't have the same problems as a risk matrix, but they introduce others—such as the mathematical no-no of applying operations like addition and multiplication to ordinal scales. As the authors have stated it in presentations on this topic, it is like saying "Birds times Orange plus Fish times Green equals High." And, of course, methods like those used in the CVSS would share the same problems of scale-response psychology (discussed earlier) as any risk matrix.

Amplifying Effects: More Studies Against the Risk Matrix (As If We Needed More)

The effects mentioned so far are compounding, meaning they work together to make risk management even more difficult than they could individually. Work from multiple sources has been done that shows the harm of combining scales and risk matrices.

In 2008 and 2009, Hubbard collected data from five different organizations regarding cybersecurity risks. Each provided separate responses from multiple individuals, with each individual providing dozens of scores for various risks. In total, there were a little over 2,000 individual responses. Hubbard found that the responses were highly clustered—about 76% of responses fell within just two values on the scale (a 3 or 4 on a 5-point scale). That is, most of the responses really boiled down to a decision between two specific values on the 5-point scale. What was meant to be a 5 × 5 matrix was mostly a 2 × 2 matrix. The net effect of the clustering was an even lower resolution—that is, an even bigger rounding error and even less information. Combined with the other research, Hubbard suspected this clustering could only exacerbate the problems found in the earlier research.

Hubbard teamed up with psychologist Dylan Evans to publish these findings in the *IBM Journal of Research & Development*. (Evans is an experienced researcher and professor who had also researched the effects of placebos and their use in clinical drug trials.) Their paper, which was published in 2010, presented a comprehensive review of the literature up to that point, and combined this with Hubbard's observations from his collection of ordinal-scale responses. In short, the paper concluded:

> The problem discussed in this paper is serious. The fact that simple scoring methods are easy to use, combined with the difficulty and time delay in tracking results with respect to reality, means that the proliferation of such methods may well be due entirely to their perceived benefits and yet have no objective value.[10]

Another more recent and (as Hubbard is happy to concede) even more comprehensive investigation, using psychological literature, theoretical issues, and original data, found similar results. In the *Economics & Management* journal of the Society of Petroleum Engineers, authors Philip Thomas, Reidar Bratvold, and J. Eric Bickel reviewed 30 different papers that described various risk matrices (mostly used in the oil and gas industry). In addition to providing a comprehensive review of all the literature (including Budescu, Cox, Hubbard and Evans, and many more), the authors also examined the effect of changing the design of the risk matrix and the ranking of various risks, and then measured how risk matrices distort data.[11]

Leveraging Cox's findings, Thomas et al. showed how the designs of these various risk matrices affected the rankings of risks in a way the matrices' designers probably did not anticipate. For example, 5 of the 30 risk matrix designs they investigated reversed the score—that is, 1 was high impact or likelihood instead of 5. These matrices would then multiply the likelihood and impact scores just as many of the other matrices did, but the lower product was considered high risk. The designers of these methods may have thought this was an arbitrary choice that would have no consequence for the risk rankings. Actually, it changed them a lot. Thomas et al. also looked at how various methods of categorizing likelihood and impact into a few discrete ordinal values (such as defining "Unlikely" as 1% to 25% or moderate impact as $100,000 to $1 million) modified risk rankings. Again, they found that these arbitrary design choices had a significant impact on ranking risks.

Thomas et al. also estimated a "Lie Factor" for each of several types of risk matrices. The Lie Factor is a measure defined by Edward Tufte and Peter Graves-Morris in 1983 based on how much data is distorted in a chart by misleading features of the chart, intentional or otherwise.[12] This is effectively a variation on the "range compression" that Cox examined in detail. Using a particular method for computing the Lie Factor, they found that the ratio of distortions of data averaged across the various risk matrix designs was in excess of 100. To get a sense of what a Lie Factor of 100 means, consider that when Edward Tufte explained this method he used an example that he classified as a "whopping lie"—it had a Lie Factor of 14.8.

Thomas et al. found that any design of a risk matrix had "gross inconsistencies and arbitrariness" embedded within it. Their conclusion is consistent with the conclusions of everyone who has seriously researched risk matrices:

> How can it be argued that a method that distorts the information underlying an engineering decision in non-uniform and uncontrolled ways is an industry best practice? The burden of proof is squarely on the shoulders of those who would recommend the use of such methods to prove that the obvious inconsistencies do not impair decision making, much less improve it, as is often claimed.

They presented these findings in a webinar that was part of Stanford's Strategic Decision and Risk Management lecture series. To drive home their finding, one of the PowerPoint slides in their presentations contained a large rectangular space titled "Heat Map Theory and Empirical Testing" (see Figure 5.2). Showing a little humor combined with a lot of seriousness, the rectangle was empty.

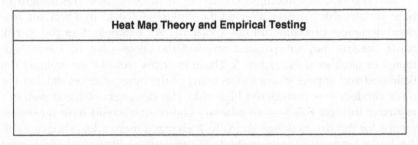

FIGURE 5.2 Heat Map Theory and Empirical Testing
Source: P. Thomas, R. Bratvold, and J. E. Bickel, "The Risk of Using Risk Matrices," *Society of Petroleum Engineers Economics & Management* 6, no. 2 (April 2014): 56–66.

Again, if you are wondering whether these findings must somehow be limited to the oil and gas industry (the target audience of the journal where this research was published), consider the NASA example briefly mentioned in Chapter 4. Recall that the research showed how Monte Carlo and statistical regression-based methods performed compared to "softer" methods. The softer method referred to was actually NASA's own version of the 5 × 5 risk matrix. The mission scientists and engineers arguably had a subject-matter advantage over the accountants—and yet, the accountants using Monte Carlo simulations and historical data were better at forecasting than the scientists and engineers using a risk matrix.

Last, these scales do not account in any way for the limitations of expert judgment as described in Chapter 4. The errors of the experts are simply further exacerbated by the additional errors introduced by the scales and matrices themselves. We agree with the solution proposed by Thomas et al. There is no need for cybersecurity (or other areas of risk analysis that also use risk matrices) to reinvent well-established quantitative methods used in many equally complex problems. Thomas et al. recommend proper decision-analysis tools that use explicit probabilities to represent uncertainty. They compare RMs (risk matrices) to decision analysis in this way:

> [T]he processes and tools drawn from decision analysis are consistent, do not carry the inherent flaws of the RMs, and provide clarity and transparency to the decision-making situation. Our best chance for providing high-quality risk-management decisions is to apply the well-developed and consistent set of processes and tools embodied in decision science.

To make this distinction clear, just compare the risk matrix to the Loss Exceedance Curve presented in Chapter 3. Recall that the LEC captures all uncertainty about impact regardless of how wide the range might be, and that the risk tolerance curve provides an explicit record of how much risk an organization's management accepts. So how does the risk matrix allow for more uncertainty about impact if impact doesn't neatly fit in one category? How does the risk matrix unambiguously capture the risk tolerance of management in a way that allows for clear evaluation of options?

Like the authors of this book, Thomas, Bratvold and Bickel state what should now be the obvious conclusion for anyone who considers all the research:

> Given these problems, it seems clear that RMs should not be used for decisions of any consequence.

Hopefully, that settles that.

Exsupero Ursus and Other Fallacies

You might have heard the old joke about two hikers getting ready for a walk into the woods. (If you have heard it—probably many times—thanks in advance for your indulgence, but there is a point.) One hiker is wearing his running shoes instead of his regular hiking boots. The other asks, "Is there something wrong with your regular boots?" to which the first hiker responds, "No, I just heard there were bears in the woods today. I wore these shoes so I could run faster."

His friend, confused, reminds him, "But you know you can't outrun a bear."

The hiker with the running shoes replies, "I don't have to outrun a bear. I just have to outrun you."

This old (and admittedly tired) joke is the basis for the name of a particular fallacy when it comes to evaluating models or decision-making methods of any kind. We call it the *Exsupero Ursus* fallacy—or, if you can do without the hokey pseudo-scholarly Latin term we just made up with Google Translate, you can call it the "beat the bear" fallacy. The basis of this fallacy goes something like this: If there is a single example of one method failing in some way or even having a minor weakness, we default to another method without ever investigating whether the alternative method has even worse weaknesses and track record.

We get many opportunities to meet managers and executives who have difficulty believing that quantitative models could possibly be an improvement over expert intuition or qualitative methods. One such person was an operational risk officer who challenged quantitative methods by asking, "How can you possibly model all the factors?" Of course, models never model or even attempt to model "all" the factors. The risk officer was committing the Exsupero Ursus fallacy. Does he believe that when he uses his own judgment or a softer score-based method that he is capturing literally all the factors? Of course not. He was simply comparing the quantitative method to some ideal that apparently captures all possible factors as opposed to comparing quantitative method to the actual alternatives: his own judgment or other methods he preferred.

Remember, the reason we are promoting the quantitative methods mentioned in this book is that we can point to specific research showing that they are superior (i.e., *measurably* superior) to specific alternatives like expert intuition. As the great statistician George Box is often quoted as saying, "All models are wrong, but some are useful." And to take it further, the research clearly shows that some models are measurably more useful than others. That is, they predict observed results better and are more likely to lead to preferred outcomes. When someone points out a shortcoming of any model, the same standard must then be applied to the proposed alternative to that model. The first model may have error, but if the alternative has even more error, then you stick with the first.

This fundamental fallacy seems to be behind several arguments against the use of quantitative, probabilistic methods. We only need to list a few and you will see how each of the objections can be countered with the same response.

Beliefs about the Feasibility of Quantitative Methods: A Hard Truth

Some cybersecurity experts in the survey (18%) said they agreed with the statement "Ordinal scales must be used because probabilistic methods are not possible in cybersecurity." This can be disproven by virtue of the fact that every method we discuss in this book has already been used in real organizations many times. Holding a belief that these methods are not practical is sort of like telling an airline pilot that commercial flight isn't practical. So where does this resistance really come from?

Our survey indicated one potential reason behind that position: Statistical literacy is strongly correlated with acceptance of quantitative methods. One set of questions in the survey tested for basic understanding of statistical and probabilistic concepts. We found that those who thought quantitative methods were impractical or saw other obstacles to using quantitative methods were much more likely to perform poorly on statistical literacy.

The statistical literacy section of the survey had 10 questions related to basic statistical literacy. Many of those survey items were based on questions that had been used in other surveys on statistical literacy by Kahneman and others. Some of the questions involved common misunderstandings of correlation, sample size, inferences from limited data, the meaning of "statistically significant," and basic probabilities (see example in Table 5.4).

TABLE 5.4 Example Stats Literacy Question

Assume the probability of an event, X, occurring in your firm sometime in 2016 is 20%. The probability of this event goes to 70% if threat T exists. There is a 10% probability that threat T exists. Which of the following statements is true?
A. If the threat T does not exist, the probability of the event X must be less than 20%.*
B. If the event X does not occur, then T does not exist.
C. Given that the event X occurs, the probability that threat T exists must be greater than 50%.
D. There is insufficient information to answer the question.
E. I don't know.

*Correct answer. (Chapter 8 covers the relevant rules—specifically rule 6.)

For further details, we put the entire survey report available for download on www.howtomeasureanything.com/cybersecurity.

We then compared stats literacy to the attitudes regarding the seven strongly anti-quantitative questions in the ATQM section of the survey. A summary of the relationship between stats literacy and positive attitudes toward the use of quantitative methods is shown in Figure 5.3.

Note that a rating in the "Median or Lower" group on pro-quant attitude doesn't necessarily mean they were generally against quantitative methods. Most people were quite supportive of quantitative methods, and so the median number of supportive responses is still more supportive than not, although it shows more reservations about quantitative methods than those who had more than the median number of pro-quant responses. For stats literacy, however, a median score (3 out of 10) was about how well someone would do if they were guessing (given the number of choices per question, randomly choosing any answer other than "I don't know" would produce 2.3 correct out of 10, on average). Those who did even worse were not only worse than guessing, they believed common misconceptions. Those who did better than the median on stats literacy were doing better than guessing.

Now that we clarified that point, you can see that those who scored above the median on stats literacy were much more likely to be above the median on "pro-quant" attitudes; likewise, those who were pro-quant were more likely to be stats literate. This is true even for what may seem like a small number of questions in this quiz. Given the number of questions and

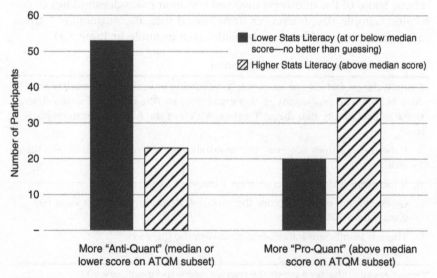

FIGURE 5.3 Stats Literacy versus Attitude toward Quantitative Methods

the number of potential choices per question, we can apply certain statistical tests. We find that—when we do the math—the relationship between stats literacy and pro-stats attitudes is statistically significant even with the small number of questions per respondent. (For the particularly stats-literate among the readers, these findings have a P-value of less than 0.01.) The survey also provided some other interesting observations.

Various Other Survey Observations Related to Stats Literacy and Acceptance

- The most anti-quantitative quartile of subjects (the bottom 25%) were twice as likely to simply skip the stats literacy quiz as those who were in the most pro-quant quartile.
- More experience in cybersecurity was associated with positive attitudes toward quantitative methods. It also appears that those who had *even tried* quantitative methods like Monte Carlo simulations were much more likely to be pro-quantitative. We found that 23% of the more pro-quant group had tried Monte Carlo simulations, while only 4% of the anti-quantitative group had done so. We aren't saying that the pro-quantitative disposition drove the desire to try Monte Carlo simulations or that trying Monte Carlo made them pro-quantitative. But the association is strong.
- Those who performed the worst on the stats literacy quiz were more likely to overestimate their skills in statistics. This is consistent with a phenomenon known as the Dunning-Kruger effect.[13] That is, there is a tendency for people who perform poorly on any test (driving, basic logic, etc.) to believe they are better than they are at the measured task. In our survey we found that 63% of individuals with below-average statistics literacy wrongly identified themselves as having average or above-average proficiency in statistics. So those who are performing poorly on stats literacy won't usually know they have misconceptions.

Actually, all this just confirms with empirical analysis the suspicions we've had based on multiple anecdotal observations. Those who believe quantitative methods are impractical in cybersecurity are not saying so because they know more about cybersecurity but because they know less about quantitative methods. If you think that you understand quantitative probabilistic methods but do not agree that these methods are feasible in cybersecurity, don't shoot the messenger. We're just reporting the observation. For those of you in the majority who believe better methods are feasible and are supportive of exploring them, we don't mean to preach to the choir. Perhaps you can use this information to diagnose internal resistance and possibly influence future training and hiring decisions to address unfamiliarity with quantitative methods in cybersecurity.

It may be a hard pill to swallow for some, but the conclusion from our survey is as unavoidable as it is harsh. Cybersecurity is a critically important topic of growing concern and we don't have the luxury of pulling punches when solving this problem. As we argued in Chapter 4 as well as earlier in this chapter, all models should be critically evaluated, including quantitative solutions, so it is not our objective to browbeat these voices into silence. But blanket objections to quantitative methods need to be recognized as nothing more than stats-phobia—born of stats illiteracy.

We are fairly sure we will get some e-mail on this point. But the math is sound and the arguments against the conclusion will contain critical flaws (we know this because we have already seen many of them). The person at Hubbard Decision Research who assisted with this analysis was one of HDR's senior quantitative analysts, Jim Clinton. He has a PhD in cognitive psychology and has published scientific research specializing in the application of advanced statistical methods to experimental psychology. So, yes, he knows what he is doing when he is assessing the statistical validity of a survey. We mention this in anticipation of objections to the survey methods, the number and type of questions we used, and the overall statistical significance. The methods, the sample size, and the correct answers to the stats literacy questions are all quite sound. But we know from past experience and the results of this survey that there will be some people who—based on an incorrect belief of their understanding of statistical methods—presume that because the findings contradict the math they do in their heads, it must be the survey that was wrong. It's not. We didn't do the math in our heads. We did the actual math. Now let's continue.

Same Fallacy: More Forms

The 29% who agreed with the statement "Ordinal scales or qualitative methods alleviate the problems with quantitative methods" were committing a type of Exsupero Ursus fallacy. The thinking here is that because quantitative methods are imperfect, therefore we must use the alternative, which somehow corrects for these errors. But what is this alleged mechanism of correction? From what we see of the research previously presented, not only do ordinal scales and risk matrices not correct for the errors of quantitative methods, they add errors of their own.

Again, we believe we should always ask tough questions of any method, including quantitative ones, and we've attempted to address this by citing overwhelming research to make our point. But we also apply the same skepticism to the preferred, softer alternatives promoted by so many standards organizations and consulting firms. We cited research that consistently finds flaws in these methods and finds a *relative* advantage in quantitative methods. So, let's use other responses in this survey to break down various sources of the anti-quantitative positions and address them one by one.

"Probabilistic methods are impractical because probabilities need exact data to be computed and we don't have exact data" is a common objection to the use of statistics in many fields, not just cybersecurity. In our survey, 23% of respondents agreed with the statement. Yet, as we mentioned in Chapter 2, you have *more* data than you think and need *less* than you think, if you are resourceful in gathering data and if you actually do the math with the little data you may have. The Exsupero Ursus fallacy here, again, is that the alternative to the proposed quantitative method somehow alleviates the lack of data. On the contrary, it appears ordinal scales and expert intuition may be useful in obfuscating the lack of data because they gloss over the entire issue. The previous research shows that ordinal scales and risk matrices might actually add error—that is, they literally *reduce* the limited information available to the intuition of the person using them.

Fortunately, like the other anti-quant-attitude questions, most respondents disagreed. They are more willing than not to try better methods. However, 23% is a significant portion of cybersecurity professionals who have a fundamental misunderstanding of why probabilistic methods are used. One of those who agreed with the statement wrote the following in an open-ended response section of the survey:

> The problem I have always had with quantifying a security risk is that when you have a vulnerability, say, an unpatched server, there is such a wide range of things that could happen if that was to be exploited . . . So, what does it mean to go to your board and say, well, this could result in a loss in the range of $0–$500 million?

Before we respond, know that this is not a personal attack on anyone—. not the person who graciously participated in our survey or anyone else who agrees with the statement. But we aren't helping cybersecurity by not providing an honest evaluation of the claim. We respect this claim enough to say it deserves a response. So here we go.

Of course, such losses are at least *possible* for organizations that are large enough, since we know of losses about that size that have happened in business. So, if this is the "possibility range," then why not make the upper bound a billion dollars or more? But clearly these outcomes are not all equally likely. In contrast, a *probability* distribution communicates the probabilities of various outcomes. We suspect that this analyst has more information than this or could at least gather more information.

If that enormous range really is the extent of uncertainty about this loss, and if everything in that range was equally likely, how does the analyst propose that, say, a conventional risk matrix would have alleviated that uncertainty? Of course, it would not. It would simply have glossed over the uncertainty. (In fact, the analyst probably would have plotted this risk in a single cell of the matrix, even though the stated range would have spanned most or all of the impact categories.)

Another interesting question is that if this were really the level of uncertainty about potential losses, then what steps is the analyst taking to reduce that uncertainty by at least some amount? Surely, any risk with such a wide range of uncertainties would merit further investigation. Or does this analyst plan on simply continuing to hide this major uncertainty from the board by using ambiguous risk terminology? Remember from Chapter 2 that it is in precisely these cases of extreme uncertainty where uncertainty reduction is both easier and most valuable. We have already presented research on how decomposing a wide range like that (by thinking through estimates of individual consequences and running a simulation to add them up) is likely to reduce uncertainty.

Those who agree with the statement that probabilistic methods need exact data misunderstand a basic point in probabilistic methods. We use quantitative, probabilistic methods *specifically because we lack perfect information*, not in spite of it. If we had perfect information, we would not need probabilistic models at all. Remember, nothing we are proposing in this book is something the authors and other colleagues haven't done many times in many environments. We have presented wide ranges many times to upper management in many firms, and we find they appreciate explicit statements of uncertainty.

We can make a similar response to the concern that cybersecurity is too complex to model quantitatively or that quantitative methods don't apply where human opponents are involved. Just like the previous questions, we have to ask exactly how risk matrices and risk scores alleviate these issues. If it is too complex to model quantitatively, how do we propose that a non-quantitative solution addresses this complexity? Remember, no matter how complex a system is, if you are making even purely subjective judgments about the system, you are modeling it. The Exsupero Ursus fallacy (i.e., *it's not a perfect method; it failed once before, so I can't use it*) still depends on failing to apply the same standard to the alternatives to probabilistic methods.

Many experts make an incorrect assumption that the more complex the problem, the worse quantitative methods will do compared to human experts. Yet, the findings of Meehl and Tetlock (reviewed in Chapter 4) show that as problems get more complex, the human experts are not doing better compared to even naïve statistical models. So the complexity of the world we model is common to both quantitative and nonquantitative models. But, unlike the risk matrix and ordinal scales, the components of even a simplified quantitative method hold up to scientific scrutiny.

Christopher "Kip" Bohn, an actuary for the insurance broker Aon, runs into this same objection and has the same reaction we do. Bohn has done a wide variety of risk analysis in many fields, but is one of a growing rank of actuaries who have been working on underwriting cybersecurity risks using the quantitative tools of analytics. He describes his response in an interview:

> In every single presentation I give in analytics I have a slide regarding how to respond to people who say you can't model that. Of course, they are actually building a model in their head when they make a decision. I tell them, "We just want the model out of your head."

Well said, Kip. Complexity, the lack of data, unpredictable human actors, and rapidly changing technology are often used as excuses for not adopting more quantitative methods. Ironically, the de facto solution is often to somehow deal with these issues in the undocumented and uncalculated intuition of the expert. If a problem is extremely complex, that's exactly the time to avoid trying to do it in your head. Aerodynamic simulations and power plant monitoring are also complex. But that is exactly why engineers don't do that analysis their heads. Cybersecurity will deal with multiple, interacting systems and controls and multiple types of losses. Some of these systems will have different types of losses than others and some events are more likely than others. Then you have to roll it up into a portfolio to determine overall risk. It's not particularly hard math (especially since we are providing spreadsheets for just about every calculation we talk about), but you still don't want to do that math in your head.

So, whenever you hear such an objection, just ask, "But how does your current method (risk matrix, ordinal scores, gut feel, etc.) alleviate this shortcoming?" It only feels like the issue is addressed in softer methods because the softer methods never force you to deal with it. And if you are uncertain—even as uncertain as the $0 to $500 million impact range mentioned earlier—then you can specifically state that uncertainty and prioritize your security controls accordingly.

The Target Breach as a Counter to Exsupero Ursus

A final objection we will mention related to Exsupero Ursus is that there are numerous examples of quantitative methods failing, and it is therefore argued that they should be avoided. The idea is that events like the 2008 financial crisis, the 2010 *Deepwater Horizon* rig explosion and oil leak in the Gulf of Mexico, the 2011 Fukushima Nuclear Power Plant disaster in Japan, and other events indicated the failure of quantitative methods. There are several problems with this objection, which Hubbard also discusses in *The Failure of Risk Management,* but we will summarize a couple of them.

First, the anecdotes presume that an actual quantitative method was being used instead of intuition and if intuition were used it somehow would have averted the disaster. There is no basis for this claim and there is actually evidence that the opposite is true. For example, greed and incentives created and then obscured the risks of investments, and in some cases (such as the AIG crisis) it was in fact the lack of actuarially sound analysis by regulators and auditors that allowed these systems to flourish.

The second problem with this objection is that they are selected anecdotes. How many examples of failures are there from methods based on pure intuition or soft methods? Even if these were legitimate examples of actual quantitative-method failure (the authors would concede there are many), we still come back to how to avoid the basic fallacy we are discussing—that is, we need to compare them to the failure rate of nonquantitative methods. The fact is there are also many failures where nonquantitative methods were used in decision making. Indeed, how well did judgment and intuition perform in the financial crisis, the design of the Fukushima plant, or the management of *Deepwater Horizon*?

The massive data breach of the retailer Target in 2013 is a case in point. This breach is well known in the cybersecurity community, but perhaps what is less widely known are the methods Target used and failed to use to assess its risks. Hubbard and Seiersen interviewed a source who was employed by Target up to about a year prior to the event. According to our source, Target was about as far from a quantitative solution to cyber risks as any organization could be. Even though there were attempts to introduce more quantitative methods, several people were entrenched in using a method based on assessing risks based on verbal "high, medium, and low" labels. There were executives who believed quantitative methods to be too complex and that they required too much time. They actually took the trouble to create a list of reasons against using quantitative methods—the items on the list that we know about are those very objections we have been refuting in this chapter. (We were told that since the breach, there has been a significant change in cybersecurity leadership.)

Eventually the company recognized that credit card records of as many as 70 million people had been breached. The combined settlements to Master Card and Visa exceeded $100 million.[14] Now, if we believed anecdotes were a sufficient basis for a comparison of methods, then we could definitely spend the time to find more examples. After all, were Anthem, Sony, Home Depot, the U.S. federal government, and other organizations that were hit by major cyberattacks using probabilistic methods instead of scales and risk matrices? We doubt it.

Of course, selected anecdotes are not the way to support the claim about which method is better. As we have done so far, the only way to properly avoid the Exsupero Ursus fallacy is to look at large sets, chosen in an unbiased manner, and systematically compare failures of *both* methods. Even if one method has failures, it should be preferred over a method that has even more. The research we presented so far (see the endnotes for this chapter and Chapter 4) supports the claim that quantitative methods outperform human expert intuition and humans using scales or risk matrices. The only research available on risk matrices, on the other hand, supports the claim that risk matrices do no good at all and may even do harm.

Communication and Consensus Objections

Last, there are objections that are neither strictly Exsupero Ursus fallacies nor based on misconceptions about quantitative methods such as the belief that we need perfect data. Some objections boil down to the presumption of other conveniences, such as the idea that nonquantitative methods are better because they are easier to explain and, therefore, easier to agree with and act on. In the survey, we saw that 31% of respondents agreed with the statement "Ordinal scales used in most information risk assessments are better than quantitative because they are easy to understand and explain." Also, a majority (64%) agreed with "Commonly used ordinal scales help us develop consensus for action."

Yet, as we saw with Budescu's research, seeming easy to understand and explain may just involve glossing over important content with ambiguous terms. We would argue that Budescu's "illusion of communication" may make someone think they have explained something, the explanation of which another someone believed they understood, and that they all agreed in the end. The authors have had multiple opportunities in many different types of firms to explain various quantitative methods to executive-level management—including in situations where we were told that the executives would not understand it. However, we find far fewer situations where people fail to understand it than some other people would have us believe. It seems we are often warned by one group that another group will not understand something quantitative (rarely does anyone admit they themselves don't understand it).

We propose the possibility that if a cybersecurity analyst says that someone else won't understand it, the problem might be their own understanding of it. We are told that management won't get "theoretical" methods (even though every method we talk about here has been used on practical problems with senior management). So we find that calling probabilistic methods theoretical really just means "I don't understand it" and perhaps "I feel threatened by it." Hopefully, the example of the simple one-for-one substitution model in Chapter 3 can help address this hurdle. We made that approach as simple as possible while still using methods that show a measurable improvement and producing actionable output.

Although a majority in the survey believed ordinal scales helped build consensus, we propose that if communication is an illusion as Budescu shows, then consensus is also an illusion. The appearance of consensus may feel satisfying but, as we stated in Chapter 1, we think it is important whether the risk assessment method actually works in a way that has been measured. Perhaps the management at Target felt that what they were doing was "working" because they believed risk was being communicated and that when they came to a consensus, they all understood what they were agreeing with. If the risk assessment itself is based on flawed methods, a little dissent should probably be preferable over illusory consensus.

Conclusion

Obstacles to the use of better quantitative methods have to be recognized as simply being misunderstandings based on common fallacies. Now let's summarize:

- Nothing is gained by the use of the popular scales and matrices. They avoid none of the issues offered as a challenge to more quantitative methods (complexity of cybersecurity, human agents, changing technology, etc.). In fact, they introduce vagueness of communication and just plain bad math. They must be abandoned in all forms of risk analysis.
- There is nothing modeled with the qualitative scales that can't be modeled with quantitative, probabilistic methods, even if we use only the same source of data as most qualitative methods (i.e., the cybersecurity expert). These methods show a measurable improvement based on previous research. Their performance can also be measured after implementation since we can use standard statistical methods to compare their risk assessments to observed reality.
- Quantitative models have been implemented in many real environments. Dismissing these methods as "theoretical" is just a way of saying that they seem threatening to the person who used that label.

Cybersecurity has grown too important to simply leave to methods that the reader—after this extensive argument—should now recognize as obviously flawed. Businesses and governments can no longer afford the misconceptions that keep them from adopting methods that work. We've spent quite a lot of text on this topic, so we appreciate your patience if you made it this far. We have cited a lot of sources on every point we make, but we thought we would end this chapter with one more voice of agreement from a leader in the cybersecurity field, Jack Jones. Read what Jack wrote in the following section, so we can put that topic to rest and get on with describing better methods.

Building Acceptance for Better Methods

By Jack Jones, Guest Contributor

Jack Jones has worked in the information security field for 26 years and has a decade of experience as a CISO. He is also the creator of the Factor Analysis of Information Risk (FAIR) framework.

Although almost everyone will agree that quantification and metrics in general are a good thing, the topic of quantifying risk in the information security realm can generate significant debate and even hostility. Many people simply don't believe it's possible or practical. That being the case, why bother trying to quantify risk? Why not just avoid the firefights and stick to counting vulnerabilities, awareness levels, and attacks against the organization? The reason is context. In other words, those and all of the other information security landscape elements you might choose to measure are only meaningful in how they affect risk (i.e., the frequency and magnitude of loss).

Inertia against risk quantification can be especially strong when you're dealing with information security professionals and auditors who have built their careers and reputations by thinking and acting in a certain way, particularly when their approach is common throughout the industry and its limitations aren't widely recognized. It's made even stronger when you include misconceptions regarding quantification, and, worse yet, when fundamental nomenclature isn't normalized (e.g., terms like "risk" don't mean the same thing to everyone). Successfully overcoming this inertia requires a combination of tactics.

Education—Normalize and Demystify

Education regarding risk quantification has at least a couple of dimensions, including:

Getting everyone on the same page regarding a meaningful definition for "risk" (hint—control deficiencies and threats aren't risks). Without this foundation in place, everything else will remain a struggle and likely not succeed. It can help to keep in mind that at the end of the day, the purpose of information security is to manage how often loss occurs and how bad it is when it does occur.

Helping people to understand that quantification is not rocket science and does not require an advanced mathematics degree. In fact,

(Continued)

(Continued)

when approached properly, it is intuitive, conceptually simple, and pragmatic. That said, quantification does require critical thinking, which can be a challenge because many people in our profession haven't done a lot of critical thinking over the years when it comes to risk measurement. Wet fingers in the air predominate. This isn't an indictment of their intelligence or innate capability for critical thinking, but it is an indictment of the methods our profession has relied on so heavily (e.g., checklist frameworks and ordinal "risk" ratings, to name two).

Small Wins, Fast

One of the big concerns many people have is that risk quantification will require too much work. The best way to disprove that misperception is to start out by analyzing smaller, more digestible problems. Instead of trying to measure something amorphous like "the risk of cloud computing," measure more tightly defined issues like "the risk associated with a particular cloud provider's service going down due to a cyberattack." These clearer, less ambiguous scenarios are much faster and easier to analyze, and can be used to quickly demonstrate the pragmatic value of quantitative risk analysis.

A series of these small analyses can also demonstrate how rapidly input data can become reusable from analysis to analysis, which can further accelerate results and efficiency.

Leverage Quants

Many organizations of any size will have business functions that specialize in quantification. Examples include some of the more mature risk disciplines (e.g., credit risk in financial institutions) and business intelligence functions. Where these functions exist you can often find well-positioned executives who appreciate and will advocate for quantitative methods. These people can be important allies when swimming through tough political waters.

Keep It Real

Some people believe risk quantification is a switch you can throw—that when an organization quantifies information security risk, it no longer sticks wet fingers in the air. This couldn't be further from the truth. No organization I've ever encountered has come close to quantifying all of the information security issues it faces. There simply aren't the resources or time. As a result, it is important to develop a triage process that helps your organization to identify when to quantify risk.

Depending on its resources and needs, an organization can choose where to start along the quantification continuum. Perhaps at first it only uses risk quantification to develop business cases for major information security expenditures, or to prioritize what it believes are its most concerning issues. The bottom line is that risk quantification can provide significant value quickly and not be a boat anchor if it is applied thoughtfully and not in an attempt to boil the ocean.

Summary

Quantifying information security risk can represent a paradigm shift within an organization and, as with almost any paradigm shift, there will be inertia and pain to overcome. One of the keys to success is to realize that the most difficult part of the transition is cultural—both within the organization and (at least today) within the information security profession as a whole. And because culture is in large part a function of beliefs, you will need to focus on changing beliefs in order to be successful.

Notes

1. Open Web Application Security Project, "OWASP Risk Rating Methodology," last modified September 3, 2015, www.owasp.org/index.php/OWASP_Risk_Rating_Methodology.
2. IEC, "ISO 31010: 2009–11," *Risk Management–Risk Assessment Techniques* (2009).
3. D. V. Budescu, S. Broomell, and H. Por, "Improving Communication of Uncertainty in the Reports of the Intergovernmental Panel on Climate Change," *Psychological Science* 20, no. 3 (2009): 299–308.
4. Richards J. Heuer, Jr., *Psychology of Intelligence Analysis* (Langley, VA: Center for the Study of Intelligence, Central Intelligence Agency, 1999).
5. Rebecca M. Blank and Patrick D. Gallagher, *Guide for Conducting Risk Assessments*, NIST Special Publication 800–30, Revision 1 (Gaithersburg, MD: National Institute of Standards and Technology, 2012), http://csrc.nist.gov/publications/nistpubs/800–30-rev1/sp800_30_r1.pdf.

6. K. E. See, C. R. Fox, and Y. Rottenstreich, "Between Ignorance and Truth: Partition Dependence and Learning in Judgment under Uncertainty," *Journal of Experimental Psychology: Learning, Memory and Cognition* 32 (2006): 1385–1402.

7. G. Moors, N. D. Kieruj, and J. K. Vermunt, "The Effect of Labeling and Numbering of Response Scales on the Likelihood of Response Bias," *Sociological Methodology* 44, no. 1 (2014): 369–399.

8. J. Chan, "Response-Order Effects in Likert-Type Scales," *Educational and Psychological Measurement* 51, no. 3 (1991): 531–540.

9. L. A. Cox Jr., "What's Wrong with Risk Matrices?" *Risk Analysis* 28, no. 2 (2008): 497–512.

10. D. Hubbard and D. Evans, "Problems with Scoring Methods and Ordinal Scales in Risk Assessment," *IBM Journal of Research and Development* 54, no. 3 (April 2010): 2.

11. P. Thomas, R. Bratvold, and J. E. Bickel, "The Risk of Using Risk Matrices," *Society of Petroleum Engineers Economics & Management* 6, no. 2 (April 2014): 56–66.

12. Edward R. Tufte and P. Graves-Morris, *The Visual Display of Quantitative Information* (Cheshire, CT: Graphics Press, 1983).

13. J. Kruger and D. Dunning, "Unskilled and Unaware of It: How Difficulties in Recognizing One's Own Incompetence Lead to Inflated Self-Assessments," *Journal of Personality and Social Psychology* 77, no. 6 (1999): 1121–1134.

14. Ahiza Garcia, "Target Settles for $39 Million over Data Breach," *CNN Money*, December 2, 2015.

PART II

Evolving the Model of Cybersecurity Risk

CHAPTER 6

Decompose It
Unpacking the Details

The everyday meanings of most terms contain ambiguities signifi-cant enough to render them inadequate for careful decision analysis.

—Ron Howard, Father of Decision Analysis[1]

Recall the cybersecurity analyst mentioned in Chapter 5 whose estimate of a loss was "$0 to $500 million" and worried how upper management would react to such an uninformative range. Of course, if such extreme losses really were a concern, it would be wrong to hide it from upper management. Fortunately, there is an alternative: Just decompose it. Surely such a risk would justify at least a little more analysis.

Impact usually starts out as a list of unidentified and undefined out-comes. Refining this is just a matter of understanding the "object" of measurement as discussed in Chapter 2. That is, we have to figure out what we are measuring by defining it better. In this chapter, we discuss how to break up an ambiguous pile of outcomes into at least a few major categories of impacts.

In Chapter 3 we showed how to make a simple quantitative model that merely makes exact replacements for steps in the familiar risk matrix, but does so using quantitative methods. This is a very simple baseline, which we can make more detailed through decomposition. In Chapter 4 we dis-cussed research showing how decomposition of an uncertainty especially helps when the uncertainty is particularly great—as is usually the case in cybersecurity. Now, in this chapter we will exploit the benefits of decom-position by showing how the simple model in Chapter 3 could be given more detail.

Decomposing the Simple One-for-One Substitution Model

Every row in our simple model shown in Chapter 3 (Table 3.2) had only two inputs: a probability of an event and a range of a loss. Both the event probability and the range of the loss could be decomposed further. We can say, for example, that if an event occurs, we can assess the probability of the type of event (was it a sensitive data breach, denial of service, etc.?). Given this information, we could further modify a probability. We can also break the impact down into several types of costs: legal fees, breach investigation costs, downtime, and so on. Each of these costs can be computed based on other inputs that are simpler and less abstract than some aggregate total impact.

Now let's add a bit more detail as an example of how you could use further decomposition to add value.

Just a Little More Decomposition

A simple decomposition strategy for impact that many in cybersecurity are already familiar with is confidentiality, integrity, and availability or "C, I, and A." As you probably know, "confidentiality" refers to the improper disclosure of information. This could be a breach of millions of records, or it could mean stealing corporate secrets and intellectual property. "Integrity" means modifying the data or behavior of a system, which could result in improper financial transactions, damaging equipment, misrouting logistics, and so on. Last, "availability" refers to some sort of system outage resulting in a loss of productivity, sales, or other costs of interference with business processes. We aren't necessarily endorsing this approach for everyone, but many analysts in cybersecurity find that these decompositions make good use of how they think about the problem.

Let's simplify it even further in the way we've seen one company do it by combining confidentiality and integrity. Perhaps we believe availability losses were fairly common compared to others, and that estimating availability lends itself to using other information we know about the system, like the types of business processes the system supports, how many users it has, how it might affect productivity, whether it could impact sales while it is unavailable, and so on. In Table 6.1, we show how this small amount of additional decomposition could look if we added it to the spreadsheet shown in the one-for-one substitution model shown in Chapter 3. To save room, we've left off columns to the right that show how they are aggregated; to see the entire spreadsheet, as always, just go to www.howtomeasureanything.com/cybersecurity. In addition to the original model shown in Chapter 3, you will also see this one.

TABLE 6.1 Example of Slightly More Decomposition

Event	Probability of event occurring in a year	Type of Event if One Occurs			Confidentiality and Integrity 90% Confidence Interval ($000)		Availability 90% Confidence Intervals			
							Duration of Outage (hours)		Cost per Hour ($000)	
		Only ConfInt	Only Availability	Both Types	Lower Bound	Upper Bound	Lower Bound	Upper Bound	Lower Bound	Upper Bound
AA	.1	.2	.7	.1	$50	$50	.25	4	$2	$10
AB	.05	.3	.5	.2	$100	$10,000	.25	8	$1	$10
AC	.01	.1	.8	.1	$200	$25,000	.25	12	$40	$200
AD	.03	0	0	1.0	$100	$15,000	.25	2	$2	$10
AE	.05	0	.6	.4	$250	$30,000	1	24	$5	$50

Notice that the first thing we've done here is decompose the event by first determining what kind of event it was. We state a probability the event was only confidentiality and integrity (ConfInt) and a probability that it was only availability (Avail). The probability that it could be both is 1-ConfInt-Avail. To show an example of how you might model this, we can use the following formula in Excel to determine which type of event it was or whether it was both. (We already determined that an event *did* occur, so we can't have a result where it was neither type of event.)

$$= If(rand() < ConfInt, 1, if(rand() < ConfInt + Avail, 2, 3))$$

The loss for confidentiality and integrity then will be added in if the value from this formula is a 1 (where confidentiality and integrity event occurred) or 3 (when both confidentiality and integrity as well as availability occurred). The same logic is applied to availability (which is experienced when the equation's output is a 2 or 3). We could also have just assessed the probabilities of the events separately instead of first determining whether an event occurred and then determining the type of event. There are many more ways to do this and so you should choose the decomposition that you find more convenient and realistic to assess.

When availability losses are experienced, that loss is computed by multiplying the hours of outage duration times the cost per hour of the outage. Just as we did in the simpler model in Chapter 3, we generate thousands of values for each row. In each random trial we randomly determine the type of event and its cost. The entire list of event costs are totaled for each of the thousands of trials, and a loss exceedance curve is generated, as we showed in Chapter 3. As before, each row could have a proposed control, which would reduce the likelihood and perhaps impact of the event (these reductions can also be randomly selected from defined ranges).

If an "event" is an attack on a given system, we would know something about how that system is used in the organization. For example, we would usually have a rough idea of how many users a system has—whether they would be completely unproductive without a system or whether they could work around it for a while—and whether the system impacts sales or other operations. And many organizations have had some experience with system outages that would give them a basis for estimating something about how long the outage could last.

Now that you can see how decomposition works in general, let's discuss a few other strategies we could have used. If you want to decompose your model using a wider variety of probability distributions, see details on a list of distributions in Appendix A. And, of course, you can download an entire spreadsheet from www.howtomeasureanything.com/cybersecurity that contains all of these random probability distributions written in native (i.e., without VBA macros or add-ins) MS Excel.

A Few Decomposition Strategies to Consider

We labeled each row in the simulation shown in Table 6.1 as merely an "event." But in practice you will need to define an event more specifically and, for that, there are multiple choices. Think of the things you would normally have plotted on a risk matrix. If you had 20 things plotted on a risk matrix, were they 20 applications? Were they 20 categories of threats? Were they business units of the organization or types of users?

It appears that most users of the risk matrix method start with an application-oriented decomposition. That is, when they plotted something on a risk matrix, they were thinking of an application. This is a perfectly legitimate place to start. Again, we have no particular position on the method of decomposition until we have evidence saying that some are better and others are worse. But out of convenience and familiarity, our simple model in Chapter 3 starts with the application-based approach to decomposing the problem. If you prefer to think of the list of risks as being individual threat sources, vulnerabilities, or something else, then you should have no problem extrapolating the approach we describe here to your preferred model.

Once you have defined what your rows in the table represent, then your next question is how detailed you want the decomposition in each row to be. In each decomposition, you should try to leverage things you know—we can call them "observables." Table 6.2 has a few more examples.

TABLE 6.2 A Few More Examples of Potential Decompositions

Decomposing into a Range for:	. . . Leverages Knowledge of the Following (Either You Know Them or Can Find Out, Even If It Is Also Just Another 90% CI)
Financial theft	You generally know whether a system even handles financial transactions. So some of the time the impact of financial theft will be zero or, if not zero, you can estimate the limit of the financial exposure in the system.
System outages	How many users a system has, how critical it is to their work, and whether outages affect sales or other operations with a financial impact can be estimated. You may even have some historical data about the duration of outages once they occur.
Investigation and remediation costs	IT often has some experience with estimating how many people work on fixing a problem, how long it takes them to fix it, and how much their time is worth. You may even have knowledge about how these costs may differ depending on the type of event.
Intellectual property (IP)	You can find out whether a given system even has sensitive corporate secrets or IP. If it has IP, you can ask management what the consequences would be if the IP were compromised (again, ranges are okay).
Notification and credit monitoring	Again, you at least know whether a system has this kind of exposure. If the event involves a data breach of personal information, paying for notification and credit monitoring services can be directly priced on a per-record basis.
Legal liabilities and fines	You know whether a system has regulatory requirements. There isn't much in the way of legal liabilities and fines that doesn't have some publicly available precedent on which to base an estimate.
Other interference with operations	Does the system control some factory process that could be shut down? Does the system control health and safety in some way that can be compromised?
Reputation	You probably have some idea whether a system even has the potential for a major reputation cost (e.g., whether it has customer data or whether it has sensitive internal communications). Once you establish that, reputation impact can be decomposed further (addressed again later in this chapter).

If we modeled even some of these details, we may still have a wide range, but we can at least say something about the relative likelihood of various outcomes. The cybersecurity professional who thought that a range for a loss was zero to a half-billion dollars was simply not considering what can be inferred from what is known rather than dwelling on all that isn't known. A little bit of decomposition would indicate that not all the values in that huge range could be equally likely. You will probably be able to go to the board with at least a bit more information about a potential loss than a flat uniform distribution of $0 to $500 million or more.

And don't forget that the reason you do this is to evaluate alternatives. You need to be able to discriminate among different risk-mitigation strategies. Even if your range was that wide and everything in the range were equally likely, it is certainly not the case that every system in the list has a range that wide, and knowing which do would be helpful. You know that some systems have more users than others, some systems handle Personal Health Information (PHI) or Payment Card Industry (PCI) data and some do not, some systems are accessed by vendors, and so on. All this is useful information in prioritizing action even though you will never remove all uncertainty.

This list just gives you a few more ideas of elements into which you could decompose your model. So far we've focused on decomposing impact more than likelihood because impact seems a bit more concrete for most people. But we can also decompose likelihood. Chapters 8 and 9 will focus on how that can be done. We will also discuss how to tackle one of the more difficult cost estimations—reputation loss—later in this chapter.

More Decomposition Guidelines: Clear, Observable, Useful

When someone is estimating the impact of a particular cybersecurity breach on a particular system, perhaps they are thinking, "Hmm, there would at least be an outage for a few minutes if not an hour or more. There are 300 users, most of which would be affected. They process orders and help with customer service. So the impact would be more than just paying wages for people unable to work. The real loss would be loss of sales. I think I recall that sales processed per hour are around $50,000 to $200,000 but that can change seasonally. Some percentage of those who couldn't get service might just call back later, but some we would lose for good. Then there would be some emergency remediation costs. So, I'm estimating a 90% CI of a loss per incident of $1,000 to $2,000,000."

We all probably realize that we may not have perfect performance when recalling data and doing a lot of arithmetic in our heads (and imagine how much harder it gets when that math involves probability distributions of different shapes). So we shouldn't be that surprised that the researchers we mentioned back in Chapter 4 (Armstrong and MacGregor) found that we are better off decomposing the problem and doing the math in plain sight. If you find yourself making these calculations in your head then stop, decompose, and (just like in school) show your math.

We expect a lot of variation in decomposition strategies based on desired granularity and differences in the information different analysts will have about their organizations. Yet there are principles of decomposition that can apply to anyone. Our task here is to determine how to further decompose the problem so that, regardless of your industry or the uniqueness of your firm, your decomposition actually improves your estimations of risk.

This is an important question because some decomposition strategies are better than others. Even though there is research that highly uncertain quantities can be better estimated by decomposition, there is also research that identifies conditions under which decomposition does not help. We need to learn how to tell the difference. If the decomposition does not help, then we are better off leaving the estimate at a more aggregated level. As one research paper put it, decompositions done "at the expense of conceptual simplicity may lead to inferences of lower quality than those of direct, unaided judgments."[2]

Decision Analysis: An Overview of How to Think about a Problem

A good background for thinking about decomposition strategies is the work of Ron Howard, who is generally credited for coining of the term "decision analysis" in 1966.[3] Howard and others inspired by his work were applying the somewhat abstract areas of decision theory and probability theory to practical decision problems dealing with uncertainties. They also realized that many of the challenges in real decisions were not purely mathematical. Indeed, they saw that decision makers often failed to even adequately define what the problem was. As Ron Howard put it, we need to "transform confusion into clarity of thought and action."[4]

Howard prescribes three prerequisites for doing the math in decision analysis. He stipulates that the decision and the factors we identify to inform the decision must be clear, observable, and useful.

- *Clear*: Everybody knows what you mean. *You* know what you mean.
- *Observable*: What do you see when you see more of it? This doesn't mean you will necessarily have already observed it but it is at least possible to observe and you will know it when you see it.
- *Useful*: It has to matter to some decision. What would you do differently if you knew this? Many things we choose to measure in security seem to have no bearing on the decision we actually need to make.

All of these conditions are often taken for granted, but if we start systematically considering each of these points on every decomposition, we may choose some different strategies. Suppose, for example, you wanted to decompose your risks in such a way that you had to evaluate a threat actor's "skill level." This is one of the "threat factors" in the OWASP standard, and we have seen homegrown variations on this approach. We will assume you have already accepted the arguments in previous chapters and decided to abandon the ordinal scale proposed by OWASP and others, and that you are looking for a quantitative decomposition about a threat actor's skill level. So now apply Howard's tests to this factor.

The Clear, Observable, and Useful Test Applied to "Threat Actor Skill Level"

- *Clear*: Can you define what you mean by "skill level"? Is this really an unambiguous unit of measure or even a clearly defined discrete state? Does saying, "We define 'average' threat as being better than an amateur but worse than a well-funded nation state actor" really help?
- *Observable*: How would you even detect this? What basis do you have to say that skill levels of some threats are higher or lower than others?
- *Useful*: Even if you had unambiguous definitions for this, and even if you could observe it in some way, how would the information have bearing on some action in your firm?

We aren't saying threat skill level is necessarily a bad part of a strategy for decomposing risk. Perhaps you have defined skill level unambiguously by specifying the types of methods employed. Perhaps you can observe the frequency of these types of attacks, and perhaps you have access to threat intelligence that tells you about the existence of new attacks you haven't seen yet. Perhaps knowing this information causes you to change your estimates of the likelihood of a particular system being breached, which might inform what controls should be implemented or even the overall cybersecurity budget. If this is the case, then you have met the conditions of clear, observable, and useful. But when this is not the case—which seems to be very often—evaluations of skill level are pure speculation and add no value to the decision-making process.

Avoiding "Over-Decomposition"

The threat skill level example just mentioned may or may not be a good decomposition depending on your situation. If it meets Howard's criteria and it actually reduces your uncertainty, then we call it an "informative" decomposition. If not, then the decomposition is "uninformative" and you were better off sticking with a simpler model.

Imagine someone standing in front of you holding a crate. The crate is about 2 feet wide and a foot high and deep. They ask you to provide a 90% CI on the weight of the crate simply by looking at it. You can tell they're not a professional weightlifter, so you can see this crate can't weigh, say, 350 pounds. You also see that they lean a bit backward to balance their weight as they hold it. And you see that they're shifting uncomfortably. In the end, you say your 90% CI is 20 to 100 pounds. This strikes you as a wide range, so you attempt to decompose this problem by estimating the number of items in the crate and the weight per item. Or perhaps there are different categories of items in the crate, so you estimate the number of categories of items, the number in each category, and the weight per item in that category. Would your estimate be better? Actually, it could easily be worse. What you have done is decomposed the problem into multiple purely speculative estimates that you then use to try to do some math. This would be an example of an "uninformative decomposition."

The difference between this and an informative decomposition is whether you are describing the problem in terms of quantities you are more familiar with than the original problem. An informative decomposition would be decompositions that utilize specific knowledge that the cybersecurity expert has about their environment. For example, the cybersecurity expert can get detailed knowledge about the types of systems in their organization and the types of records stored on them. They would have or could acquire details about internal business processes so they could estimate the impacts of denial of service attacks. They understand what types of controls they currently have in place. Decompositions of cybersecurity risks that leverage this specific knowledge are more likely to be helpful.

However, suppose a cybersecurity expert attempts to build a model where they find themselves estimating the number and skill level of state-sponsored attackers or even the hacker group "Anonymous" (about which, as the name implies, it would be very hard to estimate any details). Would this actually constitute a reduction in uncertainty relative to where they started?

Decompositions should be less abstract to the expert than the aggregated amount. If you find yourself decomposing a dollar impact into factors like threat skill level then you should have less uncertainty about the new factors than you did about the original, direct estimate of monetary loss.

However, if decomposition causes you to widen a range, that might be informative if it makes you question the assumptions of your previous range. For example, suppose we need to estimate the impact of a system availability risk where an application used in some key process—let's say order-taking—would be unavailable for some period of time. And suppose that we initially estimated this impact to be $150,000 to $7 million. Perhaps we consider that to be too uncertain for our needs, so we decide to decompose this further into the duration of an outage and the cost per hour of an outage. Suppose further that we estimated the duration of the outage to be 15 minutes to

4 hours and the cost per hour of the outage to be $200,000 to $5 million. Let's also state that these are lognormal distributions for each (as discussed in Chapter 3, this often applies where the value can't be less than zero but could be very large). Have we reduced uncertainty? Surprisingly, no—not if what we mean by "uncertainty reduction" is a narrower range. The 90% CI for the product of these two lognormal distributions is about $100,000 to $8 million—wider than the initial 90% CI of $150,000 to $7,000,000. But even though the range isn't strictly narrower, you might think it was useful because you realize it is probably more realistic than the initial range.

Now, just a note in case you thought that to get the range of the product you multiply the lower bounds together and then multiply the upper bounds together, that's not how the math works when you are generating two independent random variables. Doing it that way would produce a range of $50,000 to $20 million (0.25 hours times $200,000 per hour for the lower bound and 4 hours times $5 million per hour for the upper bound). This answer could only be correct if the two variables are *perfectly* correlated—which they obviously would not be.

So decomposition might be useful just as a reality check against your initial range. This can also come up when you start running simulations on lots of events that are added up into a portfolio-level risk, as the spreadsheet shown in Table 6.1 does. When analysts are estimating a large number of individual events, it may not be apparent to them what the consequences for their individual estimates are at a portfolio level. In one case we observed that subject matter experts were estimating individual event probabilities at somewhere between 2% and 35% for about a hundred individual events. When this was done they realized that the simulation indicated they were having a dozen or so significant events per year. A manager pointed out that the risks didn't seem realistic because none of those events had been observed even once in the last five years. This would make sense if the subject matter experts had reason to believe there would be a huge uptick in these event frequencies (it was over a couple of years ago and we can confirm that this is not what happened). But, instead, the estimators decided to rethink what the probabilities should be so that they didn't contrast so sharply with observed reality.

A Summary of Some Decomposition Rules

The lessons in these examples can be summarized in two fundamental decomposition rules:

- *Decomposition Rule #1*: Decompositions should leverage what you are better at estimating or data you can obtain (i.e., don't decompose into quantities that are even more speculative than the first).

■ *Decomposition Rule #2*: Check your decomposition against a directly estimated range with a simulation, as we just did in the outage example. You might decide to toss the decomposition if it produces results you think are absurd, or you might decide your original range is the one that needs updating.

In practice there are a few more things to remember in order to keep whatever decomposition strategy you are using informative. Decomposition has some mathematical consequences to think about in order to determine if you actually have less uncertainty than you did before:

■ If you are expecting to reduce uncertainty by multiplying together two decomposed variables, then the decomposed variables need to not only have less uncertainty than the initial range but often a *lot* less. As a rule of thumb, the ratios of the upper and lower bounds for the decomposed variables should be a lot less than a third the width of the ratio of upper and lower bounds of the original range. For the case in the previous section, the ratio of bounds of the original range was about 47 ($7 million / $150,000), while the other two ranges had ratios of bounds of 16 and 25, respectively.

■ If most of the uncertainty is in one variable, then the ratio of the upper and lower bounds of the decomposed variable must be less than that of the original variable. For example, suppose you initially estimated that the cost of an outage for one system was $1 million to $5 million. If the major source of uncertainty about this cost is the duration of an outage, the upper/lower bound ratio of the duration must be less than the upper/lower bound ratio of the original estimate (5 to 1). If the range of the duration doesn't have a lower ratio of upper/lower bounds, then you haven't added information with the decomposition. If you have reason to believe your original range, then just use that. Otherwise, perhaps your original range was just too narrow and you should go with the decomposition.

■ In some cases the variables you multiply together are related in a way that eliminates the value of decomposition unless you also make a model of the relationship. For example, suppose you need to multiply A and B to get C. In this case when A is large, B is small, and when B is large, A is small. If we estimate separate, independent ranges for A and B, the range for the product C can be greatly overstated. This might be the case for the duration and cost per hour of an outage. That is, the more critical a system, the faster you would work to get them back on line. If you decompose these, you should also model the inverse relationship. Otherwise, just provide a single overall range for the cost of the impact instead of decomposing it.

■ If you have enough empirical data to estimate a distribution, then you probably won't get much benefit from further decomposition.

A Hard Decomposition: Reputation Damage

In the survey we mentioned in Chapter 5, some cybersecurity professionals (14%) agreed with the statement "There is no way to calculate a range of the intangible effects of major risks like damage to reputation." Although a majority disagree with the statement and there is a lot of discussion about it, we have seen few attempts to model this in the cybersecurity industry. This is routinely given as an example of a very hard measurement problem. Therefore, we decided to drill down on this particular loss in more detail as an example of how even this seemingly intangible issue can be addressed through effective decomposition. Reputation, after all, seems to be the loss category cybersecurity professionals resort to when they want to create the most FUD. It comes across as an unbearable loss. But let's ask the question we asked in Chapter 2 regarding the object of measurement, or in this chapter regarding Howard's observability criterion: What do we *see* when we see a loss of reputation?

The first reaction many would have is that the observed quantity would be a long-term loss of sales. Then they may also say that stock prices would go down. Of course, the two are related. If investors (especially the institutional investors who consider the math on the effect of sales on market valuation) believed that sales would be reduced, then we would see stock prices drop for that reason alone. So if we could observe changes in sales or stock prices just after major cybersecurity events, that would be a way to detect the effect of loss of reputation, or at least the effects that would have any bearing on our decisions.

It does seem reasonable to presume a relationship between a major data breach and a loss of reputation resulting in changes in sales, stock prices, or both. Articles have been published that implied such a direct relationship between the breach and reputation, with titles like "Target Says Data Breach Hurt Sales, Image; Final Toll Isn't Clear."[5] *Forbes* published an article in September 2014 by the Wall Street analysis firm Trefis, which noted that Target's stock fell 14% in the two-month period after the breach, implying the two are connected.[6] In that article, Trefis cited the Poneman Institute (a major cybersecurity research service using mostly survey-based data), which anticipated a 6% "churn" of customers after a major data breach. Looking at this information alone, it seems safe to say that a major data breach means a significant loss of sales and market valuation.

Yet perhaps there is room for skepticism about these claims. There were multiple studies prior to 2008 showing that there was a minor effect on stock prices the same day of a breach and no longer-term effect,[7,8,9] but these studies may be considered dated since they were published long before big breaches like Target and Anthem. Since these are publicly traded companies, we thought we should just look up the data on sales before and after the breach.

Of course, we know that changes can be due to many factors and a certain amount of volatility is to be expected even if there weren't a breach. So the way to look at these sorts of events is to consider how big the changes are compared to historical volatility in sales and stock prices. Figure 6.1 shows changes—relative to the time of the breach—for the quarterly sales of three major retailers that had highly publicized data breaches: Home Depot, JCPenney, and Target. Figure 6.2 shows changes in stock prices for those firms and Anthem.

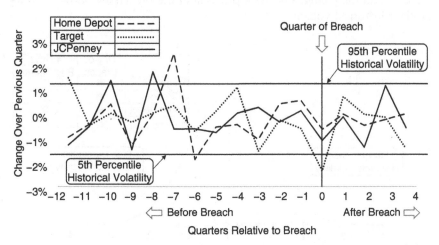

FIGURE 6.1 Quarter-to-Quarter Change in Sales for Major Retailers with Major Data Breaches Relative to the Quarter of the Breach

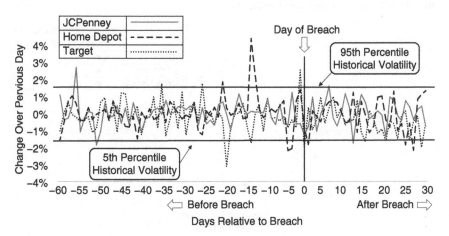

FIGURE 6.2 Day-to-Day Change in Stock Prices of Firms with Major Data Breaches Relative to Day of the Breach

Figures 6.1 and 6.2 don't appear to show significant changes after a breach compared to the volatility before the breach. To see the detail better, let's just show changes relative to historical volatility. In Figures 6.3 and 6.4, historical volatility on sales and stock prices is shown as an interval representing the fifth and ninety-fifth percentile of changes for three years up until the breach. The markers show the change after the breach compared to the range of historical volatility (the vertical dashed lines). The changes in sales and the changes in stock prices after the breach are shown *relative* to their historical volatility.

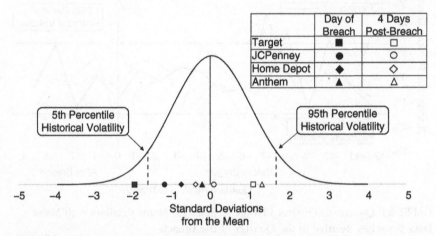

FIGURE 6.3 Changes in Stock Prices after a Major Breach for Three Major Retailers Relative to Historical Volatility

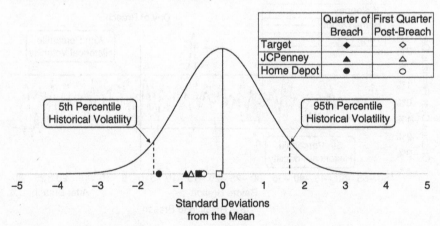

FIGURE 6.4 Changes in Seasonally Adjusted Quarterly Sales after Breach Relative to Historical Volatility

Clearly, any relationship between a major data breach and sales or stock prices—even for breaches as large as Home Depot and Target—is weak at best. While it does look like they might have resulted in some downward movement on average, the movement is explainable as the historical "noise" of day-to-day or quarter-to-quarter changes. In March 2015, another analysis by Trefis published in *Forbes* magazine indicated that while Home Depot did not actually lose business in the quarters after the breach, management reported other losses in the form of expenses dealing with the event, including "legal help, credit card fraud, and card re-issuance costs going forward."[10]

How about the 14% price drop Target experienced in the two-month period after the breach? Well, that too needs to be put in context. Earlier in the same year as the Target breach, we can find another 14% drop in Target's stock price in the two-month August-to-September period. And by November of 2014 the stock had surpassed the price just before the breach.

What about the survey indicating how customers would abandon retailers hit by a major breach? All we can say is that the sales figures don't agree with the statements of survey respondents. This is not inconsistent with the fact that what people say on a survey about their value of privacy and security does not appear to model what they actually do, as one Australian study shows.[11] Trefis even applied a caveat on the observed decline in sales for Target, saying that "industry-wide foot traffic is already declining due to gradual customer shift to online channel, where Target's presence is almost negligible."[12] Trefis also said of Home Depot:

> In spite of dealing with a case that is bigger than the data breach at Target in late 2013, Home Depot is not expected to lose out on much revenue. Part of this is because the retailer will continue to reap the benefits of an upbeat U.S. economy and housing market. Furthermore, unlike Target, where consumers moved to the likes of Costco or Kohl's, there are hardly any substitutes when it comes to buying material such as plywood, saws, cement, or the like.[13]

So apparently there could be other factors regarding whether a retailer sees any impact on customer retention. Perhaps as part of the real "loss of reputation," it is also a function of where your customers could go for the same products and services. And yet even when these factors apply, as in the case of Target, it is still hard to separate the impact from routine market noise.

Finally, when we look back at past reports about the cost of data breaches, something doesn't add up. The 2007 data breach at T.J. Maxx was estimated to cost over $1.7 *billion*.[14] Enough time has passed that we should have seen even the delayed impacts realized by now. But if anything approaching that amount were actually experienced, it seems well hidden in their financial reports. The firm was making an annual income from operations of around $700 million or so in the years prior to the breach, which went up to about $1.2 billion at some point after the breach. Annual reports present accounting data at a highly aggregated level, but an impact even half that size should be clearly visible in at least one of those years. Yet we don't see such an obvious impact in profit, expenses, or even cash or new loans. It certainly did cost T.J. Maxx something but there is no evidence it was anything close to $1.7 billion.

It's not impossible to lose business as a result of a data breach, but the fact that it is hard to tease out this effect from normal day-to-day or even quarter-to-quarter variations helps inform a practical approach to modeling these losses. Marshall Kuypers, a PhD candidate in management science and engineering at Stanford, has focused his study on these issues. As Kuypers tells the authors:

> Academic research has studied the impact of data breach announcements on the stock price of organizations and has consistently found little evidence that the two are related. It is difficult to identify a relationship because signals dissipate quickly and the statistically significant correlation disappears after roughly 3 days.

A Better Way to Model Reputation Damage: Penance Projects

We aren't saying major data breaches are without costs. There are real costs associated with them, but we need to think about how to model them differently than with vague references to reputation. The actual "reputation" losses may be more realistically modeled as a series of very tangible costs we call "penance projects" as well as other internal and legal liabilities. Penance projects are expenses incurred to limit the long-term impact of loss of reputation. In other words, companies appear to engage in efforts to control damage to reputation instead of bearing what could otherwise be much greater damage. The effect these efforts have on reducing the real loss to reputation seem to be enough that the impact seems hard to detect in sales or stock prices. These efforts include the following:

- Major new investments in cybersecurity systems and policies to correct cybersecurity weaknesses.
- Replacing a lot of upper management responsible for cybersecurity (It may be scapegoating, but it may be necessary for the purpose of addressing reputation.)

- A major public relations push to convince customers and shareholders the problem is being addressed (this helps get the message out that the efforts of the preceding bullet points will solve the problem).
- Marketing and advertising campaigns (separate from getting the word out about how the problem has been confidently addressed) to offset potential losses in business

These damage-control efforts to limit reputation effects appear to be the real costs here—not so much reputation damage itself. Each of these are conveniently concrete measures for which we have multiple historical examples. Of course, if you really do believe that there are other costs to reputation damage, you should model them. But what does reputation damage really mean to a business if you can detect impacts on neither sales nor stock prices? Just be sure you have an empirical basis for your claim. Otherwise, it might be simpler to stick with the penance project cost strategy.

So, if we spend a little more time and effort in analysis, it should be possible to tease out reasonable estimates even for something that seems as "intangible" as reputation loss.

Conclusion

A little decomposition can be very helpful up to a point. To that end, we showed a simple additional decomposition that you can use to build on the example in Chapter 3. We also mentioned a downloadable spreadsheet example and the descriptions of distributions in Appendix A to give you a few tools to help with this decomposition.

We talked about how some decompositions might be uninformative. We need to decompose in a way that leverages your actual knowledge—however limited our knowledge is, there are a few things we do know—and not speculation upon speculation. Test your decompositions with a simulation and compare them to your original estimate before the decomposition. This will show if you learned anything or show if you should actually make your range wider. We tackled a particularly difficult impact to quantify—loss of reputation—and showed how even that has concrete, observable consequences that can be estimated.

So far, we haven't spent any time on decomposing the likelihood of an event other than to identify likelihoods for two types of events (availability vs. confidentiality and integrity). This is often a bigger source of uncertainty for the analyst and anxiety for management than the impact. Fortunately, that, too, can be decomposed. We will review how to do that later in Part II.

We also need to discuss where these initial estimates of ranges and probabilities can come from. As we discussed in earlier chapters, the same expert who was previously assigning arbitrary scores to a risk matrix can also be taught to assign subjective probabilities in a way that itself has a measurable performance improvement. Then those initial uncertainties can be updated with some very useful mathematical methods even when it seems like data is sparse. These topics will be dealt with in the next two chapters, "Calibrated Assessments" and "Reducing Uncertainty with Bayesian Methods."

Notes

1. Ronald A. Howard and Ali E. Abbas, *Foundations of Decision Analysis* (New York: Prentice Hall, 2015), 62.
2. Michael Burns and Judea Pearl. "Causal and Diagnostic Inferences: A Comparison of Validity," *Organizational Behavior and Human Performance* 28, no. 3 (1981): 379–394.
3. Ronald A. Howard, "Decision Analysis: Applied Decision Theory," *Proceedings of the Fourth International Conference on Operational Research* (New York: Wiley-Interscience, 1966).
4. Ronald A. Howard and Ali E. Abbas, *Foundations of Decision Analysis* (New York: Prentice Hall, 2015), xix.
5. "Target Says Data Breach Hurt Sales, Image; Final Toll Isn't Clear," *Dallas Morning News,* March 14, 2014.
6. Trefis Team, "Home Depot: Will the Impact of the Data Breach Be Significant?" *Forbes,* March 30, 2015, www.forbes.com/sites/greatspeculations/2015/03/30/home-depot-will-the-impact-of-the-data-breach-be-significant/#1e882f7e69ab.
7. Karthik Kannan, Jackie Rees, and Sanjay Sridhar, "Market Reactions to Information Security Breach Announcements: An Empirical Analysis," *International Journal of Electronic Commerce* 12, no. 1 (2007): 69–91.
8. Alessandro Acquisti, Allan Friedman, and Rahul Telang, "Is There a Cost to Privacy Breaches? An Event Study," *ICIS 2006 Proceedings* (2006): 94.
9. Huseyin Cavusoglu, Birendra Mishra, and Srinivasan Raghunathan, "The Effect of Internet Security Breach Announcements on Market Value: Capital Market Reactions for Breached Firms and Internet Security Developers," *International Journal of Electronic Commerce* 9, no. 1 (2004): 70–104.
10. Trefis Team, "Home Depot: Will the Impact of the Data Breach Be Significant?" March 27, 2015, www.trefis.com/stock/hd/articles/286689/home-depot-will-the-impact-of-the-data-breach-be-significant/2015-03-27.

11. Wallis Consulting Group, *Community Attitudes to Privacy 2007*, prepared for the Office of the Privacy Commissioner, Australia, August 2007, www.privacy.gov.au/materials/types/download/8820/6616.
12. Trefis Team, "Data Breach Repercussions and Falling Traffic to Subdue Target's Results," August 18, 2014, www.trefis.com/stock/tgt/articles/251553/aug-20data-breach-repercussions-and-falling-traffic-to-subdue-targets-results/2014–08–18.
13. Trefis Team, "Home Depot: Will the Impact of the Data Breach Be Significant?" March 27, 2015, www.trefis.com/stock/hd/articles/286689/home-depot-will-the-impact-of-the-data-breach-be-significant/2015-03-27.
14. Ryan Singel, "Data Breach Will Cost TJX 1.7B, Security Firm Estimates," *Wired*, March 30, 2007, www.wired.com/2007/03/data_breach_wil/.

CHAPTER 7

Calibrated Estimates

How Much Do You Know Now?

*The most important questions of life are indeed, for the most part,
really only problems of probability.*

—Pierre Simon Laplace, *Théorie Analytique des Probabilités*, 1812[1]

The method described so far requires the subjective evaluation of quantitative probabilities. For example, the cybersecurity expert will need to assess a probability that an event will occur or how much will be lost if it does. This meets some resistance. Some cybersecurity experts who seem to have no issue with assigning a "medium" or a "2" to a likelihood will often wonder how it is possible to subjectively assess a quantitative probability of an event.

Of course, it is legitimate to ask whether subjective probabilities can be valid. Fortunately, as mentioned in Chapter 5, much research has already been done on this point and two findings are clear: (1) Most people are bad at assigning probabilities, but (2) most people can also be trained to be very good at it.

Yes, the validity of subjective estimates of probability can be and *has been* objectively measured (ironically, perhaps to some). To deny this is a rejection of scientifically validated facts. A cybersecurity expert can learn how to express his or her uncertainty with a subjective—but quantitative—expression of uncertainty. In this chapter we will introduce the basic idea of using subjective estimates of probabilities. We will also show how your skill at doing this can be measured and improved with practice.

This chapter is largely duplicated from the calibration chapter in the original *How to Measure Anything: Finding the Value of "Intangibles" in Business*. If the reader is already familiar with the discussion of calibrated probability assessments in that book, then this chapter can be skipped or just quickly reviewed.

Introduction to Subjective Probability

In the simplest method we have described so far, there are two types of probability assignments. One type applies to discrete "either/or" events such as whether there will be a major breach of customer credit card information by a retailer. The other type applies to ranges of values, such as, how much will be lost in sales if there is a major breach of customer credit card information. These two types of probability assignments are summarized in Table 7.1.

In Chapter 3 we used both of these methods to express uncertainty about a cybersecurity event. Whether an event occurred in the first place was a type of discrete event. We assigned a probability (1%, 15%, etc.) to the event occurring within a given period of time. The monetary impact of that event was represented as a range.

Of course, we can make lots of combinations of these two basic forms of distributions. We can have discrete events with more than just two outcomes and we can have hybrids of discrete and continuous

TABLE 7.1 Two Types of Subjective Probability Assignments Used in the Simple One-for-One Substitution Model (from Chapter 3)

Type of Probability Distribution	Description	Examples
Discrete binary (a.k.a. Bernoulli)	An either/or type of event, it happens or doesn't; expressed as a probability the event will occur	▪ A coin flip ▪ A data breach happens in a given time period ▪ A system goes down ▪ "There is a 5% chance of a data breach of PHI that will be required to be reported on the HHS website"
Continuous	A quantity with a range of possible values; expressed as a "confidence interval"	▪ The size of a future data breach ▪ The duration of a future system outage ▪ The change in sales due to a past data breach (a past event but the actual value was difficult to pin down) ▪ "The 90% confidence interval for the duration of a system outage in case X is 30 minutes to 4 hours"

distributions. We can even construct a continuous distribution from a large number of binary distributions. In practice, however, this simple distinction is useful.

To express our uncertainty about a continuous number is to think of it as a range of probable values. As noted in Chapter 3, a range that has a particular chance of containing the correct answer is called in statistics a confidence interval (CI).[2] A 90% CI is a range that has a 90% chance of containing the correct answer (there is a bit of a philosophical debate on this use of the term and for subjective probabilities in general—this will be addressed later in the chapter). Recall in Chapter 3 that we asked for a range to represent the uncertainty of a loss from a breach or other cybersecurity event. You may have computed these values with all sorts of sophisticated statistical inference methods, but you may have picked values based just on your experience. Either way, the values are a reflection of your uncertainty about this quantity.

You can also use probabilities to describe your uncertainty about specific future events, such as whether customer payment card information, personal health information, or other personal information will be stolen from the hack of a particular system. You may determine that there is a 2% chance of a data breach in the next 12 months large enough to warrant some public announcement. (Note that when putting probabilities on future events, we must *always* state the period of time or the probability is meaningless.)

Of course, if this event does not occur, was the probability "right"? Clearly with a probability that is much less than 50% we weren't expecting the event to occur, anyway. But a single event doesn't determine whether a stated probability was right or wrong. We can only look at a number of data points. We can ask, "Of the large number of events we assigned a 5% probability to for a given year, did about 5% actually occur?" Likewise, where we thought an event was 20% or 1% likely in that same time period, did the event occur 20% or 1% of the time, respectively?

Unfortunately, as we mentioned in Chapter 4, extensive studies have shown that very few people are naturally calibrated estimators. Calibrated probability assessments were an area of research in decision psychology in the 1970s and 1980s and up to very recently. As we mentioned in Chapter 4, leading researchers in this area have been Daniel Kahneman, winner of the 2002 Nobel Prize in Economic Sciences, and his colleague Amos Tversky.[3] Decision psychology concerns itself with how people actually make decisions, however irrational, in contrast to many of the "management science" or "quantitative analysis" methods taught in business schools, which focus on how to work out "optimal" decisions in specific, well-defined problems. This research shows that almost everyone tends to be biased either toward

"overconfidence" or "underconfidence" about their estimates; the vast majority being overconfident (see inset, "Two Extremes of Subjective Confidence"). Putting odds on uncertain events or ranges on uncertain quantities
is not a skill that arises automatically from experience and intuition.

Two Extremes of Subjective Confidence

Overconfidence: When an individual routinely overstates knowledge
and is correct less often than he or she expects. For example, when
asked to make estimates with a 90% confidence interval, many fewer
than 90% of the true answers fall within the estimated ranges.
Underconfidence: When an individual routinely understates knowledge and is correct much more often than he or she expects. For example, when asked to make estimates with a 90% confidence interval,
many more than 90% of the true answers fall within the estimated
ranges.

Fortunately, some of the work by other researchers shows that better
estimates are attainable when estimators have been trained to remove their
personal estimating biases.[4] Researchers discovered that odds makers and
bookies were generally better at assessing the odds of events than, say,
executives. They also made some disturbing discoveries about how bad
physicians are at putting odds on unknowns like the chance that a tumor
is malignant or that a chest pain is a heart attack. They reasoned that this
variance among different professions shows that putting odds on uncertain
things must be a learned skill.

Researchers learned how experts can measure whether they are systematically underconfident, overconfident, or have other biases about their
estimates. Once people conduct this self-assessment, they can learn several
techniques for improving estimates and measuring the improvement. In
short, researchers discovered that *assessing uncertainty is a general skill
that can be taught with a measurable improvement.* That is, when calibrated
cybersecurity experts say they are 95% confident that a system will not be
breached, there really is a 95% chance the system will not be breached.

As mentioned earlier, there are competing philosophies over the definition, and both sides of the debate include many of the greatest minds
in math, statistics, and science. We won't go into detail here about that
debate but if you want to read about it, see the original *How to Measure
Anything* book, especially the third edition. The case Hubbard makes in
that book—which merely repeats the same arguments already made by

great scientists and mathematicians like L. J. Savage, Edwin T. Jaynes, and Harold Jefferies—is that the subjectivist view of probability is actually the only one that can possibly apply in real-world decision making. For your convenience, we have summarized part of this debate in the "Purely Philo-sophical Interlude" section in this chapter.

Calibration Exercise

Let's benchmark how good you are at quantifying your own uncertainty by taking a short quiz. Table 7.2 contains ten 90% CI questions and ten binary (i.e., true/false) questions. Unless you are a *Jeopardy* grand champion, you probably will not know all of these general knowledge questions with cer-tainty (although some are very simple). But they are all questions you prob-ably have some idea about. These are similar to the exercises Hubbard gives attendees in his workshops and seminars. The only difference is that the tests he gives have more questions of each type, and he presents several tests with feedback after each test. This calibration training generally takes about half a day.

But even with this small sample, we will be able to detect some impor-tant aspects of your skills. More important, the exercise should get you to think about the fact that your current state of uncertainty is itself something you can quantify.

Table 7.2 contains 10 of each of these two types of questions.

1. *90% Confidence Interval (CI).* For each of the 90% CI questions, pro-vide both an upper bound and a lower bound. Remember that the range should be wide enough that you believe there is a 90% chance that the answer will be between your bounds.
2. *Binary.* Answer whether each of the statements is "true" or "false," then circle the probability that reflects how confident you are in your answer. For example, if you are absolutely certain in your answer, you should say you have a 100% chance of getting the answer right. If you have no idea whatsoever, then your chance should be the same as a coin flip (50%). Otherwise, it is one of the values between 50% and 100%.

Of course, you could just look up the answers to any of these questions, but we are using this as an exercise to see how well you estimate things you can't just look up (e.g., how long a system will be down next year or whether one of the systems in your firm will experience a data breach).

Important hint: The questions vary in difficulty. Some will seem easy while others may seem too difficult to answer. But no matter how

TABLE 7.2 Sample Calibration Test

| # | Question | 90% Confidence Interval | |
		Lower Bound	Upper Bound
1	In 1938, a British steam locomotive set a new speed record by going how fast (mph)?		
2	In what year did Sir Isaac Newton publish the Universal Laws of Gravitation?		
3	How many inches long is a typical business card?		
4	The Internet (then called "Arpanet") was established as a military communications system in what year?		
5	In what year was William Shakespeare born?		
6	What is the air distance between New York and Los Angeles (miles)?		
7	What percentage of a square could be covered by a circle of the same width?		
8	How old was Charlie Chaplin when he died?		
9	What is the weight, in pounds, of the first edition of *How to Measure Anything*?		
10	The TV show *Gilligan's Island* first aired on what date?		

	Statement	Answer (True/False)	Confidence That You Are Correct (Circle One)
1	The ancient Romans were conquered by the ancient Greeks.		50% 60% 70% 80% 90% 100%
2	There is no species of three-humped camels.		50% 60% 70% 80% 90% 100%
3	A gallon of oil weighs less than a gallon of water.		50% 60% 70% 80% 90% 100%

TABLE 7.2 *(continued)*

		Answer (True/False)	Confidence That You Are Correct (Circle One)
4	Mars is always farther away from Earth than Venus.		50% 60% 70% 80% 90% 100%
5	The Boston Red Sox won the first World Series.		50% 60% 70% 80% 90% 100%
6	Napoleon was born on the island of Corsica.		50% 60% 70% 80% 90% 100%
7	"M" is one of the three most commonly used letters.		50% 60% 70% 80% 90% 100%
8	In 2002, the price of the average new desktop computer purchased was under $1,500.		50% 60% 70% 80% 90% 100%
9	Lyndon B. Johnson was a governor before becoming vice president.		50% 60% 70% 80% 90% 100%
10	A kilogram is more than a pound.		50% 60% 70% 80% 90% 100%

difficult the question seems, you still know something about it. Focus on what you *do* know. For the range questions, you know of some bounds beyond which the answer would seem absurd (e.g., you probably know Newton wasn't alive in ancient Greece or in the twentieth century). Similarly, for the binary questions, even though you aren't certain, you have some opinion, at least, about which answer is more likely.

After you've finished, but before you look up the answers, try a small experiment to test if the ranges you gave really reflect your 90% CI. Consider one of the 90% CI questions, let's say the one about when Newton published the Universal Laws of Gravitation. Suppose you were offered a chance to win $1,000 in one of these two ways:

A. You win $1,000 if the true year of publication of Newton's book turns out to be between the dates you gave for the upper and lower bound. If not, you win nothing.
B. You spin a dial divided into two unequal "pie slices," one comprising 90% of the dial and the other just 10%. If the dial lands on the large slice, you win $1,000. If it lands on the small slice, you win nothing (i.e., there is a 90% chance you win $1,000). (See Figure 7.1.)

Option B:

Spin the Dial!

FIGURE 7.1 Spin to Win!

Which do you prefer? The dial has a stated chance of 90% that you win $1,000 and a 10% chance that you win nothing. If you are like most people (about 80%), you prefer to spin the dial. But why would that be? The only explanation is that you think the dial has a higher chance of a payoff. The conclusion we have to draw is that the 90% CI you first estimated is really not your 90% CI. It might be your 50%, 65%, or 80% CI, but it can't be your 90% CI. We say, then, that your initial estimate was probably overconfident. You express your uncertainty in a way that indicates you have less uncertainty than you really have.

An equally undesirable outcome is to prefer option A, where you win $1,000 if the correct answer is within your range. This means that you think there is *more* than a 90% chance your range contains the answer, even though you are representing yourself as being merely 90% confident in the range. In other words, this is usually the choice of the underconfident person.

The only desirable answer you can give is if you set your range just right so that you would be indifferent between options A and B. This means that you believe you have a 90% chance—not more and not less—that the answer is within your range. For an overconfident person (i.e., most of us), making these two choices equivalent means increasing the width of the range until options A and B are considered equally valuable. For the underconfident person, the range should be narrower than first estimated.

You can apply the same test, of course, to the binary questions. Let's say you were 80% confident about your answer to the question about Napoleon's birthplace. Again, you give yourself a choice between betting on your answer being correct or spinning the dial. In this case, however, the dial pays off 80% of the time. If you prefer to spin the dial, you are probably less than 80% confident in your answer. Now let's suppose we change the payoff odds on the dial to 70%. If you then consider spinning the dial just as good (no better or worse) as betting on your answer, then you should say that you are really about 70% confident that your answer to the question is correct.

In Hubbard's calibration training classes, he has been calling this the "equivalent bet test." (Some examples in the decision psychology literature refer to this as an "equivalent urn," involving drawing random lots from an urn.) As the name implies, it tests to see whether you are really 90% confident in a range by comparing it to a bet that you should consider to be equivalent. Research indicates that even just pretending to bet money significantly improves a person's ability to assess odds.[5] In fact, *actually* betting money turns out to be only slightly better than pretending to bet.

Methods like the equivalent bet test help estimators give more realistic assessments of their uncertainty. People who are very good at assessing their uncertainty (i.e., they are right 80% of the time they say they are 80% confident, etc.) are called "calibrated." There are a few other simple methods for improving your calibration, but first, let's see how you did on the test. The answers are shown at the end of this chapter after the citations.

To see how calibrated you are, we need to compare your expected results to your actual results. Since the range questions you answered were asking for a 90% CI, you are, in effect, saying that you expect 9 out of 10 of the true answers to be within your ranges. We need only to compare how many answers were actually within your stated ranges to your expected number, 9. If expectations closely match outcomes, then you may be well calibrated. This very small sample is not, of course, conclusive for one individual. But since tests like this have been given to over 1,000 people, a pattern can be seen even with only this many questions.

Figure 7.2 shows the actual and expected distribution of answers that were within the stated CI on 10-question tests (the data in this figure actually shows results from multiple variations of the 10-question tests and results are similar across all versions). If the entire set of respondents were perfectly calibrated, we would expect most respondents (75%) to get 8, 9, or 10 of the 10 answers within their stated 90% CIs. This is literally the distribution we would expect if we rolled a 10-sided die 10 times, counted up the number of times the result was 9 or less, and repeated that a thousand times. But instead we see that most people are providing ranges that are more like a 40% or 60% CI, not a 90% CI. Those who happened to get 8 or more answers within their stated ranges are mathematically consistent with an uncalibrated but lucky "upper tail" of the uncalibrated population, not a group of people who were already calibrated when they took the first test.

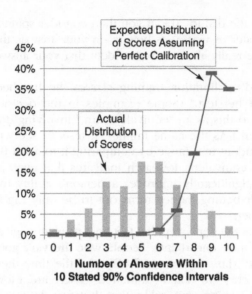

FIGURE 7.2 Distribution of Answers Within 90% CI for 10-Question Calibration Test

The expected outcome for your answers to the true/false questions, however, is not a fixed number since your confidence could be different for each answer. For each of the answers, you said you were between 50% and 100% confident. If you said you were 100% confident on all 10 questions, you are expecting to get all 10 correct. If you were only 50% confident on each question (i.e., thought your odds were no better than a coin flip), you expected to get about half of them right. To compute the expected outcome, convert each of the percentages you circled to a decimal (i.e., .5, .6, .7, .8, .9, 1 and add them up. Let's say your confidence in your answers was 1, .5, .9, .6, .7, .8, .8, 1, .9, and .7, totaling to 7.9. This means your "expected" number correct was 7.9.

If you are like most people, the number of questions you answered correctly was less than the number you expected to answer correctly. This is a very small number of questions for measuring your skill at assessing your uncertainty, but most people are so overconfident that even this small number can be illuminating.

One way to frame the performance on a test like this is to determine how likely it would be for a person who really was calibrated (i.e., each 90% CI really had a 90% chance of containing the real value) to get the observed result. A calculation would show that for such a calibrated person, there is only a 1 in 612 chance that he or she would be so unlucky as to get only 5 or fewer out of 10 of the 90% CIs to contain the real answers. See www.howtomeasureanything.com/cybersecurity for a spreadsheet example of this calculation and for examples of longer tests. But since over half of those who take these tests perform that badly (56%), we can safely conclude that it is systemic overconfidence and not a rash of bad luck combined with a small sample size. It is not just that these questions were too difficult, since these results reflect findings from a variety of tests with different questions over the past several years. Even with this small sample, if you got fewer than 7 answers within your bounds, you are probably overconfident; if you got fewer than 5 within your bounds, you are very overconfident.

People tend to fare slightly better on the true/false tests, but, on average, they still tend to be overconfident—and overconfident by enough that even a small sample of 10 can usually detect it. On average, people expect to get 74% of true/false questions like these correct, but, in reality, answer just 62% of them correct. Nearly one-third of the participants expected to get 80% to 100% correct on 10-question true/false tests like this; of those, they correctly answered only 64% of the questions. Part of the reason you may have performed better on the true/false test is because, statistically, this test is less precise. (It is easier for a calibrated person to be unlucky and for an uncalibrated person to appear calibrated in this small sample of questions.) But if your actual number correct was lower by 2.5 or more than the expected correct number, you are still probably overconfident.

Further Improvements on Calibration

The academic research so far indicates that training has a significant effect on calibration. We already mentioned the equivalent bet test, which allows us to pretend we are tying personal consequences to the outcomes. Research proves that another key method in calibrating a person's ability to assess uncertainty is repetition with feedback. To test this, we ask participants a series of trivia questions similar to the quiz you just took. They give their answers, then they are shown the true values, and they test again.

However, it doesn't appear that any single method completely corrects for the natural overconfidence most people have. To remedy this, we combined several methods and found that most people could be nearly perfectly calibrated.

Another one of these methods involves asking people to identify arguments against each of their estimates. For example, your estimate of losses due to legal liabilities may be based on another example in your firm. But when you think about how varied reported losses were in other companies and perhaps some surprising rulings by courts, you may reassess the initial range. Academic researchers found that this method by itself significantly improves calibration.[6]

Hubbard also asked experts who are providing range estimates to look at each bound on the range as a separate "binary" question. A 90% CI interval means there is a 5% chance the true value could be greater than the upper bound and a 5% chance it could be less than the lower bound. This means that estimators must be 95% sure that the true value is less than the upper bound. If they are not that certain, they should increase the upper bound until they are 95% certain. A similar test is applied to the lower bound. Performing this test seems to avoid the problem of anchoring, first mentioned in Chapter 4. Recall that anchoring is the observation that once we have a number stuck in our head, our other estimates tend to gravitate toward it. Some estimators say that when they provide ranges, they think of a single number and then add or subtract an "error" to generate their range. This might seem reasonable, but it actually tends to cause estimators to produce overconfident ranges (i.e., ranges that are too narrow). Looking at each bound alone as a separate binary question of "Are you 95% sure it is over/under this amount?" cures our tendency to anchor.

You can also force your natural anchoring tendency to work the other way. Instead of starting with a point estimate and then making it into a range, start with an absurdly wide range and then start eliminating the values you know to be extremely unlikely. If you have no idea how much losses from a breach of intellectual property (IP) data might be, start with a range of $100 to $10 billion. Then you realize that if IP is lost there will at least be an effort at evaluating the loss so you raise the lower bound. You also recognize that the value of IP can't exceed all profits from the given product and new technology reduces the longevity of IP so perhaps you lower the upper bound. And keep narrowing it from there as you eliminate absurd values.

We sometimes call this the "absurdity test." It reframes the question from "What do I think this value could be?" to "What values do I know to be ridiculous?" We look for answers that are obviously absurd and then eliminate them until we get to answers that are still unlikely but not entirely implausible. This is the edge of our knowledge about that quantity.

After a few calibration tests and practice with methods like listing pros and cons, using the equivalent bet, and anti-anchoring, estimators learn to fine-tune their "probability senses." Most people get nearly perfectly calibrated after just a half-day of training. Most important, even though subjects may have been training on general trivia, the calibration skill transfers to any area of estimation.

We've provided additional calibration tests of each type—ranges and binary—on this book's website at www.howtomeasureanything.com/cybersecurity. Using these tests, try applying the methods summarized in Table 7.3 to improve your calibration.

TABLE 7.3 Methods to Improve Your Probability Calibration

Repetition and feedback. Take several tests in succession, assessing how well you
did after each one and attempting to improve your performance on the next
one.

Equivalent bets. For each estimate, set up the equivalent bet to test if that range or
probability really reflects your uncertainty.

Consider two pros and two cons. Think of at least two reasons why you should be
confident in your assessment and two reasons you could be wrong.

Avoid anchoring. Think of range questions as two separate binary questions of
the form "Are you 95% certain that the true value is over/under (pick one) the
lower/upper (pick one) bound?"

Reverse the anchoring effect. Start with extremely wide ranges and narrow them
with the "absurdity test" as you eliminate highly unlikely values.

Conceptual Obstacles to Calibration

The methods just mentioned don't help if someone has irrational ideas
about calibration or probabilities in general. While most people in decision-making positions seem to have or are able to learn useful ideas about
probabilities, some have surprising misconceptions about these issues. We
addressed some general conceptual obstacles in Chapter 5, but let's focus
a bit further on misconceptions about the use of subjective probabilities.
Here are some comments Hubbard received while taking groups of people
through calibration training or eliciting calibrated estimates after training:

- "My 90% confidence can't have a 90% chance of being right because
  a subjective 90% confidence will never have the same chance as an
  objective 90%."
- "This is my 90% confidence interval but I have absolutely no idea if
  that is right."
- "We couldn't possibly estimate this. We have no idea."
- "If we don't know the exact answer, we can never know the odds."

The first statement was made by a chemical engineer and is indicative
of the problem he was initially having with calibration. As long as he sees
his subjective probability as inferior to objective probability, he won't get
calibrated. However, after a few calibration exercises, he did find that he
could subjectively apply odds that were correct as often as the odds implied; in other words, his 90% confidence intervals contained the correct
answers 90% of the time.

The rest of the objections are fairly similar. They are all based in part on
the idea that not knowing exact quantities is the same as knowing nothing of

any value. And, again, note that none of these types of objections would be answered in any way at all by substituting subjective—but clearly defined—probabilities and ranges with the ambiguous language of "high" or "medium" likelihood or loss. Whatever the challenges of using calibrated probability assessments might be, we can't help them by avoiding the issue with language that introduces further imprecision.

Even calibrated experts will initially need some coaching to overcome these misconceptions. The following example is based on a conversation Hubbard Decision Research had with the information security staff at the U.S. Department of Veterans Affairs (first mentioned in Chapter 2) back in 2000. The expert initially gave no range at all and instead insisted that it could never be estimated. He went from saying he knew "nothing" about a variable to later conceding that he actually is very certain about some bounds.

Analyst: If your systems are being brought down by a computer virus, how long does the downtime last? As always, all I need is a 90% confidence interval.

Security Expert: We would have no way of knowing that. Sometimes we were down for a short period, sometimes a long one. We don't really track it in detail because the priority is always getting the system back up, not documenting the event.

Analyst: Of course you can't know it exactly. That's why we only put a range on it, not an exact number. But what would be the longest downtime you ever had?

Security Expert: I don't know, it varied so much. . .

Analyst: Were you ever down for more than two entire workdays?

Security Expert: No, never two whole days.

Analyst: Ever more than a day?

Security Expert: I'm not sure . . . probably.

Analyst: We are looking for your 90% confidence interval of a future downtime. If you consider all the downtimes you've had due to a virus, are they usually more than a day?

Security Expert: I see what you mean. I would say the average is usually less than a day.

Analyst: So your upper bound for an event would be . . . ?

Security Expert: Okay, I think almost all system outages would be resolved in 24 hours.

Analyst: Great. Now let's consider the lower bound. How small could it be?

Security Expert: Some events are corrected in a couple of hours. Some take longer.

Analyst:	Okay, but does a system ever get back online in less than an hour?
Security Expert:	I suppose it has taken less than 30 minutes at times.
Analyst:	Good. So your 90% confidence interval for the duration of a single outage is 30 minutes to 24 hours?
Security Expert:	Yes, but I suppose a system could be out for three days.
Analyst:	Sure. That's why we call it a 90% confidence interval. We allow for a 5% chance it is below the lower bound and a 5% chance it is above the upper bound. In our simulations, we will get values below 30 minutes or greater than 24 hours a total of 1 in 10 times. Depending on the distribution we choose, we could get durations of a few days on rare occasions.
Security Expert:	Then I would say that sounds about right.

This is a typical conversation for a number of highly uncertain quantities. Initially the experts resist giving any range at all, perhaps because they have been taught that in business, the lack of an exact number is the same as knowing nothing, or perhaps because they will be "held accountable for a number." But *the lack of having an exact number is not the same as knowing nothing.* The security expert knew that it is definitely not true that most outages would be solved in less than 30 minutes or that most would last longer than a week. He at least knew those were rarer extremes. He was uncertain, of course, but the uncertainty was not boundless.

This example is one reason we don't like to use the word "assumption" in our analysis. An assumption is a statement we treat as true for the sake of argument, regardless of whether it is true. Assumptions are necessary if you have to use deterministic accounting methods with exact points as values. You could never know an exact point with certainty, so any such value must be an assumption. But if you are allowed to model your uncertainty with ranges and probabilities, you do not have to state something you don't know for a fact. If you are uncertain, your ranges and assigned probabilities should reflect that. If you have "no idea" that a narrow range is correct, you simply widen it until it reflects what you do know.

It is easy to get lost in how much you don't know about a problem and forget that there are still some things you *do* know. There is literally nothing we will ever need to measure where our only bounds are negative infinity to positive infinity.

The dialog is an example of the absurdity tests in the reverse-anchoring approach we mentioned earlier. We apply it whenever we get the "There is no way I could know that" response or the "Here's my range, but it's a guess" response. No matter how little experts think they know about a quantity, it always turns out that there are still values they know are absurd.

Again, the point at which a value ceases to be absurd and starts to become unlikely but somewhat plausible is the edge of their uncertainty about the quantity. As a final test, we give them an equivalent bet to see if the resulting range is really a 90% CI.

You will likely encounter more conceptual objections as you implement more quantitative methods that will rely, at some point, on subjective estimates of probabilities. As the survey in Chapter 5 showed, curious dispositions about the use of probabilities seem to affect some small percentage of professionals in cybersecurity. One more example of this observed by Hubbard is the case where the expert responded that every event was 100% likely. His own colleagues argued with him regarding what seemed like an obviously absurd position. He responded that he had to act *as if* each of these events was going to happen. His colleagues sitting next to him pointed out that if that were the case, he would have to treat every event as equally likely, and since his resources were limited, he would have to assign them arbitrarily. He seemed to be conflating the likelihood of the event with risk tolerance and what to do about it.

A Purely Philosophical Interlude

Does 90% Confidence Mean 90% Probability?

All possible definitions of probability fall short of the actual practice.
—William Feller (1906–1970), American mathematician[7]

It is unanimously agreed that statistics depends somehow on probability. But, as to what probability is and how it is connected with statistics, there has seldom been such complete disagreement and breakdown of communication since the Tower of Babel.
—L. J. Savage (1917–1971), American mathematician[8]

Throughout this book, we will refer to a 90% CI as a range of values (indicated by an upper and lower bound) that has a 90% probability of containing the true value. We will use this definition regardless of whether the CI was determined subjectively or—as Chapter 9 will show—with sample data. By doing so, we're using a particular interpretation of probability that treats it as an expression of the uncertainty or "degree of belief" of the person providing the estimate.

Some (not all) statistics professors hold a different interpretation that contradicts this. If we computed the 90% CI of, say, the estimate of the population of users following a security protocol correctly, to be 25% to 40%, they would argue that it is incorrect to say there is a 90% probability that the true population mean is within the interval. They would say the true population mean is either in the range or not.

This is one aspect of what is called the "frequentist" interpretation of confidence intervals. Students and many scientists alike find this a confusing position. A frequentist would argue that the term "probability" can apply only to events that are purely random, "strictly repeatable," and have an infinite number of iterations. These are three conditions that, if we pin a frequentist down on the definitions, make probability a purely mathematical abstraction that never applies to any situation in practical decision making.

Most decision makers, however, behave as if they take the position we use in this book. They are called "subjectivists," meaning that they use probabilities to describe a personal state of uncertainty, whether or not it meets criteria like being "purely random." This position is also sometimes called the "Bayesian" interpretation (although this interpretation and the Bayes formula we will discuss in Chapter 8 often have nothing to do with each other). To a subjectivist, a probability merely describes what a person knows, whether or not the uncertainty involves a fixed fact, such as the true mean of a population, as long as it is unrevealed to the observer. Using probabilities (and confidence intervals) as an expression of uncertainty is the practical approach for making risky decisions.

Suppose you and a colleague bet on how many people will lose a laptop next month (we're not proposing you start such betting pools; this is just an example). You state your 90% CI for laptops lost is between 2 and 10 next month. Suppose you also have the choice to make a bet instead, on a spin of a dial where you have a 90% chance of winning. Whatever bet you would be willing to make on one you would be willing to make on the other. Until new information, such as the true number of lost laptops, is revealed to you, you treat the confidence in a confidence interval as a probability. If real money was on the line, we suspect an experiment involving frequentist statisticians betting on various confidence intervals and dial-spins would show they would also act like subjectivists.

In many published works in the empirical sciences, physicists,[9] epidemiologists,[10] and paleobiologists[11] explicitly and routinely describe a confidence interval as having a *probability* of containing the estimated value. Yet it appears that nobody has ever had to retract an article because of it—nor should anyone. It is important to note, however, that

(*Continued*)

(Continued)

either interpretation is pure semantics and is not a function of mathematical fundamentals or empirical observation that can be proven true or false. This is why these positions are called merely "interpretations" and not "theorems" or "laws."

But there is one pragmatic, measurable, real-world difference between these two interpretations: Students find the frequentist interpretation much more confusing. *Some* statistics professors understand this perfectly well and therefore teach both the subjectivist and frequentist interpretations. Like most decision scientists, we will act as if a 90% confidence interval has a 90% probability of containing the true value (and we never run into a mathematical paradox because of it).

The Effects of Calibration

One of the authors, Doug Hubbard, started calibrating people in 1995, gathering data on how well people do on trivia tests and even how well-calibrated people do in estimating real-life uncertainties after those events have come to pass. The calibration methods and tests have evolved but have been fairly consistent since 2001. Since then, Hubbard and his team at Hubbard Decision Research have trained well over 1,000 people in calibration methods and have recorded their performance, both their expected and actual results on several calibration tests, given one after the other during a half-day workshop.

The data gathered over these participants gave some insight into the aggregated data often published in various peer-reviewed scientific studies. The academic research usually shows aggregated results for all the participants in the research, so we can see only an average for a group. When Hubbard aggregated the performance of participants in the same way, he got a result very similar to the prior research. But because he could break down the data by specific subjects, he saw another interesting phenomenon. Hubbard observed that most perform superbly by the end of the training; it is a few poor performers who bring down the average.

To determine who is calibrated we have to allow for some deviation from the target, even for a perfectly calibrated person. Also, an uncalibrated person can get lucky. Accounting for this statistical error in the testing, fully 80% of participants are ideally calibrated after the fifth calibration exercise. They are neither underconfident nor overconfident. Their 90% CIs have about a 90% chance of containing the correct answer.

Another 10% show significant improvement but don't quite reach ideal calibration. And 10% show no significant improvement at all from the first test they take.[12] The analysis shows there are different groups of performance among the individuals, which does not fit the model of everyone being slightly uncalibrated. This group cannot be explained as just randomly unlucky participants, and those who were calibrated cannot just be a lucky but uncalibrated majority. Why is it that about 10% of people are apparently unable to improve at all in calibration training? Whatever the reason, it turns out not to be that relevant. Every single person we ever relied on for actual estimates was in the first two groups, and almost all were in the first, ideally calibrated group. Those who seemed to resist any attempt at calibration were, even before the testing, never considered to be the relevant expert or decision maker for a particular problem. It may be that they were less motivated, knowing their opinion would not have much bearing. Or it could be that those who lacked aptitude for such problems just don't tend to advance to the level of the people we need for the estimates. Either way, it's academic.

We see that training works very well for most people. But does proven performance in training reflect an ability to assess the odds of real-life uncertainties? The answer here is an unequivocal yes. Hubbard tracked how well-calibrated people do in real-life situations on multiple occasions, but one particular controlled experiment done in the IT industry still stands out. In 1997, Hubbard was asked to train the analysts of the IT advisory firm Giga Information Group (since acquired by Forrester Research, Inc.) in assigning odds to uncertain future events. Giga was an IT research firm that sold its research to other companies on a subscription basis. Giga had adopted the method of assigning odds to events it was predicting for clients, and it wanted to be sure it was performing well.

Hubbard trained 16 Giga analysts using the methods described earlier. At the end of the training, the analysts were given 20 specific IT industry predictions they would answer as true or false and to which they would assign a confidence. The test was given in January 1997, and all the questions were stated as events occurring or not occurring by June 1, 1997 (e.g., "True or False: Intel will release its 300 MHz Pentium by June 1," etc.). As a control, the same list of predictions was also given to 16 of their chief information officer (CIO) clients at various organizations. After June 1 the actual outcomes could be determined. Hubbard presented the results at Giga World 1997, their major IT industry symposium for the year. Figure 7.3 shows the results. Note that some participants opted not to answer all of the questions, so the response counts on the chart don't add up to 320 (16 subjects times 20 questions each) in each of the two groups.

The horizontal axis is the chance the participants gave to their prediction on a particular issue being correct. The vertical axis shows how

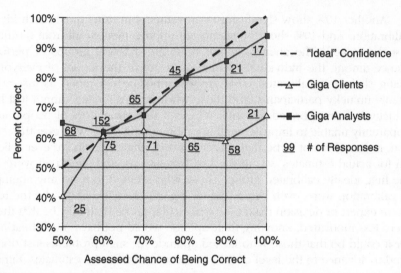

FIGURE 7.3 Calibration Experiment Results for 20 IT Industry Predictions in 1997
Source: Hubbard Decision Research

many of those predictions turned out to be correct. An ideally calibrated person should be plotted right along the dotted line. This means the person was right 70% of the time he or she was 70% confident in the predictions, 80% right when he or she was 80% confident, and so on. You see that the analysts' results (where the points are indicated by small squares) were very close to the ideal confidence, easily within allowable error. The results appear to deviate the most from perfect calibration at the low end of the scale, but this part is still within acceptable limits of error. (The acceptable error range is wider on the left of the chart and narrows to zero at the right.) Of all the times participants said they were 50% confident, they turned out to be right about 65% of the time. This means they might have known more than they let on and—only on this end of the scale—were a little underconfident. It's close; these results might be due to chance. There is a 1% chance that 44 or more out of 68 would be right just by flipping a coin.

The deviation is a bit more significant—at least statistically if not visually—at the other end of the scale. Where the analysts indicated a high degree of confidence, chance alone would have allowed for only slightly less deviation from expected, so they are a little overconfident on that end of the scale. But, overall, they are very well calibrated.

In comparison, the results of clients who did not receive any calibration training (indicated by the small triangles) were very overconfident. The numbers next to their calibration results show that there were 58 instances when a particular client said he or she was 90% confident in a particular prediction. Of those times, the clients got less than 60% of those predictions correct. Clients who said they were 100% confident in a prediction in 21 specific responses got only 67% of those correct. All of these results are consistent with what has typically been observed in a number of other calibration studies over the past several decades.

Equally interesting is the fact that the Giga analysts didn't actually get more answers correct. (The questions were general to the IT industry, not focusing on analyst specialties.) They were simply more conservative—but not overly conservative—about when they would put high confidence on a prediction. Prior to the training, however, the calibration of the analysts on general trivia questions was just as bad as the clients were on predictions of actual events. The results are clear: The difference in accuracy is due entirely to calibration training, and the calibration training—even though it uses trivia questions—works for real-world predictions.

Many of Hubbard's previous readers and clients have run their own calibration workshops and saw varying results depending on how closely they followed these recommendations. In every case where they could not get as many people calibrated as observed in Hubbard's workshops, it was found that they did not actually try to teach all of the calibration strategies mentioned in Table 7.3. In particular, they did not cover the equivalent bet, which seems to be one of the most important calibration strategies. Those who followed these strategies and practiced with them on every exercise invariably saw results similar to those observed by Hubbard.

Motivation and experience in estimating may also be a factor. Hubbard usually gives his training to experienced managers and analysts, most of whom knew they would be called on to make real-world estimates with their new skills. Dale Roenigk of the University of North Carolina–Chapel Hill gave this same training to his students and noticed a much lower rate of calibration (although still a significant improvement). Unlike managers, students are rarely asked for estimates; this may have been a factor in their performance. As observed in Hubbard's own workshops, those who did not expect their answers to be used in the subsequent real-world estimation tasks were almost always those who showed little or no improvement.

There is one other extremely important effect of calibration. In addition to improving one's ability to subjectively assess odds, calibration seems to eliminate objections to probabilistic analysis in decision making. Prior to calibration training, people might feel any subjective estimate was useless. They might believe that the only way to know a CI is to do the math they vaguely remember from first-semester statistics. They may distrust probabilistic analysis in general because all probabilities seem arbitrary to them. But it is rare for a person to offer such challenges after being calibrated. Apparently, the hands-on experience of being forced to assign probabilities, and then seeing that this was a measurable skill in which they could see real improvements, addresses these concerns. Although this was not an objective when Hubbard first started calibrating people, it became clear how critical this process was in getting them to accept the entire concept of probabilistic analysis in decision making.

You now understand how to quantify your current uncertainty by learning how to provide calibrated probabilities. This skill is critical to the next steps in measurement.

Notes

1. P. Laplace, *Théorie analytique des probabilités* (Paris: Courcier, 1812), translated by F. W. Truscott and F. L. Emory as *A Philosophical Essay on Probabilities* (Mineola, NY: Dover, 1952), 16–17.
2. Some proponents of the alternative "frequentist" interpretation of probability will find it necessary to differentiate between a confidence interval and a "credibility interval" or "credence interval." This distinction is unnecessary for our purposes since we take a Bayesian view of probability—that is, it is ultimately an expression of a personal state of uncertainty. See the "Purely Philosophical Interlude" in this chapter for further discussion.
3. D. Kahneman and A. Tversky, "Subjective Probability: A Judgment of Representativeness," *Cognitive Psychology* 4 (1972): 430–454; and D. Kahneman and A. Tversky, "On the Psychology of Prediction," *Psychological Review* 80 (1973): 237–251.
4. B. Fischhoff, L. D. Phillips, and S. Lichtenstein, "Calibration of Probabilities: The State of the Art to 1980," in *Judgment under Uncertainty: Heuristics and Biases*, ed. D. Kahneman and A. Tversky (New York: Cambridge University Press, 1982).
5. Ibid.
6. Ibid.
7. William Feller, *An Introduction to Probability Theory and Its Applications* (New York: John Wiley & Sons, 1957), 19.
8. L. J. Savage, *The Foundations of Statistics* (New York: John Wiley & Sons, 1954), 2.
9. Frederick James, *Statistical Methods in Experimental Physics,* 2nd ed. (Hackensack, NJ: World Scientific Publishing, 2006), 215; and Byron P. Roe, *Probability and Statistics in Experimental Physics,* 2nd ed. (New York: Springer Verlag, 2001), 128.
10. C. C. Brown, "The Validity of Approximation Methods for the Interval Estimation of the Odds Ratio," *American Journal of Epidemiology* 113 (1981): 474–480.

11. Steve C. Wang and Charles R. Marshal, "Improved Confidence Intervals for Estimating the Position of a Mass Extinction Boundary," *Paleobiology* 30 (January 2004): 5–18.
12. Note that this is slightly different from the figures in the editions of *How to Measure Anything: Finding the Value of "Intangibles" in Business* because we continued to gather new samples (i.e., participants in calibration training).

Answers to Trivia Questions for Calibration Exercise

Confidence Intervals: (1) 203 (2) 1685 (3) 8.9 (4) 1969 (5) 1564 (6) 3,944 (7) 78.5% (8) 88 (9) 0.56 (10) 1964 True/False: (1) True (2) True (3) True (4) False (5) True (6) True (7) False (8) True (9) False (10) True

CHAPTER 8

Reducing Uncertainty with Bayesian Methods

We are now in possession of proven theorems and masses of worked-out numerical examples. As a result, the superiority of Bayesian methods is now a thoroughly demonstrated fact in a hundred different areas.

—E. T. Jaynes, Quantum Physicist and Outspoken Bayesian Proponent, in *Probability Theory: The Logic of Science: Principles and Elementary Applications*

The previous chapter showed how the performance of subjective probabilities are objectively measurable—and they have been measured thoroughly in published scientific literature. These subjective "prior probabilities" ("priors" for short) are the starting point of all of our analyses. This is the best way to both preserve the special knowledge and experience of the cybersecurity expert and produce results that are mathematically meaningful and useful in simulations. Stating our current uncertainty in a quantitative manner allows us to update our probabilities with new observations using some powerful mathematical methods.

The tools we are introducing in this chapter are part of Bayesian methods in probability and statistics, named after the original eighteenth-century developer of the idea, Reverend Thomas Bayes. It has multiple advantages that are particularly well suited to the problems the cybersecurity expert faces. First, it exploits existing knowledge of experts. This is in contrast to conventional methods the reader may have been exposed to in first-semester statistics, which assume that literally nothing else is known about a measurement before the sample data was acquired. Second, because it uses this prior knowledge it can make inferences from very little data. These inferences may be just slight reductions in the cybersecurity expert's uncertainty, but they can still have a big impact on risk mitigation decisions. If you do have a lot of data, the Bayesian solution and the measurements from basic sampling methods that ignore prior knowledge will converge.

In this chapter we will introduce some of the basic Bayesian reasoning and how it might apply to one problem in cybersecurity. We will, for now, focus on fundamental mechanics to lay a foundation. The basics we are covering will be trivial for some. We assume nothing more than that the reader is familiar with basic algebra. But there is a lot of detail to cover, so, if you find this trivial, feel free to skim quickly. If you find it overwhelming, bear in mind that you still, as always, have access to the calculations done for you in our downloadable spreadsheet (www .howtomeasureanything.com/cybersecurity). If you can make it through this chapter, the reward is access to some very powerful tools in the next chapter.

We will put this in context by starting with an example of a concern to everyone in cybersecurity—the major data breach.

A Major Data Breach Example

Imagine this hypothetical, and overly simplified, scenario. As CISO for company ABC, you find yourself responsible for securing a large portfolio of cloud-deployed products. These products all process critical data—data that must be secure. The associated databases include financial data and even sensitive data. Let's say this is a large organization and each of the cloud applications process millions of records of critical data daily. Also, the company has 500 developers updating code regularly from several global locations. Your company additionally has embraced a DevOps approach, which supports multiple software-feature releases on a daily basis in rapid succession. Last, you have invested in a series of security defenses and security staff.

In short, you have lots of risk in your systems, you create a lot of new risk daily via development, but you also are heavily armored and believe you are ready for battle. Unexpectedly, you have been asked into the CEO's office for a quick talk.

CEO: I just heard about financial company XYZ getting hacked right through the front door of their website—huge data loss and a lot of liability! What is the chance that someone can hack any one of our websites and steal our customers' data?

CISO: You pull out your mobile device and open the Naïve Bayesian Calculator spreadsheet you downloaded from www.howtomeasureanything .com/cybersecurity. You say, "1.24% over the next year, but I reserve the right to update that number after our next comprehensive third-party penetration test."

CEO: That sounds like an impossibly precise number.

CISO: Actually it's a probability. It represents my uncertainty about what the "precise" outcome will be. In this case, this probability was derived from other subjective probability estimates I've provided. My staff and I have been calibrated so we've measured how good we are at assessing subjective probabilities.

CEO: You now have me curious. How much will you change your mind if your test finds something? Or, what if your test finds nothing— would you change that rather specific number?

CISO: We've done other pen tests, but now the pen testers are looking for a particular set of remotely exploitable vulnerabilities. If they find them in our cloud products and are able to steal protected data without us knowing about it, then I would say my belief in possible future loss goes up to 24%. If the pen testers get no treasure, then 1.01%. The bigger question is, if they succeed or even get close, what is the likelihood that we have already been breached? And, perhaps even more importantly, when should we take our forensics to determine if there was a loss? Forensics is very expensive. . .

CEO: Please let me know the results of the test and your recommended decisions in light of those results. Let's make it fast . . . we have an opportunity here. Now, let me see that spreadsheet, I have a lot of other questions for it!

Questions like the CEO's about future loss are normal. When big breaches like Sony, JPMorgan, Target, and RSA happen, executives naturally wonder, "Could that be us?" They are wondering about a highly uncertain, and possibly dangerous, future loss. Reframing the question in quantitative terms such as "What is the probability of having a massive data breach?" is reasonable.

To make this example real, imagine we've identified three specific terms (defined well enough that they meet our clarity tests), downloaded the aforementioned spreadsheet, and entered those terms accordingly.

Defining the Binary Terms

We are introducing the idea of modifying a probability based on a condition. That is, you have a probability that something will happen, learn one new thing, and you update that probability. We are actually introducing a way to decompose that a little further by showing that the condition itself can be an uncertain state that is also conditional on something else.

In this simple example we will limit the analysis to three discrete, binary states—each is something that is either true or false. The three terms we are defining are:

- The occurrence in a given year of a "major data breach" (MDB)
- The existence of a currently unknown but possible "remotely exploitable vulnerability" (REV)
- A result on a penetration test that would indicate the existence of some remotely exploitable vulnerability, called a "positive pen test" (PPT)

Let's assume MDB, REV, and PPT have been defined for us in unambiguous terms that are clear, observable, and useful for practical decisions. In this simple case, the CEO and other stakeholders (decision makers) wanted to evaluate the risk of an MDB like the ones they read about in the news. They agreed that to be considered a massive data breach it must be 1 million records or more. Also, they agreed on specific terms for what REV means by identifying types of weaknesses in their web application, cloud infrastructure, and/or security operations that would allow an external malicious party to steal data remotely. Finally, the penetration test is a defined campaign with potential results and the meaning of those results are specifically identified.

If our stakeholders know precisely what the terms mean, how they are observed, and what consequences they would have for action, then we have a useful decomposition of the problem. If we decomposed this risk to "nation-state threat actor wielding a zero day," we would have made the error of "useless decompositions," in which case what we do, and how we know for sure, are put far out of reach.

The Bayesian example we are going to describe involves two "stages" of analysis. The existence of a remotely exploitable vulnerability changes the probability of a major data breach. Furthermore, the outcome of a penetration test changes the probability of a remotely exploitable vulnerability. In this way, we have made a simple decomposition of the likelihood of a major data breach. But otherwise, this example is contrived to make the Bayesian solution as simple as we can make it.

A Brief Introduction to Bayes and Probability Theory

> *The claim has often been correctly made that Einstein's equation*
> *$E = mc^2$ is of supreme importance because it underlies so much of*
> *physics. . . . I would claim that Bayes equation, or rule, is equally*
> *important because it describes how we ought to react to the acquisition*
> *of new information.*

—Dennis V. Lindley[1]

In our model, we started with the CISO's beliefs about our key variables and how they relate. Specifically, he provided a calibrated estimate for the probability for having a massive data breach in light of a remotely exploitable vulnerability.

The Language of Probabilities: A Basic Vocabulary

If we give you a little notation now, we can avoid longer and potentially more confusing verbal expressions. This may be trivial to some readers, but if you are the least bit rusty, look this over to get back up to speed on how to write in the language of probabilities. For now, we will just mention a few handy rules from probability theory. This is not the complete list of fundamental axioms from probability theory, and it's definitely not a comprehensive list of all theorems that might be useful. But it is enough to get through this chapter.

1. How to write "Probability."

    P(A) = probability of A. P(A) has to be some value between 0 and 1, inclusive.

    P(~A) = the probability of *not* A. Read the "~" sign as "no," "not," or "is/will not."

    If P(MDB) is the probability of a major data breach in a given year, then P(~MDB) is the probability there won't be a major data breach.
2. The "Something has to be true but contradictory things can't both be true" rule.

    The probabilities of all mutually exclusive and collectively exhaustive events or states must add up to 1. If there are just two possible outcomes, say A or not A, then:

    P(A) + P(~A) = 1

    For example, either there will be a major data breach or not. If we defined this term unambiguously (which we assume we have in this specific case), it has to be one or the other and it can't be both (i.e., we can have MDB happen and NOT happen)

3. How to write the probability of "More than one thing happens."

P(A,B) means both A and B are true. If A and B are "independent," meaning the probability of one does not depend on the other, then P(A,B) = P(A)P(B). This may not be the case for MDB, REV, and PPT, so we can't say P(MDB,REV,PPT) = P(MDB)P(REV)P(PPT).

4. How to write, and compute, probability when "It depends" (conditional probability).

P(A | B) = conditional probability of A given B. For example, P(MDB | REV) is how we can write the probability of a major data breach given a remotely exploitable vulnerability. It is also true that P(A | B) = P(A,B) / P(B). If A can change based on two or more things, we can write P(A | B,C).

5. How to decompose "More than one thing happens" into a series of "It depends."

We can use rule 4 to turn a larger joint probability of two things into P(A,B)=P(A|B)P(B) and if we have a joint probability of three things we can write P(A,B,C)=P(A|B,C)P(B|C)P(C) and so on. This is called the "chain rule."

6. How to add up "It can happen different ways" rule.

We can extend Rule 4 to working out the probability based on all the conditions under which it could happen and the probabilities of each of those conditions.

P(A) = P(A | B)P(B) + P(A | ~B)P(~B)

For example, a positive penetration test has some bearing on the probability of a major data breach. Using this rule, the probability of a major data breach can be written like this:

P(MDB) = P(MDB | PPT)P(PPT) + P(MDB | ~PPT) P(~PPT)

7. How to "flip" a conditional probability: Bayes's Rule

We will often want to "flip" a conditional probability. That is, we might start out with P(A | B) but what we really want is P(B | A). These two things are only equal if P(A) = P(B), which is often not the case. So in order to flip them we have to apply Bayes's Rule, which is written as:

P(A | B) = P(A)P(B | A) / P(B)

Sometimes the form of this is referred to as the "general" form of Bayes by computing P(B) according to the rule stated in Rule 3. If we consider just two conditions for P(B), then Rule 4 allows us to substitute P(B) so that:

P(A | B) = P(A)P(B | A)/[P(B | A)P(A) + P(B | ~A)P(~A)]

In our particular case, we want to know the probability of a major data breach given some additional information, like the discovery of a particular remotely exploitable vulnerability. We can write this as:

$$P(MDB \mid REV) = \frac{P(MDB)P(REV \mid MDB)}{P(REV \mid MDB)P(MDB) + P(REV \mid \sim MDB)P(\sim MDB)}$$

In short, Bayes's Rule allows you to determine P(MDB | REV) from P(REV | MDB) or vice versa. This means that you can determine the probability of your evidence given an event and, conversely, the probability of an event given your evidence. To see how these are different, consider the following:

- "What is the probability we have had a breach in light of the fact that we found several malware specimens that were beaconing to blacklisted command and control servers for the last six months?"

  Written: P(Breach | Malware Beaconing To Blacklisted Server)

- Equally important is, "What is the probability that we have malware beaconing to blacklisted servers owned by organized crime given that we discovered millions of corporate e-mails, user IDs, Social Security numbers, and other protected data being sold in the netherworld by organized crime—that is, that we had a breach?"

  Written: P(Malware Beaconing To Blacklisted Server | Breach)

Did you see how these are different? The first led with asking, "What is the probability of the event (Breach) given the evidence?" The second is asking, "What is the probability of the evidence given the fact that the event has occurred?" (Getting these two confused is also known as the "Prosecutor's Fallacy" if you want to study this further.)

This "flip" is what Bayes's Rule is all about, and we will find it becomes a very important foundation of reasoning under uncertainty. Bayesian probability becomes a "consistency" yardstick for measuring *your* beliefs about some uncertain event as you get more data. In particular, it makes the process of updating those beliefs reasonable.

A Brief Note on Priors

All of the operations just described require some source of an input. In this example, we will be using the calibrated estimates of the CISO. Since the CISO is using his previous experience and his calibrated probability-assessment skill to generate the inputs, we call them an "informative prior." Again, "prior" is short for "what you already believe about something." An informative prior is a fancy way for saying that your prior is generated by a subject matter expert who knows *something*, is well calibrated, and is willing to state how some things are more likely than others.

We could also start with an "uninformative prior." The idea here is to have a prior that assumes a maximum possible level of uncertainty at first; any changes to that will be informed by the data. It is considered a more conservative starting point since it can't be influenced by the mistaken beliefs of the expert—on the other hand, it can't take into account perfectly legitimate beliefs, either.

It could be argued that an uninformative prior on a discrete binary event is 50%. There is actually a philosophical debate about this, which we won't get into, but, mathematically speaking, that is the most uncertainty we can have in a system with only two possible states. Of course, the selection of a prior in either case is subjective. The uninformative prior is considered more conservative by some people but it is probably also less realistic than the informative (i.e., you usually don't really have *zero* prior information). Whatever the mix you have on the subjective to objective scale, probability theory can help make your reasoning far more consistent.

Proving Bayes

If you've absorbed all of that to the point of its being intuitive, there are some more concepts you can pick up if you understand where Bayes's Rule comes from. To do that let's expand on the chain rule (item #5 in the basic vocabulary list).

Consider all the possible combinations of remotely exploitable vulnerability and major data breach, such as both are true (REV, MDB), neither is true (~REV, ~MDB), and one or the other is true but not both, (~REV, MDB) and (REV,~MDB). Think of these as branches on a "chain rule tree" as shown in Figure 8.1.

Starting from the left, a branch in each level is multiplied by a single branch in the next level, leading to all four combinations we need. From left to right, following the top branch, we get P(REV)P(MDB | REV) = P(REV,MDB). It shows the flow of probability from left to right using multiplication. Each branch ends in what decision analysts call "elemental probabilities." This is just another way to decompose a probability similar to what we did with impacts

Elemental Probabilities

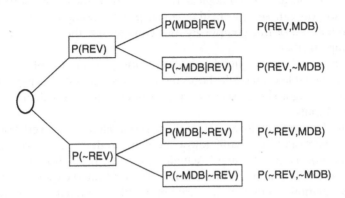

FIGURE 8.1 A Chain Rule Tree

in Chapter 6. You don't have to use it explicitly, but you can see how by fill-ing in some of the nodes of this tree, you can infer others. So now let's look at how we come up with Bayes's Rule in the first place.

Proving Bayes

1. P(MDB,REV) = P(REV,MDB)—Same as 3 × 2 = 2 × 3 or the "commuta-tive property"
2. P(MDB,REV) = P(MDB)P(REV | MDB)—See tree in Figure 8.1, first branch
3. P(REV,MDB) = P(REV)P(MDB | REV)—True because of 1 and 2.
4. P(MDB)P(REV | MDB) = P(REV)P(MDB | REV)—True because of 1, 2, and 3
5. P(REV | MDB) = P(REV)P(MDB | REV) / P(MDB)—Divide #4 by P(MDB)
6. P(MDB | REV) = P(MDB)P(REV | MDB) / P(REV)—Divide #4 by P(REV)

Please don't feel you need to memorize these; just understand them as sub-rules. We reference these throughout our analysis.

Bayes Applied to the Cloud Breach Use Case

Now that you have the basics of probability manipulation in hand, we will analyze how the calculator builds its outputs using all the equations we have provided. We have added a larger chain rule tree as a crutch for understanding the flow of probability. If you get all of this, which requires no more than seventh-grade algebra, you will be well on your way toward modeling using any technological medium. Also, these are purposefully simple so you can see the mathematical proofs. Computational tools we provide hide all of this complexity, but you can use them to study the relationships further.

Figure 8.2 shows a spreadsheet calculation you can download from the website. The table on the left shows the inputs of calibrated experts and the table on the right shows some derived values that were calculated based on those inputs.

Before we get into how each of these probabilities is derived, you might ask why we would necessarily know the items in the "Calibrated Expert Inputs" and not "Derived Values." Actually, we could have chosen many combinations of different inputs and outputs. The calibrated expert simply starts with the quantities they feel they are better able to estimate. Or, if they feel they have some idea for many of the derived values, they can check to see if their estimates of probabilities in the second table are at least consistent with those in the first.

We also could have decided to estimate P(MDB | PPT) directly without using REV as a middle step. But we wanted to show how uncertainties about different states can be linked together. Now let's show how we did the math with these values one-by-one for each of the values shown in "Derived Values" in Figure 8.2.

Calibrated Expert Inputs		Derived Values	
P(MDB|REV)	25.00%	P(REV|MDB)	20.15%
P(MDB|~REV)	1.00%	P(REV|~MDB)	0.76%
P(REV|PPT)	95.00%	P(~MDB|REV)	75.00%
P(REV|~PPT)	0.05%	P(MDB)	1.24%
P(PPT)	1.00%	P(REV)	1.00%
		P(MDB|PPT)	23.80%
		P(MDB|~PPT)	1.01%

FIGURE 8.2 Major Data Breach Decomposition Example with Conditional Probabilities

1. What is the probability of this remotely exploitable vulnerability?

   P(REV) = P(PPT)P(REV | PPT) + P(~PPT)P(REV | ~PPT)

   = (.01)(.95) + (1 − .01)(.0005) = 1.0%

2. What is the probability of P(MDB)?

   P(MDB) = P(REV)P(MDB | REV) + P(~REV)P(MDB | ~REV)

   = (.01)(.25) + (1 − .01)(.01) = 1.24%

3. What is the probability of a remotely exploitable vulnerability given the probability there is a massive data breach?

   P(REV | MDB) = P(MDB | REV)P(REV)/P(MDB)

   = (.25)(.01)/(.0124) = 20.16%

Note: You can now see that P(MDB | REV) ≠ P(REV | MDB), as we pointed out before.

4. Probability of a remotely exploitable vulnerability given the probability there isn't a massive data breach?

   P(REV | ~MDB) = P(~MDB | REV)P(REV)/P(~MDB)

   Using the complements of the calibrated probabilities we were given by the CISO—that is, P(~MDB | REV) = 1 − P(MDB | REV) and P(~MDB) = 1 − P(MDB)—we continue with

   = (1 − .25)(.01) / (1 − .0124) = 0.76%

Now here is what we really wanted to know all along: How much should the penetration test results change our probability of a massive data breach?

5. Probability of a massive data breach given a positive penetration test.

   P(MDB | PPT) = P(REV | PPT) P(MDB | REV) + (1 − P(REV | PPT)) P(MDB | ~REV)

   = (.95)(.25) + (.05)(.01) = 23.8%

6. Probability of a massive data breach given the penetration test failed.

   P(MDB | ~PPT) = P(REV | ~PPT)P(MDB | REV) + (1 − P(REV | ~PPT)) P(MDB | ~REV)

   = (.0005)(.25) + (1 − .0005)(.01) = 1.01%

Knowing the outcome of the penetration test was informative since P(MDB | PPT) > P(MDB) > P(MDB | ~PPT). Think of informative conditions like a teeter-totter with the original prior in the middle. If a condition increases the probability, the opposite of that condition must decrease it, and vice versa. (By the way, this is the reason for the stats literacy answer shown in Chapter 5, Table 5.4.)

We just showed how a Bayesian analysis can be applied to update a prior probability of a major data breach based on an observed pen test. To make it as simple as possible, the entire calculation has been provided in a spreadsheet. This spreadsheet, and all others, can be found at www .howtomeasureanything.com/cybersecurity. We first applied the clarity test to our three variables (REV, MDB, and PPT), but this is only a launching point into advanced models that combine beliefs with evidence for the purpose of reducing uncertainty.

Note

1. Dennis V. Lindley, *Understanding Uncertainty* (Hoboken, NJ: John Wiley & Sons, 2006).

CHAPTER 9

Some Powerful Methods Based on Bayes

If one fails to specify the prior information, a problem of inference is just as ill-posed as if one had failed to specify the data . . . In realistic problems of inference, it is typical that we have cogent prior information, highly relevant to the question being asked; to fail to take it into account is to commit the most obvious inconsistency of reasoning, and it may lead to absurd or dangerously misleading results.

—Edwin T. Jaynes

Recall that in our survey, 23% of respondents agreed with the statement "Probabilistic methods are impractical because probabilities need exact data to be computed and we don't have exact data." This is just a minority, but even those who rejected that claim probably have found themselves in situations where data seemed too sparse to make a useful inference. In fact that may be why the majority of the survey takers also responded that ordinal scales have a place in measuring uncertainty. Perhaps they feel comfortable using wildly inexact and arbitrary values like "high, medium, and low" to communicate risk while ironically still believing in quantitative approaches. Yet someone who thoroughly believed in using quantitative methods would roundly reject ordinal scales when measuring highly uncertain events. When you are highly uncertain you use probabilities and ranges to actively communicate your uncertainty—particularly when you are relying on subject matter expertise. Having read the earlier research in this book, you know how even subjective estimates can be decomposed and made more consistent before any new "objective" data is applied, and how even a single data point (such as the outcome of one penetration test) can be used to update that belief.

Now that we've laid some groundwork of Bayesian empirical methods with an (admittedly) oversimplified example, we can show solutions to slightly more advanced—and more realistic—problems.

Computing Frequencies with (Very) Few Data Points: The Beta Distribution

Here is a slightly more elaborate derivative of Bayes's Rule that should come up frequently in cybersecurity. Let's say you are one of the big retailers we discussed in Chapter 6, and again we would like to assess the probability of a major data breach. In this case our new empirical data is not the outcome of some penetration test, but the observed (in fact, widely publicized) major data breaches themselves. Of course, you would like to leverage these news reports to estimate the chance that your firm would have such a breach. In a perfect world, you would have the equivalent cybersecurity version of an actuarial table as used in insurance products like life, health, and property. You would have thousands of firms in your own industry diligently reporting data points over many decades. You would use this to compute a data breach "rate" or "frequency." This is expressed as the percentage of firms that will have a data breach in a given year. As in insurance, we would use that as a proxy for the chance of your firm having such an event.

For your actuarial table of breaches, you don't have that many data points. Fortunately, we may need less data than we think if we use a particular statistical tool known as the beta distribution. With the beta distribution, we can make an inference about this annualized rate of a breach even with what seems like very little data.

And, as we first said in Chapter 2, you have more data than you think. In the case of reputation loss, for example, saying that we lack data about major data breaches is curious since we actually have all the data. That is, every major, large-retail data breach with massive costs that has occurred was public. Many of the costs are, in fact, *because* it was widely publicized. (If there was a major data breach that was somehow not public, then that retailer has, so far, avoided some or most of the main costs of a breach.)

If we look at the Verizon Data Breach Investigations Report (DBIR) and other sources of data on breaches, we can see a number of breaches in each industry. But that information alone doesn't tell us what the probability of a breach is for a single firm in a given industry. If there were five breaches in a given industry in a given year, is that 30% of the industry or 5%? If we want to compute this, we need to know (decompose) the size of the population those firms were drawn from, including those that didn't have breaches.

Now, this is where some cybersecurity experts (who recall just enough stats to get it all wrong) will give up on this by saying that the few breaches are not "statistically significant" and that no inferences could be made. Others (especially those, we hope, who have read this book) will not give up so easily. The fact is that, again, we have more data than we think and need less than we think—especially if we have access to the beta distribution.

Calculations with the Beta Distribution

The beta distribution is useful when you are trying to estimate a "population proportion. A population proportion is just the share of a population that falls in some subset. If only 25% of employees are following a procedure correctly, then the "25%" refers to a population proportion. Now suppose you don't know whether it is exactly 25% but you would like to estimate it. If we could conduct a complete census of the population we would know the proportion exactly. But you may only have access to a small sample. If I were only able to sample, say, 10 people, would that tell me anything? This is where beta distribution comes in. And you may be surprised to find that, according to the beta distribution, we may not need very many samples to tell us something we didn't know already.

As counterintuitive as this might sound, you can use a beta distribution to estimate a range for a population proportion even with very little data. This would apply to many situations in cybersecurity, including the likelihood of a risk that relatively few organizations have experienced. A beta distribution has just two parameters that seem at first to be a little abstract: alpha and beta (we will explain them shortly). In Excel we write this as =betadist(x,alpha,beta), where x is the population proportion you want to test. The formula produces the probability that the population proportion is less than x—we call this the "cumulative probability function" (cpf) since for each x it gives the cumulative probability up to that point.

There is also an "inverse probability function" in Excel for the beta distribution written as =beta.inv(p,alpha,beta), where p is a probability, and the formula returns the population proportion just high enough such that there is a p probability that the true population proportion is lower.

The alpha and beta parameters in the beta distribution seem very abstract and many stats texts don't offer a concrete way to think about them. However, there is a very concrete way to think of alpha and beta if we think of them as being related to "hits" and "misses" from a sample. A "hit" in a sample is, say, a firm that had a breach in a given time period, and a "miss" is a firm that did not.

To compute alpha and beta from hits and misses we need to establish our prior probability. Again, an informative prior probability could simply be a calibrated subject matter expert estimate. But if we want to be extremely conservative, we can use an uninformative prior by simply using a uniform distribution of 0% to 100%. This can be done with the beta distribution by

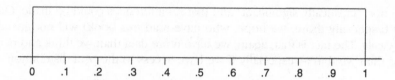

FIGURE 9.1 A Uniform Distribution (a Beta Distribution with alpha=beta=1)

setting both alpha and beta to a value of 1. This approach indicates we have almost no information about what a true population proportion could be. This is the "uninformative" prior. All we know is the mathematical constraint that a proportion of a population can't be less than 0% and can't exceed 100%. Other than that, we're simply saying everything in between is equally likely as shown in Figure 9.1.

Note that this figure shows the uniform distribution in the more familiar "probability density function" (pdf) where the area under the curve adds up to 1. Since the betadist() function is a cumulative probability, we have to slice up a bunch of increments by computing the difference between two cumulative probability functions close to each other. Just think of the height of a point on a pdf to represent the relative likelihood compared to other points. Recall that a normal distribution is highest in the middle. This just means that values near the middle of a normal distribution are more likely. In the case of this uniform distribution, we show that all values between the min and max are equally likely (i.e., it is flat).

Now, if we have a sample of some population, even a very small sample, we can update the alpha and beta with a count of hits and misses. You can download the beta distribution spreadsheet from howtomeasureanything .com/cybersecurity to do this calculation. Again, consider the case where we want to estimate the share of users following certain security procedures. We randomly sample six and find that only one is doing it correctly. Let's call the one a "hit" and the remaining five "misses." I simply add hits to our prior alpha and misses to our prior beta to get:

$$=\text{betadist}(x, \text{prior alpha} + \text{hits}, \text{prior beta} + \text{misses})$$

Figure 9.2 shows what a pdf would look like if we added a sample of 6 with one "hit" to our prior uniform distribution. To create this picture you can use the calculation below:

$$=\text{betadist}(x+i/2, \text{prior alpha} + \text{hits}, \text{prior beta} + \text{misses}) - \text{betadist}(x-i/2, \text{prior alpha} + \text{hits}, \text{prior beta} + \text{misses})$$

where "i" is the size of an increment we are using (the increment size is arbitrary but the smaller you make it the finer detail you get in your pictures of distributions). Again, you have an example in the spreadsheet if you need help.

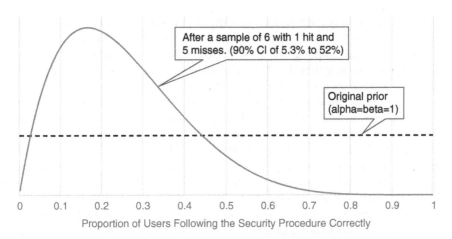

After a sample of 6 with 1 hit and 5 misses. (90% CI of 5.3% to 52%)

Original prior (alpha=beta=1)

Proportion of Users Following the Security Procedure Correctly

FIGURE 9.2 A Distribution Starting with a Uniform Prior and Updated with a Sample of 1 Hit and 5 Misses

How does the beta distribution do this? Doesn't this contradict what we learned in first semester statistics about sample sizes? No. The math is sound. In effect, the beta distribution applies Bayes's Rule over a range of possible values. To see how this works, consider a trivial question, like, "What is the probability of getting 1 hit out of 6 samples if only 1% of the population were following the procedure correctly?" If we assume we know a population proportion and we want to work out the chance of getting so many "hits" in a sample, we apply something called a binomial distribution. The binomial distribution is a kind of complement to the beta distribution. In the former, you estimate the probabilities of different sample results given the population proportion. In the latter, you estimate the population proportion given a number of sample results. In Excel, we write the binomial distribution as =binomdist(hits,sample size,probability,0). (The "0" means it will produce the probability of that exact outcome, not the cumulative probability up to that point.)

This would give us the chance of getting the observed result (e.g., 1 out of 6) for one possible population proportion (in this case 1%). We repeat this for a hypothetical population proportion of 2%, 3%, and so on up to 100%. Now Bayes lets us flip this into what we really want to know: "What is the probability of X being the population proportion given that we had 1 hit out of 6?" In other words, the binomial distribution gave us P(observed data | proportion) and we flip it to P(proportion | observed data). This is a neat trick that will be very useful, and it is already done for us in the beta distribution.

One more thing before we move on: Does 5.3% to 52% seem like a wide range? Well, remember you only sampled six people. And your previous range was even wider (on a uniform distribution of 0% to 100%, a 90% CI is 5% to 95%). All you need to do to keep reducing the width of this range is to keep sampling and *each* sample will slightly modify your range. You could have gotten a distribution even if you had zero hits out of three samples as long as you started with a prior.

If you need another example to make this concrete, let's consider one Hubbard uses in *How to Measure Anything*. Imagine you have an urn filled with red and green marbles. Let's say you think the proportion of red marbles could be anywhere between 0% and 100% (this is your prior). To estimate the population proportion, you sample 6 marbles, one of which was red. We would estimate the result as we did in the security procedure example above—the range would be 5.3% to 52%. The reason this range is wide is because we know we could have gotten 1 red out of 6 marbles from many possible population proportions. We could have gotten that result if just, say, 7% were red and we could have gotten that result if half were red. Now let's see how to extrapolate this example to breaches.

Applying the Beta to Breaches

Think of a breach as drawing a red marble from the urn example. Every firm in your industry is randomly drawing from the "breach urn" every year. Some firms draw a red marble, indicating they were breached. But there could have been more and there could have been less. You don't really know breach frequency (i.e., the portion of marbles that are red). But you can use the observed breaches to estimate the proportion of red marbles. Now, we have a list of reported breaches from the DBIR, but it doesn't tell us the size of the population. This is sort of like knowing there are 100 red marbles in the urn but without knowing the total number of marbles we can't know the population proportion of red marbles. However, we could still randomly sample a set of marbles and just use the number of red marbles in that sample compared to the size of the *sample* instead of the unknown total population size. Likewise, knowing that there were X breaches in our industry only helps if we know the size of the industry. So we find another source—not the DBIR—for a list of retailers. It could be the retailers in the Fortune 500 or perhaps a list from a retailers association. That list should have nothing to do with whether an organization had a breach reported in the DBIR, so many of those in that list will not have been mentioned in the DBIR. That list is our sample (how many marbles we draw from the urn). Some of those, however, will be mentioned in the DBIR as having experienced a breach (i.e., drawing a red marble).

Let's say we found 60 retailers in an industry list that would be relevant to you. Of that sample of 60, you find that in the time period between the start of 2014 and the end of 2015, there were two reported major data breaches. Since we are estimating a per year chance of a breach, we have to multiply the number of years in our data by the number of firms. To summarize:

- Sample Size: 120 "company years" of data (60 firms × 2 years)
- Hits: 2 breaches in that time period
- Misses: 118 company years where there was no major breach
- Alpha: prior + hits = 1 + 2 = 3
- Beta: prior + misses = 1 + 118 = 119

When we plug this into our spreadsheet we get a distribution like the one shown in Figure 9.3.

Think of the observed breaches as a sample of *what could have happened*. Just because we drew 120 marbles and two of them were red, that doesn't mean that exactly 1.67% of the marbles in the urn were red. If we drew that from the urn, we would estimate that there is a 90% chance that the true population proportion of red marbles in the urn is 0.7% to 5.1%. Likewise, just because we had 2 breaches out of 60 firms in two years (120 company years), doesn't mean we treat the per-year annual breach frequency as exactly 1.67%. We are only estimating the probability of different frequencies from a few observations. Next year we could be more lucky or less lucky even if the long-term frequency is no different.

Even the mean of the beta distribution isn't exactly 1.67% since the mean of a beta distribution is alpha / (alpha + beta) or 2.46%. The reason

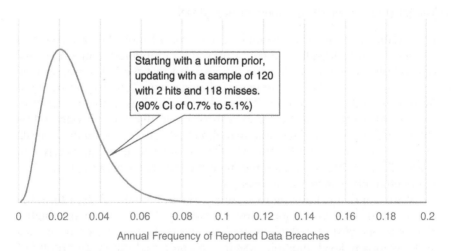

Starting with a uniform prior, updating with a sample of 120 with 2 hits and 118 misses. (90% CI of 0.7% to 5.1%)

Annual Frequency of Reported Data Breaches

FIGURE 9.3 The Per-Year Frequency of Data Breaches in This Industry

these are different is because the beta distribution is affected by your prior. Even if there were no breaches, the beta would have an alpha of 1 and a beta of 121 (120 misses + 1 for the prior beta), giving us a mean of 0.8%.

Another handy feature of the beta distribution is how easily it is updated. Every year that goes by—in fact every day that goes by—either with or without data breaches can update the alpha and beta of a distribution of breaches in your relevant industry population. For every firm where an event occurred in that period we update the alpha, and for every firm where it didn't occur we update the beta parameter. Even if we observe no events for a whole year, we still update the beta parameters and, therefore, our assessment of the probability of the event.

Note that you don't *have* to use an uninformative prior like a uniform distribution. If you have reason to believe, even before reviewing new data, that some frequencies are much less likely than others, then you can say so. You can make up a prior of any shape you like by trying different alphas and betas until you get the distribution you think fits your prior. You can start finding your prior by starting with alpha and beta equal to 1 and then, if you think the frequency is closer to zero, add to beta. Keep in mind the mean you want must be alpha / (alpha + beta). You can also add to alpha to move the frequency a little further away from zero. The larger the total alpha + beta, the narrower your range will be. Test your range by using the inverse probability function for beta in Excel: =beta.inv(.05,alpha,beta) and =beta.inv(.95,alpha,beta) will be your 90% confidence interval. After that, updating your distribution based on new information follows the same procedure—add hits to alpha and misses to beta.

The Effect of the Beta Distribution on Your Model

If we didn't use the beta distribution and instead took the observed frequency of 1.67% literally, we could be seriously underestimating risks for this industry. If we were drawing from an urn that we knew was exactly 1.67% red marbles (the rest are green), then we would still expect variation from draw to draw. If we drew 120 marbles, and assumed that the proportion of red marbles was 1.67%, we can compute that there is only a 14% chance that we would draw more than three red marbles (using the formula in Excel: 1-binomdist(3,120,.0167,1)). On the other hand, if we merely had a 90% CI that 0.7% to 5.1% are red, then the chance of drawing more than three red marbles increases to over 33%.

If we apply this thinking to security risks in an industry or a firm, the chance of multiple events increases dramatically. This could mean a higher chance in one year of multiple major breaches in the industry or, using data at the company level, multiple systems compromised out of a portfolio of many systems. In effect, this "rotates" our loss exceedance curve counterclockwise as shown in Figure 9.4. The mean is held constant while the risk

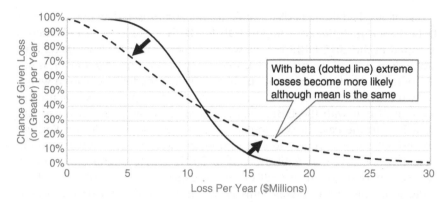

FIGURE 9.4 Example of How a Beta Distribution Changes the Chance of Extreme Losses

of more extreme losses increases. This may mean that your risk tolerance is now exceeded on the right end of the curve.

We believe this may be a major missing component of risk analysis in cybersecurity. We can realistically only treat past observations as a sample of possibilities and, therefore, we have to allow for the chance that we were just lucky in the past.

To see how we worked this out in detail, and to see how a beta distribution can be used in the simple one-for-one substitution and how it might impact the loss exceedance curve, just download the spreadsheet for this chapter on the website.

A Beta Distribution Case: AllClear ID

AllClear ID, a leading firm in customer-facing breach response in the cybersecurity ecosystem, uses a beta distribution to estimate cybersecurity risks using industry breach data. The company offers three solutions: AllClear Reserved Response™, Customer Communication services that include customer support and notification, and Identity Protection services for consumers. They handle incidents of all sizes including some of the biggest data breaches that have happened in recent history.

The capacity to respond to incidents is guaranteed for Reserved Response clients, making risk estimation critical to ensuring adequate resources are in place to meet service requirements. To help estimate the risk of a major breach, not just for a single client, but for their entire client base, AllClear ID contacted Doug Hubbard's firm, Hubbard Decision Research, to model the data breach risks in all of the industries they support, including the chance that multiple large clients could experience breaches in overlapping periods of time. This model is one of the many tools used by AllClear ID in their risk estimation analysis.

HDR applied the beta distribution to industry breach data in the Verizon Data Breach Investigations Report (DBIR). There were 2,435 data breaches reported in the 2015 DBIR but, as we explained earlier in this chapter, this alone does not tell us the per-year frequency of breaches for a given number of firms. Applying the same method explained earlier, we started with a known list of firms from the industries AllClear ID supports. We then cross referenced that with the DBIR data to determine how many of those had breaches. In the case of one industry, there were 98 firms in the Fortune 500 list. Of those, several had a breach in the two-year period between the beginning of 2014 and until the end of 2015. So, 98 organizations over a two-year period give us a total of 196 "organization years" of data where there were "hits" and "misses" (misses are firms that did not have a breach in a year). Now we can estimate the probability of a breach for the Fortune 500 firms in that industry.

In a Monte Carlo simulation, HDR used a beta distribution with an alpha and a beta. This produced a 90% confidence interval for the annual frequency of events per client. If the rate of breaches is at the upper bound, then the chance of multiple client breaches overlapping goes up considerably. The Monte Carlo model showed there is a chance that the peak activity period of multiple Reserved Response clients would overlap. This knowledge is one input to help AllClear ID to plan for the resources needed to meet the needs of clients even though the exact number and timing of breaches cannot be known with certainty.

Although breaches are unpredictable events, the simulation gave us invaluable insight into the risks we could potentially encounter and the intelligence to help mitigate those risks.

—Bo Holland, Founder & CEO of AllClear ID

Decomposing Probabilities with Many Conditions

In the Chapter 8 examples we were using a conditional probability with just one condition at a time. But often we want to consider a lot more conditions than that, even in the simplest models. One way to address this is to create what is called in Bayesian methods a "node probability table" (NPT). An expert is given every combination of conditions and is asked to provide a calibrated estimate of a probability of some defined event. Table 9.1 shows what just a few of the rows in such a table could look like.

TABLE 9.1 A Few Rows from a (Much Larger) Node Probability Table

P(Event | A,B,C,D) per Year with Cost Greater than $10K	A: Standard Security Controls Applied	B: Sensitive Data*	Multi-Factor Authentication	Corp DMZ Internet Facing, Third Party/Cloud, Internal Only
.008	Yes	No	No	DMZ
.02	No	Yes	Yes	Cloud
.065	No	No	No	Internal
.025	Yes	No	No	Cloud
.015	No	Yes	No	Internal
.0125	No	Yes	Yes	Cloud

*This may be data related to include Payment Card Industry (PCI), Protected Health Information (PHI), Personally Identifiable Information (PII), intellectual property, and so on.

The columns in Table 9.1 are just an example. We have seen companies also consider the type of operating system, whether software was internally developed, whether a vendor has access, the number of users, and so on. We leave it up to you to determine the ideal considerations. They just need to be values that meet Ron Howard's conditions of clear, observable, and useful (in this case, useful means it would cause you to change your estimate). For now, we will just focus on how to do the math regardless of what the indicators of risk might turn out to be.

Now suppose we continued the conditions (columns) on Table 9.1 to more than just four. Our previous modeling experience in cybersecurity at various firms generated 7 to 11 conditions. Each of those conditions would have at least two possible values (i.e., sensitive data or not), but some, as the example shows, could have three, four, or more. This leads to a large number of combinations of conditions. If, for example, there were just seven conditions, three of which had two possible values and the rest of which had three, then that is already 648 rows on an NPT ($2 \times 2 \times 2 \times 3 \times 3 \times 3 \times 3$). In practice the combinations are actually much larger since there are often multiple conditions with four or more possible values. The models that have been generated at some HDR clients would have produced thousands or tens of thousands of possible combinations.

Ideally, we would have data for many instances of failures. For measurements we prefer more data points, but cybersecurity professionals would like to keep the number of breaches, denial of service, and other such events low. As always, if we lack the data we can go back to our subject matter experts, who could provide an estimate of an event given each of the conditional states. We could ask for the estimate of a probability given that standard security controls are applied, it contains PHI data, it does not use multi-factor authentication, and the data is kept in a domestic data center owned by their firm. Then they would do the next combination of conditions, and so on. Obviously, as we showed with the number of possible combinations of conditions in even a modest-sized NPT, it would be impractical for subject matter experts to estimate each probability with a typical NPT.

Fortunately, there are two useful methods for experts to fill in an entire NPT—no matter how large—just by estimating a limited set of condition combinations. These methods are the log odds ratio method and the Lens method.

The One Thing at a Time Approach: The Log Odds Ratio

The log odds ratio (LOR) method provides a way for an expert to estimate the effects of each condition separately and then add them up to get the probability based on all the conditions. This is a variation on what is known as "logistic regression" in statistics. But we are going to use it in a fairly simple form.

An LOR of a probability $P(x)$ is simply $\log(P(x)/(1-P(x)))$. (Often, we assume the log is a natural log "$\ln()$" but it works in other logs, too.) This produces a negative value when the $P(x) < .5$, a positive value when $P(x) > .5$, and a zero when $P(x) = .5$. Computing an LOR is useful because an LOR allows you to "add up" the effects of independent different conditions on a probability. The procedure below goes into the details of doing this. It gets detailed but, as always, you can find a spreadsheet for this entire calculation at www.howtomeasureanything.com/cybersecurity

1. Identify participating experts and calibrate them.

2. Determine a baseline probability of a particular asset experiencing some defined event in a given period of time, assuming no additional information is available other than that it is one of your organization's assets (or applications, or systems, or threats, etc. depending on the framework of your decomposition). This is P(Event).

   Example: P(Event) per year given no other information about the asset is .02

3. Estimate the conditional probability of the asset having this defined event *given* that some condition had a particular value. We can write this as $P(E \mid X)$; that is, the probability of event E, given condition X.

   Example: P(Event | Sensitive Data) = .04

4. Estimate the conditional probability of the asset having this defined event given some *other* value to this condition. Repeat this step for every possible value of this condition.

   Example: P(Event | No Sensitive Data) = .01

5. Convert the baseline probability and each of the conditional probabilities to LOR. We will write it as L(Probability).

   Example:

   LOR(P(Event)) = ln(P(Event)) / (1 − P(Event)) = ln(.02 / .98)
   = −3.89182

   LOR(P(Event | Sensitive Data)) = ln(.04 / .96)= −3.17805

   . . . and so on for each condition

6. Compute the "delta LOR" for each condition; that is, the difference between the LOR with a given condition and the baseline LOR.

   Example: delta LOR(Sensitive Data) = L(P(Event | Sensitive Data)) − LOR(P(Event))= −(−3.18) − (−3.89) = +.71

7. Repeat steps 3 to 6 for each condition.

8. When delta LOR has been computed for all possible values of all conditions, set up a spreadsheet that will look up the correct delta log odds for each condition when a value is chosen for that condition. When a set of condition values are chosen, all delta LOR for each condition are added to the baseline LOR to get an adjusted LOR.

   Example: Adjusted LOR = −3.89 + .71 + .19 − .45 + 1.02 = −2.42

9. Convert the adjusted LOR back to a probability to get an adjusted probability.

   Example: Adjusted probability = 1 / (1 + 1 / exp(−2.42)) = .08167

10. If any condition makes the event certain or makes it impossible (i.e., P(Event | Condition) = either 0 or 1) then skip computing LOR for the condition and the delta log odds (the calculation would produce an error, anyway). Instead, you can simply apply logic that overrides this.

    Example: If condition applies, then adjusted probability = 0

    When the condition does not occur, then compute the adjusted probability as shown in previous steps.

Again, if someone tells you this or anything else we discuss isn't pragmatic, be aware that we've had an opportunity to apply this and many other methods in many situations, including several in cybersecurity. When someone says this isn't pragmatic, they often just mean they don't know how to do it. So to illustrate how it can be done, we will show another conversation between an analyst and a cybersecurity expert. The analyst will check the expert's estimates for consistency by using the math we just showed. Of course, he is using a spreadsheet to do this (available on the website).

Risk Analyst: As you recall, we've broken down our risks into a risk-by-asset approach. If I were to randomly select an asset, what is the probability of a breach happening next year?

Cybersecurity Expert:	Depends on what you mean by breach—it could be 100%. And there are a lot of factors that would influence my judgment.
Risk Analyst:	Yes, but let's say all you know is that it is one of your assets. I just randomly picked one and didn't even tell you what it was. And let's further clarify that we don't just mean a minor event where the only cost is a response from cybersecurity. It has to interfere with business in some way, cause fines, and potentially more—all the way up to one of the big breaches we just read about in the news. Let's say it's something that costs the organization at least $50K but possibly millions.
Cybersecurity Expert:	So how would I know the probability of an event if I don't know anything about the asset?
Risk Analyst:	Well, do you think all of your assets are going to have a significant event of some sort next year?
Cybersecurity Expert:	No, I would say out of the entire portfolio of assets there will be some events that would result in losses of greater than $50,000 just if I look at system outages in various business units. Maybe a bigger breach every couple of years.
Risk Analyst:	Okay. Now, since we have 200 assets on our list, you don't expect half of the assets to experience breaches at that level next year, right?
Cybersecurity Expert:	No. The way I'm using the term "breach" I might expect it to happen in 3 to 10.
Risk Analyst:	Okay, then. So if I simply randomly chose an asset out of the list there wouldn't be a 10% chance of it having a breach. Maybe closer to 1% or 2%.
Cybersecurity Expert:	I see what you mean. I guess for a given asset and I didn't know anything else, I might put the probability of a breach of some significant cost at 2%.
Risk Analyst:	Great. Now, suppose I told you just one thing about this asset. Suppose I told you it contained PCI data. Would that modify the risk of a breach at all?
Cybersecurity Expert:	Yes, it would. Our controls are better in those situations but the reward is greater for attackers. I might increase it to 4%.

Risk Analyst:	Okay. Now suppose I told you the asset did not have PCI data. How much would that change the probability?
Cybersecurity Expert:	I don't think that would change my estimate.
Risk Analyst:	Actually, it would have to. Your "baseline" probability is 2%. You've described one condition that would increase it to 4%. To make sure this balances out, the opposite condition would have to reduce the probability so that the average still comes out to 2%. I'll show you a calculation in a moment so you can see what I mean.
Cybersecurity Expert:	Okay, I think I see what you mean. Let's call it 1%.
Risk Analyst:	Okay, great. Now, what percentage of all assets actually have PCI data?
Cybersecurity Expert:	We just completed an audit so we have a pretty good figure. It's 20 assets out of 200.
Risk Analyst:	So that's 10% of the assets we are listing. So in order to see if this adds up right, I have to compute the baseline probability based on these conditional probabilities and see if it agrees with the baseline you first gave me.

The Risk Analyst computes a baseline as: P(Event | PCI)*P(PCI)+P(Event | No PCI)*P(No PCI) = .04*.1+.01*.9=.013. (A spreadsheet at www .howtomeasureanything.com/cybersecurity will contain this calculation and the other steps in this interview process, including computing delta LOR.)

| **Risk Analyst:** | So our computed baseline is a bit lower than what you originally had. The probabilities we have so far aren't internally consistent. If we can make our estimates consistent, then our model will be better. We could say the original probability was wrong and we just need to make it 1.3%. Or we could say the conditional probabilities could both be a little higher or that the share of assets with PCI is too low. What do you feel makes more sense to change? |
| **Cybersecurity Expert:** | Well, the share of PCI assets is something we know pretty well now. Now that I think about it, maybe the conditional probability without PCI could be a little higher. What if we changed that to 1.5%? |

Risk Analyst: (Doing a calculation) Well, if we make it 1.8% then it comes out to almost exactly 2%, just like your original estimate of the baseline.

Cybersecurity Expert: That seems about right. But if you would have asked me at a different time, maybe I would have given a different answer.

Risk Analyst: Good point. That's why you aren't the only person I'm asking. Plus when we are done with all of the conditions, we will show you how the adjusted probability is computed and then you might decide to reconsider some of the estimates. Now let's go to the next condition. What if I told you that the asset in question was in our own data center . . .

And so on.

Some caveats on the use of LOR. It is a very good estimate of the probability given all conditions if the conditions are independent of each other. That is, they are not correlated and don't have complex interactions with each other. This is often not the case. It may be the case, for example, that some conditions have a much bigger or much smaller effect given the state of other conditions. The simplest solution to apply is that if you think conditions A and B are highly correlated, toss one of them. Alternatively, simply reduce the expected effects of each condition (that is, make the conditional probability closer to the baseline). Check that the cumulative effect of several conditions doesn't produce more extreme results (probabilities that are too high or too low) than you would expect.

The Lens Method: A Model of an Expert That Improves on the Expert

We have another very useful way to fill in a large NPT by sampling some of the combinations of conditions and having our subject matter experts estimate those. This approach requires that we build a type of statistical model that is based purely on emulating the judgments of the experts—not by using historical data. Curiously, the model of the experts seems to be better at forecasting and estimating than the experts themselves.

This involves using "regression" methods—specifically, a "logistic regression." Discussing regression methods in enough detail to be useful is outside the scope of this book so we make the following suggestion: If you are not familiar with regression methods, then stick with the LOR method explained above. If you already understand regression methods, then we believe we can describe this approach in just enough detail that you can figure it out without requiring that we go into the mechanics.

With that caveat in mind, let's provide a little background. This method dates back to the 1950s, when a decision psychology researcher named Egon Brunswik wanted to measure expert decisions statistically. Most of his colleagues were interested in the hidden decision-making process that experts went through. Brunswik was more interested in describing the decisions they actually made. He said of decision psychologists: "We should be less like geologists and more like cartographers." In other words, they should simply map what can be observed externally and not be concerned with what he considered hidden internal processes.

This became known as the "Lens Model." The models he and subsequent researchers created were shown to outperform human experts in various topics such as the chance of repayment of bank loans, movement of stock prices, medical prognosis, graduate student performance, and more. Hubbard has also had the chance to apply this to forecasting box office receipts of new movies and battlefield logistics and, yes, in cybersecurity. In each case, the model was at least as good as human experts, and in almost all cases, it was a significant improvement.

As discussed back in Chapter 4, human experts can be influenced by a variety of irrelevant factors yet still maintain the illusion of learning and expertise. The linear model of the expert's evaluation, however, gives perfectly consistent valuations. Like LOR, the Lens Model does this by removing the error of judge inconsistency from the evaluations. Unlike LOR, it doesn't explicitly try to elicit the estimation rules for each variable from the experts. Instead, we simply observe the judgments of the experts given all variables and try to infer the rules statistically.

The seven-step process is simple enough. We've modified it somewhat from Brunswik's original approach to account for some other methods we've learned about since Brunswik first developed this approach (e.g., calibration of probabilities). Again, we are providing just enough information here so that someone familiar with different regression methods could figure out how this is done.

1. Identify the experts who will participate and calibrate them.
2. Ask them to identify a list of factors relevant to the particular item they will be estimating (e.g., like the factors we showed in the NPT), but keep it down to 10 or fewer factors.
3. Generate a set of scenarios using a combination of values for each of the factors just identified—they can be based on real examples or purely hypothetical. Make 30 to 50 scenarios for each of the judges you are surveying. Each of these will be a sample in your regression model.
4. Ask the experts to provide the relevant estimate for each scenario described.
5. Average the estimates of the experts together.
6. Perform a logistic regression analysis using the average of expert estimates as the dependent variable and the inputs provided to the experts as the independent variable. Depending on the input variables

used, you may need to codify the inputs or use multinomial regression methods. Since in this case you are estimating a probability, logistic regression methods may apply. (This is technical language but if you know regression methods, you know what this means.)

7. The best fit formula for the logistic regression becomes the Lens Model.

When you have completed the procedure above, you will be able to produce a chart like the one shown in Figure 9.5. This shows the regression model estimate of average expert judgment vs. the average of expert judgments themselves for each of the scenarios. You can see that the model, of course, doesn't exactly match the expert judgments but it is close. In fact, if you compare this to the measure of expert inconsistency *you will usually find that most of the deviation of the model from expert judgments is due to expert inconsistency.* That means the Lens Model would agree even better if only the experts were more consistent. This inconsistency is eliminated by the Lens method.

If you decided to tackle the Lens method, the model you just produced is actually better than a single expert in several ways. *It is actually an emulation of the average of your best calibrated experts if they were perfectly consistent.*

To estimate inconsistency we can use the "duplicate pair" method we showed back in Chapter 4. On several conditions instead of asking experts for the effect of individual conditions, for example, the seventh scenario in the list may be identical to the twenty-ninth scenario in the list. After looking at a couple of dozen scenarios, experts will forget that they already answered the same situation and often will give a slightly different answer. Thoughtful experts are fairly consistent in their evaluation of scenarios. Still, as we showed in Chapter 4, inconsistency accounts for about 21% of the total variation in expert judgments (the remaining 79% due to the data the

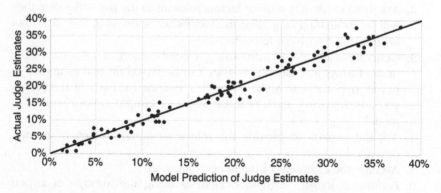

FIGURE 9.5 Example of Regression Model Predicting Judge Estimates

experts were provided to base their judgments on). This error is completely removed by the Lens method.

Comparing the Lens Method and LOR

There are pros and cons to these two methods of decomposing multiple conditions in an estimate of likelihood:

1. LOR takes (a little) less time. The Lens method requires experts to answer a large number of samples in order to make it possible to build a regression model.
2. The Lens method can pick up on more complex interactions between variables. The experts' responses could indicate that some variables only matter if other variables have a particular value.
3. LOR is a bit simpler. The Lens method depends on building a regression model that predicts the judgments of experts well. While Excel has tools to simplify this, actually building a good regression often requires several approaches. Perhaps you should make it a nonlinear model by having two variables show a compounding effect. Perhaps you should combine some of the discrete values of a variable (e.g., does "server location" really need to differentiate domestic managed by us, domestic managed by third party, or foreign instead of "we manage it" and "somebody else manages it"?). This is not technically difficult, especially for people who may have the background for this, but it can still be a bit time consuming. Also, all the math you will need for the LOR method is in one spreadsheet at www.howtomeasureanything .com/cybersecurity.
4. The LOR tends to give much more variation in estimates than the Lens method. The experts will sometimes be surprised how the effects of multiple conditions quickly add up to make an estimated likelihood very high or very small. When the same expert estimates likelihoods in a Lens method, they will tend to vary their answers a lot less. Perhaps the expert is underestimating the cumulative effect of independent variables in the LOR method, or perhaps they are being too cautious in modifying their estimates based on the information they are given for a Lens method. It will be up to you to decide which is more realistic.
5. Both methods help reduce inconsistency, but the Lens method provides a more convenient way to measure it. As mentioned earlier, measuring inconsistency is useful because we know that this error is eliminated by the quantitative model and, if we eliminate it, we can estimate how much error was reduced. Since the Lens method requires multiple estimates (at least dozens), then inconsistency can be easily estimated with the duplicate pair method.

The bottom line is that if you are looking for a quick solution, use the LOR method for decomposing probabilities based on multiple conditions. But check how much the answers vary when you change conditions between two extremes (one where all conditions are set to values that increase the likelihood, and one where all conditions are set to values that decrease likelihood). If the extremes seem entirely unrealistic, then you might consider reducing the estimates of effects of individual variables, as mentioned earlier.

There is some evidence that people tend to overreact to signals when there are several signals, especially when they are highly correlated. One study calls this a "correlation neglect" when considering conditional probabilities.[1] If two signals A and B are perfectly correlated (i.e., if you tell me the value for one, I know exactly the value for the other), then you don't need to know both A and B to estimate some probability X: $P(X \mid A,B) = P(X \mid A) = P(X \mid B)$. However, even when someone is told that A and B are highly correlated, they tend to view them as independent (and therefore reinforcing) signals and they will overreact when estimating the new conditional probability of X. As we mentioned with LOR earlier, if you suspect two conditions are highly correlated, the simplest fix is to just not use one of them.

Still, even when we use a Lens method, we have found it useful to start with LOR just to get the cybersecurity experts to start thinking how knowledge of individual conditions can modify their probabilities. It also helps to eliminate some conditions the experts originally thought might be informative. For example, suppose we are in a workshop and the cybersecurity team is listing conditions they think could be informative for an estimate in a Lens Model. One of the participants in a workshop might say they think the type of operating system an asset uses could inform the probability of a breach of the data on that asset. To test this, we employ the LOR process described earlier by asking how much the experts would change the baseline probability (the probability of a cybersecurity event given no information about the asset other than it was one of their own) if they were told that the operating system was Linux, and then what they would change it to if they were told the operating system was Microsoft. They might realize that this information would not have caused them to modify the baseline probability. If so, then we can eliminate it from the Lens Model.

Both the Lens and LOR methods raise interesting conceptual obstacles for some experts. They may lack confidence in the process because they have a misunderstanding of how it works. We do not find that most experts we have worked with will have an objection to the process based on one of these misconceptions, but some will. If we know how to address them, then we can help them better understand why their input is needed.

Let's consider the following reaction: "With the Lens method, I feel like I am picking answers at random." If this were the case for most people, we would not see the data that we see. If people who are estimating probabilities used in the Lens method truly were picking values at random, then we would be unable to find correlations that are as strong as we typically find in these models. It would also be a mystery as to why experts—who have plenty of disagreement—actually agree as much as they do. Clearly, different experts working independently who were picking estimates at random would not agree with each other about how much one condition or another changes the likelihood of an event. And yet we do observe some level of agreement, and the level is far beyond what could be explained by chance. So the expert who has this concern may be expressing that when he or she is faced with individual situations, he or she could have estimated a 5% chance or perhaps 2% or 8%. This is no doubt true. The individual choice seems like you could have estimated a slightly different value and still be satisfied. But, of course, the Lens method does not depend on a single estimate or even a single expert. When a large number of data points are brought together a pattern inevitably forms, even when the experts felt they had some randomness in their responses for individual cases.

We may also hear the reaction "These variables alone tell me nothing. I need a lot more information to make an estimate." Whether answering how a single condition can change a probability for a LOR method, or answering how estimates changed based on multiple (but still just a few) conditions, some experts will object that without knowing more—indeed, some will say without knowing everything—they cannot provide an estimate. In other words, "Knowing how frequent patches are made will only tell me something about a probability if I also know several other [usually unidentified and endless] things." This can't be true and it can be disproven mathematically. There is a more formal version of this proof in the original *How to Measure Anything*, but for now, just know that this position isn't mathematically logical. Another problem with this position is that we know relatively simple models will turn out to be decent predictors of expert judgment. Often, we even end up eliminating one or more variables from a model because they turned out to be unnecessary to predict the expert's judgment. This means that a variable the experts at one point thought was something they considered in their judgments does not appear to have any bearing on their judgment at all. They just discovered what we called in previous chapters an "uninformative decomposition." We all tend to imagine that our subjective judgments are a result of fairly elaborate and deliberate processing of options. A more realistic description of our judgment is more like a small set of variables in a very simple set of rules added to a lot of noise and error.

Reducing Uncertainty Further and When To Do It

We don't have to rely on calibrated estimates and subjective decompositions alone. Ultimately, we want to inform estimates with empirical data. For example, conditional probabilities can be computed based on historical data. Also, the beta distribution and other methods for computing conditional probabilities can be combined in interesting ways. We can even make rational decisions about when to dive deeper based on the economic value of the information.

Estimating the Value of Information for Cybersecurity: A Very Simple Primer

Hubbard's first book, *How to Measure Anything*, gets into a lot more detail about how to compute the value of information than we will cover here. But there are some simple rules of thumb that still apply and a procedure we can use in a lot of situations specific to cybersecurity.

Information has value because we make decisions with economic consequences under a state of uncertainty. That is, we have a *cost* of being wrong and a *chance* of being wrong. The product of the chance of being wrong and the cost of being wrong is called the Expected Opportunity Loss (EOL). In decision analysis, the value of information is just a reduction in EOL. If we eliminate uncertainty, EOL goes to zero and the difference in EOL is the entire EOL value. We also call this the Expected Value of Perfect Information (EVPI). We cannot usually eliminate uncertainty, but the EVPI provides a useful upper limit for what additional information might be worth. If the EVPI is only $100, then it's probably not worth your time for any amount of uncertainty reduction. If the EVPI is $1 million, then reducing uncertainty is a good bet even if you can reduce it only by half for a cost of $20,000 (the cost could simply be your effort in the analysis).

In cybersecurity, the value of information will always be related to decisions you could make to reduce this risk. You will have decisions about whether to implement certain controls, and those controls cost money. If you choose to implement a control, the "cost of being wrong" is spending money that turns out you didn't need to spend on the control. If you reject the control, the cost of being wrong is the cost of experiencing the event the control would have avoided.

In www.howtomeasureanything.com/cybersecurity we have also provided a spreadsheet for computing the value of information. Table 9.2 shows how values in the spreadsheet's payoff table would be structured. Note that we've taken a very simple example here by assuming that the proposed control eliminates the possibility of the event. But if we wanted we could make this a bit more elaborate and consider the possibility that the event still happens (presumably with a reduced likelihood and/or impact) if the control is put in place.

The same spreadsheet also captures conditional probabilities like the ones we computed before: P(MDB), P(MDB | PPT), and P(MDB | ~PPT).

TABLE 9.2 Cybersecurity Control Payoff Table

	Event Didn't Occur	Event Occurs
Decided to Implement the Control	The cost of the control	The cost of the control
Decided against the Control	Zero	The cost of the event

(Recall from Chapter 8 that MDB means "Massive Data Breach" and PPT means "Positive Penetration Test.") The calculation is simple. Based on the P(MDB), the cost of the control, and the cost of an event without the control, we compute an EOL for each strategy—implementing or not implementing the control. That is, based on the strategy you choose, we simply compute the cost of being wrong and the chance of being wrong for each strategy.

You can try various combinations of conditional probabilities, costs of events, and costs of controls in the spreadsheet. But it still comes down to this: If you reject a control, the value of information could be as high as the chance of the event times the cost of the event. If you accept a control, then the cost of being wrong is the chance the event won't occur times the cost of the control. So the bigger the cost of the control, the bigger the event it is meant to mitigate, and the more uncertainty you have about the event, the higher the value of additional information.

Futher Reducing Uncertainty by Using Empirical Data to Derive Conditional Probabilities

Let's suppose we've built a model, computed information values, and determined that further measurements were needed. Specifically, we determined that we needed to reduce our uncertainty about how some factor in cybersecurity changes the likelihood of some security event. You have gathered some sample data—perhaps within your own firm or perhaps by looking at industry data—and you organized it as shown in Table 9.3. We can call

TABLE 9.3 Table of Joint Occurrences of an Event and a Condition

Defined Security Event Occurred on This Server	A Stated Condition Exists on That Server
1	0
1	1
0	0
0	1
1	1
1	1
0	1

the occurrence of the event Y and the condition you are looking at X. Using this, we can compute the conditional probability P(Y | X) by dividing the number of rows where Y = Yes and X = No by the total number of rows where X = No. That is, P(Y | X) = count of Y and X / count of X (as shown in Rule 4—the "it depends" rule—in Chapter 8).

This could be a list of servers for each year showing whether some event of interest occurred on that server and, say, whether it was located offshore or perhaps the type of operating system it had. Or perhaps we wanted to estimate the probability of a botnet infestation on a server based on some continuous value like the amount of traffic a server gets. (One of our guest contributors, Sam Savage, has shown an example of this in Appendix B.)

If you are handy with pivot tables in Excel, you could do this analysis without too much trouble. But we propose an even easier analytical method using the Excel function =countifs(); the Countifs() formula counts the rows in a table where a set of conditions are met. If we count the rows where both columns are equal to "1," we have the number of times both the event and the condition occurred. This is different from "Countif()" (without the "s") which only counts the number in a given range that meet *one* crite-rion. Countifs(), on the other hand, can have multiple ranges and multiple criteria. We need both to compute a conditional probability from a set of historical data.

Counting just the number of 1's in the second column gives us all of the situations where the condition applies regardless of whether the secu-rity event occurred. So, to compute the conditional probability of an event given a condition, P(Event | Condition) in Table 9.3 we use the following calculation:

= countifs(column A, "=1", column B, "=1")/countif(column B,"=?1")

(Note, where we say "column A" or "column B" insert the range where your data resides in Excel.)

Now you are empirically estimating a conditional probability. Again, we've provided a spreadsheet on the website to show how to do this. There is quite a lot of interesting analysis you can do with this approach once you get handy with it.

We've already put as many detailed statistical methods into this book as we think most cybersecurity experts would want to deal with—but the reader could go much further if motivated to do so. Instead of loading more methods at this point, let's just paint a picture of where you could go from here if you feel you are mastering the methods discussed so far.

First, we can combine what we've talked about in much more elaborate and informative ways. For example, instead of using calibrated estimates as inputs for the LOR method, we can use conditional probabilities computed from data in this way as inputs. As with LOR before, as long as the conditions are independent we can add up the conditional probability with a large number of conditions.

We can also leverage the beta distribution with the empirically derived conditional probability using the data in Table 9.3. If we are using simple binary outcomes (Y) and conditions (X) we can think of them as "hits" and "misses." For example, you could have a data center where you have layers of controls in place from the network on the host: Network Firewalls, Host Firewalls, Network Intrusion Prevention Systems, Host Intrusion Prevention, and so forth. Lots of investments either way. Suppose we define the outcome variable "Y" as "security incident." This is very general, but it could be malware, hacking, denial of service, and so on. X, of course, represents the "conditions" we just articulated in terms of layers of controls. If we count 31 cases where Y and X occur together (security event and controls in place) and 52 total cases of X, then we can estimate the conditional probability with the beta distribution using 31 hits and 21 misses, added to your prior. This allows us to think of our data, again, as just a sample of possibilities and not a reflection of the exact proportion. (More specifically to our example case, we can start forecasting what our controls are saying about the probability of having security incidents.) Instead of adding LORs for fixed conditional probabilities, we randomly draw from a beta distribution and compute the LOR on that output. (This will also have the effect of rotating your LEC in a way that increases the chance of extreme losses).

Think about how handy this can be if you deal with multiple massive data centers deployed globally. You want to have a sense of the probability of incidents in light of controls. It's an easy step then to determine EVPI in relationship to making a potential strategic change in defenses in light of the simple sample data. Again, you have more data than you think!

Once again, we have provided the spreadsheets at www.howtomeasureanything.com/cybersecurity for detailed examples.

Leveraging Existing Resources to Reduce Uncertainty

Recall the measurement maxims: It's been measured before, you have more data than you think, and you need less data than you think. In this chapter so far we've focused a bit more on the last maxim. Now let's spend a little bit of time on the other two.

If you are aware of some of the resources you have available to you, you will realize that there is quite a lot of data and that some very clever people have already analyzed this data for you. Some of it is even public domain. Each of the examples that follow was submitted by contributors to this book.

■ Vivosecurity, Inc. collects mostly publicly available data on breaches and other cybersecurity incidents. Using data from the U.S. Department of Health and Human Services Breach Portal website (a.k.a. the HHS "Wall of Shame"), they've found an interesting relationship between number of employees in a firm and the chance of a breach. The HHS Breach Portal[2] shows PHI record breaches of 500 records or more. This data can be downloaded into a spreadsheet. The rate of data breaches as of 2015 appears to be about a 14% chance per 10,000 employees per year (this is higher than data on major data breaches since it includes breaches as small as 500 records). This is up slightly from about 10% in 2012. Vivosecurity's detailed analysis is shown in Appendix B.

■ Anton Mobley, a data scientist at GE Healthcare (and a colleague of one of the authors, Richard Seiersen, at GE), has done an interesting analysis of the effect of password strength policy and probability of password compromise. His analysis is based in part on empirical surveys of passwords (e.g., passwords like "password" or "work") and the rules they adhere to, and the relative difficulty of finding those passwords with widely available password-search algorithms. He also shows empirical data on the types of password hints people use that make such searches much easier (e.g., "my last name" or "my company's street"). He shows that a firm with 2,000 employees is virtually certain to have a password compromised if they don't enforce password standards. The same company would have about a 5% chance of being compromised if there was a requirement for 15-letter, multi-type passwords (e.g., "AnNtx5#undR70!z"). Anton has also provided a detailed analysis of this in Appendix B.

■ Marshall Kuypers (who we met in Chapter 6 and who, at the time of this writing, was finishing his PhD at Stanford, specializing in the statistical data analysis of cybersecurity), along with Dr. Paté-Cornell of Stanford, presented a statistical analysis at SIRACon 2015 that showed multiple interesting trends (a few of which are shown in Figure 9.6) that can inform much cybersecurity risk analysis:

◆ The rate at which data has been compromised due to lost or stolen devices has been constant over the last several years and is proportional with the number of employees. The numbers are consistent with what the authors observed based on an analysis of HHS data.

◆ The rate of malware is going down but not the impact of malware, which has a "fat-tailed" distribution.

◆ The investigation time of incidents follows a highly consistent "power law" pattern (the power law is a distribution where the log of the frequency of an event and the log of the impact create

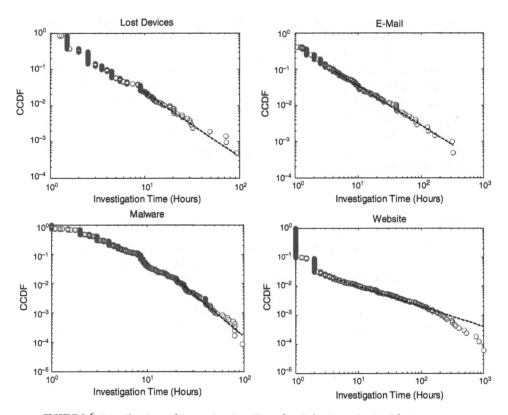

FIGURE 9.6 Distribution of Investigation Time for Cybersecurity Incidents

a straight, downward-sloping line—this distribution is described in Appendix A).

Wrapping Up Bayes

These last two chapters were an introduction to some simple and then some slightly more advanced empirical methods using Bayes. By leveraging already developed spreadsheets for some of the more detailed explanations, we covered quite a lot of ground.

We've shown how the use of Bayesian methods and its derivatives allow cybersecurity to update initial calibrated estimates with new information. We've shown how the use of the Bayesian methods can apply to a simple update problem but we've also shown how much more elaborate methods like the beta distribution can still be practically employed by using existing features of Excel. We've shown how multiple conditions can be combined using LOR methods and the Lens method, and we've shown how LOR and beta can be combined.

You don't have to adopt all of this at once. Take a one-step-at-a-time approach if necessary and add new methods as you master them. You have a variety of choices for how you model something and how you leverage new information—all of which are surely better than guessing or using methods without any mathematical foundation. Now, Part III will introduce some additional concepts and discuss practical considerations in rolling out these methods in an organization.

Notes

1. Benjamin Enke and Florian Zimmermann, "Correlation Neglect in Belief Formation," Discussion Paper No. 7372 (Bonn, Germany: Institute for the Study of Labor, 2013), http://ftp.iza.org/dp7372.pdf.
2. U.S. Department of Health and Human Services, Office for Civil Rights, Breach Portal, "Breaches Affecting 500 or More Individuals," accessed March 21, 2016, https://ocrportal.hhs.gov/ocr/breach/breach_report.jsf.

Cybersecurity Risk Management for the Enterprise

PART III

CHAPTER 10

Toward Security Metrics Maturity

A s you look to improve in any endeavor, it helps to have a view of where you are and a vision for where you need to go. This improvement will need to be continuous and will need to be measured. The requirement of being "continuous and measurable" was stated as one of the main outcomes of this how-to book. Continuous measurements that have a goal in mind are called "metrics." To that end, this chapter provides an operational security-metrics maturity model. Different from other analytics-related maturity models (yes, there are many), ours starts and ends with predictive analytics.

This chapter will begin to introduce some issues at a management and operations level. Richard Seiersen, the coauthor who is familiar with these issues, will use this chapter and the next to talk to his peers using language and concepts that they should be familiar with. Richard will only selectively introduce more technical issues to illustrate practical actions. To that end, we will cover the following topics:

- *The Operational Security Metrics Maturity Model*: This is a maturity model that is a matrix of standard questions and data sources.
- *Sparse Data Analytics (SDA)*: This is the earliest metrics stage, which uses quantitative techniques to model risk based on limited data. This can specifically be used to inform new security investments. We provide an extended example of SDA using the R programming language at the very end of this chapter. This is optional material that demonstrates analytics outside of Excel as well as illustrates SDA.
- *Functional Security Metrics*: These are subject-matter-specific metrics based on early security investments. Most security metrics programs stop at this point of maturation.
- *Security Data Marts*: This section focuses on measuring across security domains with larger data sets. The following chapter will focus on this topic.
- *Prescriptive Security Analytics*: This will be a brief discussion on an emerging topic in the security world. It is the amalgam of decision and data science. This is a large, future book-length topic.

Introduction: Operational Security Metrics Maturity Model

Predictive analytics, machine learning, data science—choose your data buzzword—are all popular topics. Maturity models and frameworks for approaching analytics abound. Try Googling images of "Analytics Maturity Models"; there are plenty of examples. Our approach (see Figure 10.1) is different. We don't require much data or capability to get started. And in fact, the practices you learned in previous chapters shine at this early stage. They help define the types of investments you will need to make to mature your program. So, there is no rush to invest in a "big data" solution and data science. Don't get us wrong—we are big advocates of using such solutions when warranted. But with all these "shiny" analytics concepts and technology come a lot of distractions—distractions from making decisions that could protect you from the bad guys now. To that end, our perspective is that any analytic maturity model and framework worth its salt takes a decision-first approach—always.

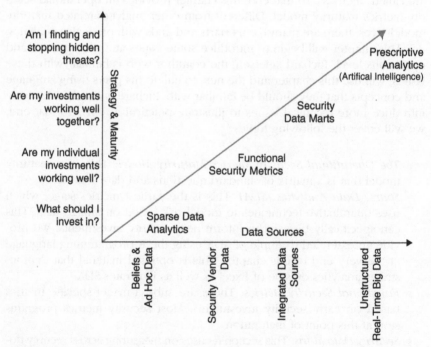

FIGURE 10.1 Security Analytics Maturity Model

Sparse Data Analytics

N (data) is never enough because if it were "enough" you'd already be on to the next problem for which you need more data. Similarly, you never have quite enough money. But that's another story.

—Andrew Gelman[1]

You can use predictive analytics *now*. Meaning, you can use advanced techniques although your security program may be immature. All of the models presented in Chapters 8 and 9 fit perfectly here. Just because your ability to collect broad swaths of security evidence is low does not mean that you cannot update your beliefs as you get more data. In fact, the only data you may have is subject matter expert beliefs about probable future losses. In short, doing analytics with sparse evidence is a mature function but is not dependent on mature security operations.

From an analytics perspective, Sparse Data Analytics (SDA) is the exclusive approach when data are scarce. You likely have not made an investment in some new security program. In fact, you may be the newly hired CISO tasked with investing in a security program from scratch. Therefore, you would use SDA to define those investments. But, once your new investment (people, process, technology) is deployed, you measure it to determine its effectiveness to continually improve its operation. For a more technical example of SDA please refer to the "SDA Example Model: R Programming" at the end of the chapter.

Functional Security Metrics

After you have made a major investment in a new enterprise-security capability, how do you know it's actually helping? Functional security metrics (FSMs) seek to optimize the effectiveness of key operational security areas. There will be key performance indicators (KPIs) associated with operational coverage, systems configuration, and risk reduction within key domains. There are several security metrics books on the market that target this level of security measurement. One of the earliest was Andrew Jaquith's *Security Metrics*.[2] It brought this important topic to the forefront and has a solid focus on what we would call "coverage and configuration" metrics. Unfortunately, most companies still do not fully realize this level of maturity. They indeed may have tens, if not hundreds, of millions of dollars invested in security staff and technology. People, process, and technology for certain silo functions may in fact be optimized, but a view into each security domain with isometric measurement approaches is likely lacking.

Most organizations have some of the following functions, in some form of arrangement:

- malware defense
- vulnerability management
- penetration testing
- application security
- network security
- security architecture
- identity and access management
- security compliance
- data loss prevention
- incident response and forensics
- and many more

Each function may have multiple enterprise and standalone security solutions. In fact, each organization ideally would have sophisticated security metrics associated with each of their functions. These metrics would break out into two macro areas:

1. *Coverage and Configuration Metrics*: These are metrics associated with operational effectiveness in terms of depth and breadth of enterprise engagement. Dimensions in this metric would include time series metrics associated with rate of deployment and effective configuration. Is the solution actually working (turned on) to specification and do you have evidence of that? You can buy a firewall and put it in line, but if its rules are set to "any:any" and you did not know it—you likely have failed. Is logging for key applications defined? Is logging actually occurring? If logging is occurring, are logs being consumed by the appropriate security tools? Are alerts for said security tools tuned and correlated? What are your false positive and negative rates, and do you have metrics around reducing noise and increasing actual signal? Are you also measuring the associated workflow for handling these events?

2. *Mitigation Metrics*: These are metrics associated with the rate at which risk is added and removed from the organization. An example metric might be "Internet facing, remotely exploitable vulnerabilities must be remediated within one business day, with effective inline monitoring or mitigation established within 1 hour."

Security Data Marts

Note: *Chapter 11 is a tutorial on security data mart design. The section below only introduces the concept as part of the maturity model.*

"Data mart" is a red flag for some analysts. It brings up images of bloated data warehouses and complex ETL (extraction, transformation, load) programs. But when we say "data mart" we are steering clear of any particular implementation. If you wanted our ideal definition we would say it is "a subject-matter-specific, immutable, elastic, highly parallelized and atomic data store that easily connects with other subject data stores." Enough buzzwords? Translation: super-fast in all its operations, scales with data growth, and easy to reason over for the end users. We would also add, "in the cloud." That's only because we are not enamored with implementation and want to get on with the business of managing security risk. The reality is that most readers of this book will have ready access to traditional relational database management system (RDBMS) technology—even on their laptops.

Security Data Marts (SDM) metrics answer questions related to cross-program effectiveness. Are people, process, and technology working together effectively to reduce risk across multiple security domains? (Note: When we say "security system" we typically mean the combination of people, process, and technology.) More specifically, is your system improving or degrading in its ability to reduce risk over time? An example question could be "Are end users who operate systems with security controls XYZ less likely to be compromised? Or, are there certain vendor controls, or combinations of controls, more effective than others? Is there useless redundancy in these investments?" By way of example related to endpoint security effectiveness, these types of questions could rely on data coming from logs like the following:

- Microsoft's Enhanced Mitigation Experience Toolkit (EMET)
- Application whitelisting
- Host intrusion prevention systems
- File integrity monitoring
- System configuration (CIS benchmarks, etc.)
- Browser security and privacy settings
- Vulnerability management
- Endpoint reputation
- Antivirus
- Etc. . . .

Other questions could include "How long is exploitable residual risk sitting on endpoints prior to discovery and prioritization for removal? Is our 'system' fast enough? How fast should it be and how much would it cost to achieve that rate?"

Data marts are perfect for answering questions about how long hidden malicious activity exists prior to detection. This is something security information and event management (SIEM) solutions cannot do—although they can be a data source for data marts. Eventually, and this could be a long "eventually," security vendor systems catch up with the reality of the bad guys on your network. It could take moments to months if not years. For example, investments that determine the good or bad reputation of external systems get updated on the fly. Some of those systems may be used by bad actors as "command and control" servers to manage infected systems in your network. Those servers may have existed for months prior to vendor acknowledgment. Antivirus definitions are updated regularly as new malware is discovered. Malware may have been sitting on endpoints for months prior to that update. Vulnerability management systems are updated when new zero-day or other vulnerabilities are discovered. Vulnerabilities can exist for many years before software or security vendors know about them. During that time, malicious actors may have been exploiting those vulnerabilities without your knowledge.

This whole subject of measuring residual risk is a bit of an elephant in the room for the cybersecurity industry. You are always exposed at any given point in time and your vendor solutions are by definition always late. Ask any security professional and they would acknowledge this as an obvious non-epiphany. If it's so obvious, then why don't they measure it with the intent of improving on it? It's readily measurable and should be a priority. Measuring that exposure and investing to buy it down at the best ROI is a key practice in cybersecurity risk management that is facilitated by SDM in conjunction with what you learned in previous chapters. In Chapter 11, we will introduce a KPI called "survival analysis" that addresses the need to measure aging residual risk. But here's a dirty little secret: If you are not measuring your residual exposure rate, then it's likely getting worse. We need to be able to ask cross-domain questions like these if we are going to fight the good fight. Realize that the bad guys attack across domains. Our analytics must break out of functional silos to address that reality.

Prescriptive Analytics

As stated earlier, prescriptive analytics is a long book-length topic in and of itself. Our intent here is to initialize the conversation for the security industry. Let's describe prescriptive analytics by first establishing where it belongs among three categories of analytics:

- *Descriptive Analytics*: The majority of analytics out there are descriptive. They are just basic aggregates like sums and averages against certain groups of interest like month-over-month burn up and burn down of certain classes of risk. This is a standard descriptive analytic. Standard Online Analytical Processing (OLAP) fares well against descriptive analytics. But as stated, OLAP business intelligence (BI) has not seen enough traction in security. Functional and SDM approaches largely consist of descriptive analytics except when we want to use that data to update our sparse analytic models' beliefs.

- *Predictive Analytics*: Predictive analytics implies predicting the future. But strictly speaking, that is not what is happening. You are using past data to make a forecast about a potential future outcome. Most security metrics programs don't reach this level. Some security professionals and vendors may protest and say, "What about machine learning? We do that!" It is here that we need to make a slight detour on the topic of machine learning, a.k.a. data science versus decision science.

   Using machine learning techniques stands a bit apart from decision analysis. Indeed, finding patterns via machine learning is an increasingly important practice in fighting the bad guy. As previously stated, vendors are late in detecting new attacks, and machine learning has promise in early detection of new threats. But probabilistic signals applied to real-time data have the potential to become "more noise" to prioritize. "Prioritization" means determining what next when in the heat of battle. That is what the "management" part of SIEM really means—prioritization of what to do next. In that sense, this is where decision analysis could also shine. (Unfortunately, the SIEM market has not adopted decision analysis. Instead, it retains questionable ordinal approaches for prioritizing incident-response activity.)

- *Prescriptive Analytics*: In short, prescriptive analytics runs multiple models from both data and decision science realms and provides optimized recommendations for decision making. When done in a big data and stream analytics context, these decisions can be done in real time and in some cases take actions on your behalf—approaching "artificial intelligence."

Simply put, our model states that you start with decision analysis and you stick with it throughout as you increase your ingestion of empirical evidence. At the prescriptive level, data science model output becomes inputs into decision analysis models. These models work together to propose, and in some cases dynamically make, decisions. Decisions can be learned and hence become input back into the model. An example use case for prescriptive analytics would be in what we call "chasing rabbits down holes." As stated, much operational security technology revolves around detect, block, remove, and repeat. At a high level this is how antivirus software and various inline defenses work. But when there is a breach, or some sort of outbreak, then the troops are rallied. What about that gray area that precedes breach and/or may be an indication of an ongoing breach? Meaning, you don't have empirical evidence of an ongoing breach, you just have evidence that certain assets were compromised and now they are remediated.

For example, consider malware that was cleaned successfully, but prior to being cleaned, it was being blocked from communicating to a command-and-control server by inline reputation services. You gather additional evidence that compromised systems were attempting to send out messages to now blocked command and control servers. This has been occurring for months. What do you do? You have removed the malware but could there be an ongoing breach that you still don't see? Or, perhaps there was a breach that is now over that you missed? Meaning, do you start forensics investigations to see if there is one or more broader malicious "campaigns" that are, or were, siphoning off data?

In an ideal world, where resources are unlimited, the answer would be "yes!" But the reality is that your incident response team is typically 100% allocated to following confirmed incidents as opposed to "likely" breaches. It creates a dilemma. These "possible breaches" left without follow-up could mature into full-blown, long-term breaches. In fact, you would likely never get in front of these phenomena unless you figure out a way to prioritize the data you have. We propose that approaches similar to the ones presented in Chapter 9 can be integrated near real time into existing event detection systems. For example, the Lens Model is computationally fast by reducing the need for massive "Node Probability Tables." It's also thoroughly Bayesian and can accept both empirical evidence coming directly from deterministic and non-deterministic (data science) based security systems and calibrated beliefs from security experts. Being that it's Bayesian, it can then be used for learning based on the decision outcomes of the model itself—constantly updating its belief about various scenario types and recommending when certain "gray" events should be further investigated. This type of approach starts looking more and more like artificial intelligence applied to the cybersecurity realm. Again, this is a big, future book-length topic and we only proposed to shine a light on this future direction.

SDA Example Model: R Programming

We want to give you yet another taste for SDA. In this case we will use the R programming language. (You could just as easily do this in Excel, Python, etc.) This will not be an exhaustive "R How-To" section. We will explain code to the extent that it helps explain analytic ideas. An intuitive understanding of the program is our goal. The need for intuition cannot be overemphasized. Intuition will direct your creativity about your own problems. To that end, we believe Excel and scripting are great ways for newcomers to risk analytics to develop intuition for analytics quickly. In fact, if any concepts in previous chapters still seem opaque to you, then take more time with the Excel tools. A picture, and a program, can be worth several thousand words. That same concept applies here: Download R and give it a spin; all of this will make much more sense if you do.

We recommend you use the numerous books and countless online tutorials on R should your interest be piqued. We will be leveraging an R library, "LearnBayes," that in and of itself is a tutorial. The author of this module, Jim Albert, has a great book[3] and several tutorials all available online that you can reference just as we have done here. If you don't have R, you can go here to download it for your particular platform: https:// cran.rstudio.com/index.html. We also recommend the RStudio; it will make your R hacking much easier: https://www.rstudio.com/products/rstudio/ download/.

Once you have downloaded R Studio, you will want to fire it up. Type install.packages("LearnBayes") at the command line.

For our scenario, here are the facts:

- You are now part of a due diligence team that will evaluate a multibillion-dollar acquisition.
- The company in question has a significant global cloud presence.
- You were told that they have several hundred cloud applications servicing various critical industries with millions of users.
- You have been given less than one week, as your CEO says, to "determine how bad they are, find any 'gotchas,' and moreover how much technical debt we are absorbing from a security perspective."
- Your organization is one of several that are making a play for this company. It's a bit of a fire sale in that the board of the selling company is looking to unload quickly.
- You will not have all the disclosures you might want. In fact, you will not get to do much of any formal assessment.

Since you want your work to be defensible from a technical assessment perspective, you choose to focus on a subset of the Cloud Security Alliances Controls Matrix. It's correlated to all the big control frameworks like ISO, NIST, and so forth. You reduce your list to a set of five macro items that represent "must haves." Lacking any one of these controls could cost several hundreds of thousands of dollars or more per application to remediate.

After a bit of research, you feel 50% confident that the true proportion of controls that are in place is less than 40%. Sound confusing? It's because we are trying to explain a "proportional picture." The best way to think about this is in shape terms on a graph. You see a bell shape that has its highest point slightly to the left of center—over the 40% mark on the x-axis. You are also 90% sure that the true value (percentage controls in place) is below the 60% mark on the graph. This moves things a bit further to the left on the graph. If you were 90% sure that the controls state was below 50%, that would make your prior look thinner and taller—denser around the 40% mark.

Let's assume you conduct your first set of audit/interviews for 10 applications. You find that 3 of the 10 applications have basic controls in place. With this, you input your "prior beliefs" about the company and add the newly acquired data into R:

```
> library(LearnBayes)
>
> beta.par <- beta.select(list(p=0.5, x=0.40), list(p=0.90, x=.60))
> triplot(beta.par, c(3,7))
```

As stated, your prior beliefs show that you think the control state for most of the cloud applications in question bunch up around 40%. As you get more data, your ideas start "taking shape." That is what the posterior reflects. The posterior is what you get after you run your analytics. The posterior, if used as input into another analysis, would then be called your "prior." The data you start with in your prediction is "prior" to getting your output, which is the "posterior." Your beliefs are getting less dispersed; that is, denser and hence more certain. Of course this is only after 10 interviews.

Note the "Likelihood" plot. It is a function that describes how likely it is, given your model (hypothesis), that you observed the data. Formally this would be written: P(Data | Hypothesis). In our case, we had 3 passes and 7 fails. If our model is consistent, then the probability that our model reflects our data should be relatively high.

In terms of the preceding code, the *beta.select* function is used to create (select) two values from our prior probability inputs. The two values go by fancy names: *a* and *b* or alpha and beta. They are also called "shape parameters." They shape the curve, or distribution, seen in Figure 10.2. Think of a distribution as clay and these two parameters as hands that shape the clay. As stated in Chapter 9, the formal name of this particular type of distribution (shape) is called the "beta distribution." As *a* and *b* get larger, our beliefs, as represented by the beta distribution, are getting taller and narrower. It just means there is more certainty (density) regarding your beliefs about some uncertain thing. In our case, that uncertain

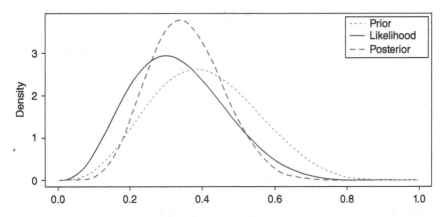

FIGURE 10.2 Bayes Triplot, beta(4.31, 6.3) prior, s=3, f=7

thing is the state of controls for roughly 200 cloud applications. You can see how the two lists hold the beliefs the CISO had: *beta.select(**list(p=0.5, x=0.40), list(p=0.90, x=.60)**)*. Those inputs are transformed by the *beta. select* function into **a** and **b** values and stored into the beta.par variable. We can print these values to screen by typing the following:

```
> beta.par
[1] 4.31 6.30
```

From your vantage point you are only dealing with your beliefs and the new data. The alpha and the beta values work in the background to shape the beta distribution as you get more data. We then use the *triplot* function to combine our new information (3,7; 3 successes and 7 fails) with our prior beliefs to create a new posterior belief:

```
> triplot(beta.par, c(3,7))
```

Let's assume you conduct 35 total audits with only 5 cloud applications meeting the most fundamental "defense in depth" controls requirements. There are over 200 applications that did not get audited. You now update your model with the new data (see Figure 10.3).

```
> triplot(beta.par, c(5,30))
```

You still have a lot of uncertainty about the real state of the company's cloud security posture. In fact, it's looking significantly worse than you had guessed. Therefore, to help your inferences you decide to simulate a large number of outcomes based on your new beliefs (posterior). That's a fancy way of saying, "I don't have time to audit everything. What if I use what I know as input into a simulation machine? This machine would simulate 1,000 audits

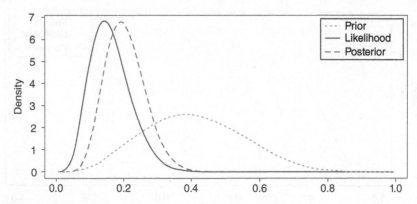

FIGURE 10.3 Bayes Triplot, beta(4.31, 6.3) prior, s=5, f=30

and give me an idea where my future audit results might fall, constrained by what I already know." Additionally, you frame up your result in terms of your 90% CI, meaning, "I am 90% confident that the true value of company XYZ's cloud security state is between x% and y%." Let's get our 90% CI first:

```
> beta.post.par <- beta.par + c(5, 30)
> qbeta(c(0.05, 0.95), beta.post.par[1],beta.post.par[2])
[1] 0.1148617 0.3082632
```

Pretty straightforward—we get the alpha and beta from our new posterior and feed it into a simple function called qbeta. The first parameter c(0.05,0.95) simply tells us the 90% CI. Now that we have that, let's simulate a bunch of trials and get the 90% CI from that for thoroughness.

```
> post.sample <- rbeta(1000, beta.post.par[1], beta.post
.par[2])
> quantile(post.sample, c(0.05, 0.95))
 5%  95%
0.1178466 0.3027499
```

It looks like the proportion in question is likely (90% confident) to land between 12% and 30%. We can take this even further and try to predict what the results might be on the next 200 audits. We run that this way:

```
> num <- 200
> sample <- 0:num
> pred.probs <- pbetap(beta.post.par, num, sample)
> discint(cbind(sample, pred.probs), 0.90)
> [1] 0.9084958
> $set
 [1] 17 18 19 20 21 22 23 24 25 26 27 28 29 30 31 32 33 34 35
[20] 36 37 38 39 40 41 42 43 44 45 46 47 48 49 50 51 52 53 54
[39] 55 56
```

Your model is telling you that you should be 91% confident that the next 200 audits will have between 17 and 56 successful outcomes. You have some financial modeling to do both in terms of remediation cost and the probability of breach. This latter issue is what is most disconcerting. How much risk are you really inheriting? What is the likelihood that a breach may have occurred or may be occurring?

This was a very simple example. It could have easily been done in Excel, Python, or on a smart calculator. But the point is that you can start doing interesting and useful measurements now. As a leader, you will use this type of analytics as your personal form of hand-to-hand combat far more than any other types of metric.

Notes

1. Andrew Gelman, "N Is Never Large," *Statistical Modeling, Causal Inference, and Social Science* (blog), July 31, 2005, http://andrewgelman.com/2005/07/31/n_is_never_larg/.
2. Andrew Jaquith, *Security Metrics: Replacing Fear, Uncertainty, and Doubt* (Upper Saddle River, NJ: Pearson Education, 2007).
3. Jim Albert, *Bayesian Computation with R* (New York: Springer Science & Business Media, 2009).

CHAPTER 11

How Well Are My Security Investments Working Together?

In Chapter 10, we shared an operational security-metrics maturity model. The model started with sparse data analytics. That really is the main theme of this book: "how to measure and then decide on what to invest in when you have a lot of uncertainty caused by limited empirical data." Chapters 8 and 9 represent the main modeling techniques used in sparse data analytics. The goal is to make the best *decision* given the circumstances. And as you may recall, a decision is an "irrevocable allocation of resources." In short, you know you've made a decision when you have written a check. Is measurement all over once you have made an investment? Certainly not!

What do you measure once you have made a decision (i.e., an investment)? You determine if your investment is meeting the performance goals you have set for it. For the security professional this is the realm of operational security metrics. Once you have made a security investment, you need to measure how well that investment is doing against certain targets. That target is often considered a KPI.

Assuming you have made a serious outlay of cash, this would warrant some form of continuous "automated" measurement for optimization purposes. Likely you may have made a number of investments that work together to affect one or more key risks. When it comes to integrating data sources for the purpose of measuring *historical performance,* we are now talking security metrics that start to look more like business intelligence (BI). There are many great books on business intelligence. Most of them large and in some cases cover multiple volumes. So why do we need more on this topic, and what could we hope to achieve in just one chapter?

Specifically, we are not aware of any books that advocate BI for cybersecurity metrics. This is a profound shame. In fact, Jaquith's book *Security Metrics* advocated against such an approach. Over 10 years ago we too might have held the same opinion. (Although at that time one of the authors was rolling out security data marts like hotcakes.) But risks and technology have evolved, and we need to as well. Analytic technology has improved, particularly open source, and more and more security systems "play well with others." Most all enterprise security solutions have APIs and/or direct database connectivity to extract well-formed and consistent data. It could not be any easier. So our first goal is to expose and encourage the reader to investigate this classical form of process modeling.

Our goal in this chapter is to give a basic, intuitive explanation in terms of a subset of business intelligence: dimensional modeling.

Dimensional modeling is a logical approach to designing physical data marts. Data marts are subject-specific structures that can be connected together via dimensions like Legos. Thus they fit well into the operational security metrics domain.

Figure 11.1 is the pattern we use for most of our dimensional modeling efforts. Such a model is typically referred to as a "cube" of three key dimensions: time, value, and risk. Most operational security measurement takes this form, and in fact the only thing that changes per area is the particular risk you are studying. Time and value end up being consistent connective tissue that allows us to measure across (i.e., drill across) risk areas. Just remember that this is a quick overview of dimensional modeling. It's also our hope that dimensional approaches to security metrics will grow over time. With the growth of big data and related open source analytic-based applications, now is the right time.

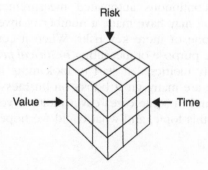

FIGURE 11.1 The Standard Security Data Mart

Addressing BI Concerns

At the mention of BI, many readers may see images of bloated data ware-houses with complex ETLs (extraction, transformation, and load). And indeed ETLs and even visualizations can take quarters to deliver value. That problem stems from the complexities underlying relational database infrastructure. It also stems from how analytic outcomes are framed. On the infrastructure side of things, this has largely been solved. Most cloud providers have big data solutions. Specifically, companies like Amazon, Google, and Microsoft have mature cloud database products that scale. Even Excel is apparently getting more batteries, as it is able to scale up to billions of records using the "PowerPivot" feature.

If you want to stay clear of a single vendor, then open source solu-tions like Apache Drill provide a unified SQL (Structured Query Language) interface to most all data stores, including NoSQL databases, various file types (CSV, JSON, XML, etc.), and Open Database Connectivity connectors for legacy databases (including Excel). The idea is to completely remove end user analytics barriers caused by complex ETLs. This is similar to what we saw over a decade ago in data visualization. Visualization tools brought the barrier to entry for end user analytics way down. Of course, this presupposed a well-formed and readily understandable data source. Unfortunately, recent maturations in data sources like Hadoop and other NoSQL stores largely did not solve this issue. In fact, data access complex-ity actually increased. But now that same "no friction" approach seen in visualization is materializing for data access. In summary, the technical barriers in terms of size, speed, and interface are completely eroding. What persists after the technical concerns are resolved? The logical fram-ing of analytic problems and selecting the right approaches for those problems.

In terms of prejudices toward an analytic approach, you may have heard the following about business intelligence: "BI is like driving the busi-ness forward by looking through the rear view mirror." You may also hear things like, "Business intelligence is dead!" But to us this is like saying, "Descriptive analytics is dead!" or "Looking at data about things that hap-pened in the past is dead!" What's dead, or should be, is slow, cumbersome approaches to doing analytics that add no strategic value. Those who make those declarations are simply guilty of the "Beat the Bear" or "Exsupero Ursus" fallacy we mentioned in Chapter 5. Of course, all predictive analyt-ics are predicated on things that happened in the past so as to forecast the future! In short, there is always some latency when it comes to observable facts that make up a predictive model. We are even seeing stream analytic solutions that create micro-cubes (mini–data marts) in memory. It's an excit-ing time for business intelligence!

Now that we have hopefully blown up any prejudice associated with BI versus big data versus NoSQL versus predictive analytics, we can get on with the true core of this chapter: how to determine if security investments are working well together by using dimensional modeling.

Just the Facts: What Is Dimensional Modeling and Why Do I Need It?

When you are asking *dimensional* questions about historical *facts* that allow for both aggregation and drilling down to atomic events, then you are doing BI. A meta-requirement typically includes data consistency, meaning that the problem you are modeling requires some consistency from a time-series perspective: day to day, month to month, and so forth. Many modeling exercises don't have time series consistency as a goal. Security metrics measure operational processes and require some amount of consistency; thus they are perfect for BI. Now, if you use that data to simulate or forecast how the data will be shaped in the future, then you are indeed doing predictive analytics—or as we like to call it, "statistics." But your underlying source for those predictions was based on BI, and the design process for doing BI is dimensional modeling.

Dimensional modeling is a logical design process for producing data marts. It deals with two macro objects: facts and dimensions. A grouping of dimensions that surround a list of facts is a data mart. Figure 11.2 is a simple logical data mart for vulnerabilities. Note that it follows the same pattern from Figure 11.1. Vulnerability in this case is a particular risk dimension. Asset is a value dimension, value being something that is worth protecting. We also have a date dimension, which exists in most all models.

In the middle of your dimensional tables is something called a "fact table." A fact table holds pointers to the dimension tables. The fact table could be in the millions if not billions of rows. If your asset dimension is in the hundreds of thousands if not millions, and that is exclusively what one of the authors has modeled, then your fact table would certainly be in the billions. Do the math; there could be N vulnerabilities per asset that exist at a given time. Also note that we said "logical." This is a reminder that we will not necessarily create physical objects like dimension tables and fact tables. With modern approaches, when you query against various data sources it may be all virtualized into one simple in-memory data object. So, don't let these various schemas fool you; they are just for our brains so we can get clear about our metrics questions.

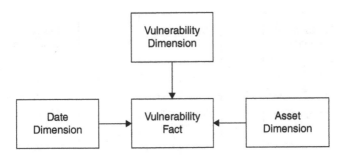

FIGURE 11.2 Vulnerability Mart

Conforming or shared dimensions allow you to connect data marts together to ask new and interesting questions. Probably the most popular conforming dimension is "date time." The second most popular, at least in security, would be "asset." Asset can be decomposed in a variety of manners: portfolio, application, product, server, virtual server, container, micro service, data, and so on. An asset represents value that gets protected by controls, attacked by malicious threats, and used for intended purposes by authorized users. To that end, you will likely want to have data marts related to the state of vulnerabilities, configurations, and mitigation. Each of those data marts may share the same concept of asset. That "sharing" across security domains is what allows us to ask both horizontal and vertical questions. Or, as we like to say in the BI world, conforming dimensions allow us to drill across.

In terms of a drill-across use case, let's say you have a metric called "full metal jacket." A full metal jacket, as shown in Figure 11.3, represents a series of macro-hardening requirements for certain classes of assets. Specifically, you have KPIs in terms of least privilege (config), patch status, speed of mitigations to end points, and availability of blocking controls on the network. This is all really control coverage metrics in relationship to some concept of value (asset). The simple structure below would give you guidance in that regard. You could determine where you have completely unmitigated, known-exploitable, residual risk versus what is controlled via configuration or mitigation.

What is missing from this model is some concept of "threat": how well your macro concept of protecting value (full metal jacket) is doing against certain vectors of threat. Here, in Figure 11.4, is a simple extension of the model. In this case, you integrate your malware-analysis data mart to your conforming data marts. This is simple, because your malware mart conforms on asset and date.

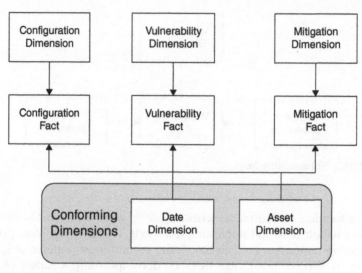

FIGURE 11.3 Expanded Mart with Conforming Dimensions

This mart could answer hundreds if not thousands of questions about the value of various forms of defense against malware. For example, on the mitigation dimension, you could ask questions about the performance of host-based versus inline defenses against spearfishing. Or, in the same vein, how often did

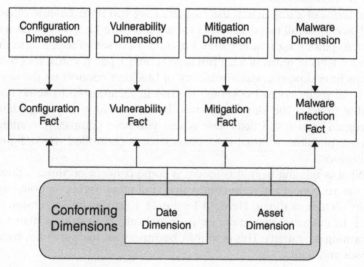

FIGURE 11.4 Malware Dimension

application whitelisting have impact where all other controls failed—that is, is there a class of malware where application whitelisting is the last line of defense? (*Note, application whitelisting is a control that only allows approved applications to run. Thus, if something malicious attempts to install itself or run, in theory, the application whitelisting control would stop it.*) Is it *increasingly* the last line of defense, meaning other investments are deteriorating? Or are there new strains of malware that all your protections are failing at finding in a timely manner, thus hinting at a possible new investment and/or de-investment opportunity? In short, are you getting the ROI on whitelisting you predicted when you modeled it as an investment? With models like this it becomes obvious which protections are underperforming, which stand out and deserve more investment, and which are retirement candidates, providing opportunity for new, innovative investments to address unmitigated growing risks.

Interestingly, in dimensional modeling, a fact in a fact table is also known as a "measure." They're called a measure because they measure a process at the atomic level. "Atomic" means you cannot decompose the event being measured any further. A typical fact in business would be the sale of some product like a can of beans. The measure in this fact would be the sale price. You might want to know how much of a particular product you sold at a particular time and place. Additionally you may want to watch its sales performance quarter by quarter. Perhaps you want to compare the profitability of a certain product versus another, given certain geographical markets and/or store placements, and so forth. This is all traditional BI.

What is a "security fact"? It is simply an event that happened. It could be that a firewall rule was changed, or it could be that an intrusion prevention system blocked a particular attack. It could be the state of a particular piece of software in a cloud application at a particular time. The point is that we are recording that an event (or state change) happened or did not happen. State could change by the millisecond or by the year. Because of this on/off metric, as opposed to a monetary measure, the security fact is said to be "factless." You are essentially summing up a bunch of "1"s as opposed to dollars and cents. A fact table in the traditional sense would look something like Table 11.1, for a simple vulnerability data mart.

TABLE 11.1 A Fact Table with Multiple Vulnerabilities for One Asset at a Given Time

Vuln_Dim_ID	Asset_Dim_ID	Date_Dim_ID	Event
1	43	67987	1
2	43	67987	1
3	43	67987	1
4	43	67987	1

TABLE 11.2 Vulnerability Facts with Dimensional References Resolved

Vulnerability	Asset	Date	Event
CVE-2016–0063	10.0.10.10	1455148800	1
CVE-2016–0060	10.0.10.10	1455148800	1
CVE-2016–0061	10.0.10.10	1455148800	1
CVE-2016–0973	10.0.10.10	1455148800	1

In old school data marts the first three columns are IDs that are references to dimensional tables. You would sum(event) based on dimensional criteria. While perhaps going into a little optional technical detail, Table 11.2 is what that same data structure might look like with the IDs revolved (note that date is an epoch).

We have various CVEs, which is short for "common vulnerabilities and exposures." The vulnerability dimension table would hold all the salient characteristics of the vulnerability that could additionally constrain a query. We have an IP address, but yet again there could be an additional 100 characteristics in the asset dimension we might use for our interrogation. Last, there is the timestamp.

A dimension is a decomposition of something of interest. It's a bunch of descriptive characteristics of some fact that allow you to ask many and varied questions. For example, in our asset dimension we could also have things like operating system or service pack version. In fact, if storage is no object you could in theory track a complete list of installed software and its versions related to a particular concept of asset over time. This asset could in turn become one or more data marts with facts that you track. You just need to be sure that you have an analytic that requires that level of decomposition. While BI is getting significantly easier, this is an area where useless decompositions can lead to a lot of wasted effort. Brainstorm with your stakeholders and shoot for agile results first. Apply the KISS model (Keep It Simple, Stupid).

Table 11.3 is a small example of what a dimension object might look like; note that it could be 100 or more columns wide.

TABLE 11.3 Asset Dimension

Asset_ID	IP	FQDN	OS	Type	Service Pack	BuildNum
1	10.0.0.1	thing1.foo.org	Win10	Laptop	n/a	14257
2	10.0.0.2	thing2.foo.org	Win10	Laptop	n/a	14257
3	10.0.0.3	thing3.foo.org	Win10	Laptop	n/a	14257
4	10.0.0.4	thing4.foo.org	Win10	Laptop	n/a	14257

Now that we have covered some of the very basics of dimensional modeling, we are going to create a dimensional model. Our goal in this case is to keep the explanation simple, intuitive, and nontechnical. No need to create the Dimensional Model to Rule the Universe that anticipates any and all possible questions. You can add those values as you have need for them.

Dimensional Modeling Use Case: Advanced Data Stealing Threats

For this use case let's assume you developed a KPI around a new distinction you are calling "Advanced Data Stealing Threats" or ADST for short. Your definition of this threat is "malware that steals data and that your commercial off-the-shelf security solutions originally miss," meaning the ADST is active for some time prior to your investments "catching up" and stopping it. Let's assume you used Excel, R, or Python to do a quick analysis on a few samples of ADST over the last year. Specifically you performed what is called a "survival analysis" to get the graph shown in Figure 11.5.

What is survival analysis? It's the analysis of things that have a life span, for which there is eventually some change in status inclusive of end of life. While survival analysis originates in the medical sphere, it has application to engineering, insurance, political science, business management, economics, and even security. The heart of survival analysis is the survival function. In our case, this ends up being a curve that maps a time variable to a

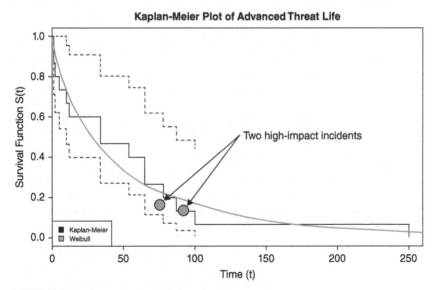

FIGURE 11.5 Days ADST Alive Before Being Found

proportion. This way we can make inferences about the life expectancy of certain phenomena, like ADSTs.

Note the two instances called out, where financial impact occurred. For a lack of better options you decide you want to "improve the overall curve," particularly in relationship to those two losses. So your KPI becomes "Improve on 20% of advanced threats surviving for 70 days or greater." You have decided that this is something that you should be measuring closely for the foreseeable future. (*This is indeed something we do recommend measuring as a fundamental security metric.*) How do you move from a strategic analytic model that informed some new investments to security metrics? To get there we will need to apply some dimensional design thinking.

Fortunately enough, the dimensional models we have been working on thus far do have application here. To that end, we list the various "dimensions" we have and how they would accommodate an ADST survival analysis mart (see Table 11.4). Our goal is to understand how what we have invested in is actually stopping ADST or not. Is there an opportunity to optimize a particular solution based on what we are learning? Is a particular vendor solution outperforming others, or is one lagging? More specifically, was there a configuration change, a patched vulnerability, a new mitigating control, or a new piece of anti-malware particularly effective in stopping ADSTs?

TABLE 11.4 ADST Dimension Descriptions

Dimension	Description
Asset	An asset could be a computer, an application, a web server, a database, a portfolio, or even data. While it's tempting to capture every potential jot and tittle related to the concept of an asset, we recommend only selecting a minimal subset of fields to start with. To that end, we're looking to focus on the end user's system. This is not to say that server-class and/or larger applications are out of scope over time. Therefore this dimension will solely focus on desktop and laptop computers and/or any other systems on the network that browse, get mail, and so forth.
HTTP Blocked	This is a list of all known bad-reputation sites that your reputation systems are aware of. At a previous engagement we built a dimensional table for this same purpose that tracked pure egress web traffic. It was well over 100 billion records. This sort of table that just logs endlessly and is used to create other dimensions is formally called a "junk dimension." The idea is that you are throwing a lot of "junk" into it without much care. This "junk dimension" looks backward in HTTP history to see when a particular asset first started attempting communication with a now known malicious command-and-control server.

TABLE 11.4 *(continued)*

Dimension	Description
Vulnerability	This is a standard vulnerability dimension, typically all of the descriptive data coming from a vulnerability management system. Perhaps it's something coming from a web application scanner like Burp Suite or some other form of dynamic analysis. One of the authors has built vulnerability dimensions well in excess of 50 fields.
Configuration	We put this here as a loose correlation, but the reality is that this would be a drill-across for meta metrics. This is why there is a dotted line in the dimensional model in Figure 11.6. You could have 100–200 controls per control area be it OS, Web Server, Data Base and so forth. If you have 100,000 assets, and you track changes over time, this would certainly be in the several hundreds of millions of records quickly.
Mitigation	This is a complete list of all dynamic blocking rules from various Host Intrusion Prevention Systems (HIPS), Network Intrusion Prevention Systems (NIPS), Reputation Services, Web Application Firewalls (WAF), local Firewall (FW) rules, etc. and when they fired in relationship to the ADST.
Malware:	A list of all malware variants that various malware systems are aware of. Anti-malware could in theory be lumped into mitigations, but it is a large enough subject that it likely warrants its own mart.

The data mart as shown in Figure 11.6 leverages the existing marts and brings in HTTP-related data from web proxies. This mart would suffice for complete ADST analysis.

In looking at Table 11.5, you can see how simple our fact table ends up being. Dimensions tend to be wide and facts are relatively thin. Here is how the fact table works:

- If mitigation is responsible for blocking, then the mit_id field will be populated with the ID of the particular mitigation vendor solution that was responsible for thwarting the attack; otherwise it will be 0. The mitigation ID points back to the mitigation dimension.
- If malware defense is responsible for closure, then the mal_id will be populated with the ID for the particular piece of anti-malware coming from the malware dimension.
- The http_id points to the URL for the particular command-and-control server that the asset was attempting to talk to at the time of being thwarted.

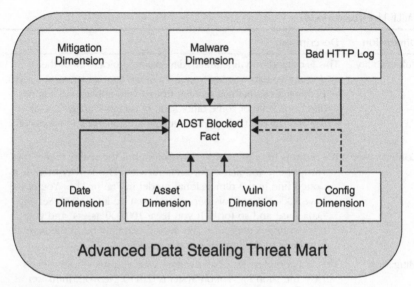

FIGURE 11.6 ADST High Level Mart

TABLE 11.5 ADST Blocked Fact

mit_id	mal_id	http_id	date_http_start_id	date_http_end_id	asset_id	vuln_id

- date_http_start_id points to the date dimension indicating when the ADST was first noticed. Nine times out of ten this will require querying back through HTTP proxy logs after the mitigation system and/or the malware system becomes aware of the threat. This is easily automated, but as previously stated the logs would likely be in a big data system.
- date_https_end_id would be the same as the previous but for when the ADST was thwarted.
- asset_id points to the asset in question.
- vuln_id is populated if there is a correlation to a known vulnerability. If it is the only populated ID, other than the date and asset fields, then it would indicate that a patch was responsible for thwarting the ADST instance.

Modeling People Processes

Dimensional models are perfect for security metrics because they are designed to measure processes, and security absolutely is a process. Of course the ADST use case is a technical process. But what if you have a need to measure processes that are more people based? What if the process has multiple gates and/or milestones? This, too, is easily modeled dimensionally. This particular type of model is called an "accumulating snapshot." What you "accumulate" is the time that each process phase has been running.

From a security perspective this is key for measuring pre- and post-product development, remediation activity, or both. For example, if you have implemented a Security Development Lifecycle program (and we hope you have), then you will likely want to measure its key phases. The macro phases are Secure by Design, Secure by Default (development), and Secure in Deploy. And it does not matter if you are using waterfall, agile, or a mix of both that looks more "wagile." You can instrument the whole processes. Such instrumentation and measurement is key if you are operating in a continuous integration and continuous development (CICD) context. CICD supports an ongoing flow of software deploys daily. New development and remediation occur continuously. This is one of many functions that can and likely should be dimensionally modeled, measured, and optimized ad infinitum.

In Figure 11.7 we have a high-level logical accumulating snapshot for security remediation. It could be one large data mart across a variety of risks, or associated with a particular risk type. For example, one of these could model system vulnerability remediation. Perhaps another could model web application remediation, and so forth. The risk dimension is just a generalization for any sort of vulnerability type that could be substituted here. "Asset" also is generalized. It could be an application or perhaps even an OS. The remediation dimension presupposes some sort of enterprise ticketing system that would contain a backlog of items, including data on the various people involved with the remediation. Time is the most complex in this case. You can see that there are four gates that are measured and one overarching gate. There are well over 20 dates associated with this measurement. In each of the five groups there is a final field like: "Days_ Existing" or "Analysis_Days_Reviewing." These are accumulators that add days by default while something is still open and then stop when the final data field for each area is filled in with a date. The accumulator makes for much faster queries and additional aggregates when analyzing remediation processes.

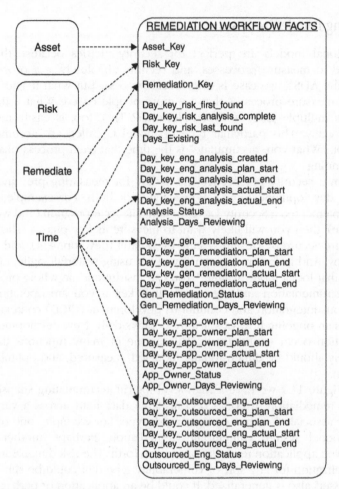

FIGURE 11.7 Remediation Workflow Facts

This model becomes a simple template that can be reused to model a number of security processes with multiple steps. It leverages dimensions that you use to model your technical solutions as well. Thus we stay close to the KISS model, agility and reuse.

In this chapter we provided a very brief glimpse into a powerful logical tool for approaching operational security metrics: dimensional modeling. This level of effectiveness metrics is little practiced in security, which as stated is a crying shame. We think analyzing the effectiveness of your investments is a close second to using predictive analytics when deciding on investments. We, in fact, would say that you are giving advantage to both the enemy and underperforming vendors when you don't go about measuring operations this way. With the advent of big data and simplification in data access, high-dimensional security metrics should become the main approach for measurement and optimization.

This chapter attempted to explain, at a very high level, a much needed approach for cybersecurity metrics. Our hope is that your interest has been piqued.

The final chapter will focus on the people side of "cybersecurity risk management" for the enterprise. It will outline various roles and responsibilities, and give perspectives for effective program management.

CHAPTER 12

A Call to Action

How to Roll Out Cybersecurity Risk Management

There are three general themes to this book:

1. What measurement is
2. How to apply measurement
3. How to improve measurement

What distinguishes this tome from its predecessors, *How to Measure Anything: Finding the Value of "Intangibles" in Business* and *The Failure of Risk Management,* is that this book is domain focused. More than that, it's designed to be a road map for establishing cybersecurity risk management as *the* C-level strategic technology risk practice. To this point, we believe cybersecurity as an operational function should be redefined around quantitative risk management. This book has provided more evangelism and proof to that quantitative end. If you are of the mind that cybersecurity risk management (CSRM) should be a program as opposed to a grab bag of quantitative tricks, then this chapter is a high level proposition to that end. We will lay out what such an organization might look like, and how it could work alongside other technology risk functions.

Establishing the CSRM Strategic Charter

This section answers the question "What should the overarching corporate role be for CSRM?" What we are framing as the CSRM function should become the first gate for executive, or board-level, large-investment consideration. Leaders still make the decisions, but they are using their quantitative napkins to add, multiply, and divide dollars and probabilities. Ordinal scales and other faux risk stuff should not be accepted.

The CSRM function is a C-level function. It could be the CISO's function, but we actually put this role as senior to the CISO and reporting directly to the CEO or board. Of course, if the CISO reports to those functions then this may work, but it requires an identity shift for the CISO. "Information and Security" are subsumed by "Risk" and that risk is exclusively understood as likelihood and impact in the manner an actuary would understand it. In terms of identity or role changes we have seen titles like "chief technology risk officer" (CTRO); this also could be a "chief risk officer" (CRO) function. Unfortunately, the latter is typically purely financial and/or legal in function. Whatever the job title, it should not be placed under a CIO/CTO. That becomes the fox watching the henhouse. A CSRM function serves at the pleasure of the CEO and board, and is there to protect the business from bad technology investments.

The charter, simply put, is as such:

- The CSRM function will report to the CEO and/or board of directors. The executive title could be CTRO, CRO, or perhaps CISO, as long as the role is quantitatively redefined.
- The CSRM function reviews all major initiatives for technology risk inclusive of corporate acquisitions, major investments in new enterprise technology, venture capital investments, and the like. "Review" means to quantitatively assess and forecast losses, gains, and strategic mitigations and related optimizations.
- The CSRM function will also be responsible for monitoring and analysis for existing controls investments. The purpose is optimization of technology investments in relation to probable future loss. The dimensional modeling practices and associated technology covered in Chapter 11 are key. Operationally the goal of this function is answering "Are my investments working well together in addressing key risks?"
- The CSRM function will use *proven* quantitative methods inclusive of probabilities for likelihoods and dollars as impact to understand and communicate risk. Loss exceedance curves will be the medium for discussing and visualizing risks and associated mitigation investments in relationship to tolerance. This includes risks associated with one application and/or a roll-up of one or more portfolios of risk.
- The CSRM is responsible for maintaining corporate risk tolerances in conjunction with the office of the CFO, General Counsel, and the board. Specifically, "risk tolerance exceedance" will be the KPI used to manage risk.
- The CSRM function will be responsible for managing and monitoring technology exception-management programs that violate risk tolerances.

■ The CSRM function will maintain cyberinsurance policies in conjunction with other corporate functions like legal and finance. CSRM provides the main parameters that inform the insurance models.

Organizational Roles and Responsibilities for CSRM

Figure 12.1 shows an example of an organizational structure for cybersecurity risk. The structure is more appropriate for a large (Fortune 1000) organization that is managing hundreds of millions of dollars, if not many billions of dollars, at risk. It presupposes that technology investments are key strategic initiatives, which is easy enough in this day and age. It also presupposes that cybersecurity risks are considered a top-five, if not top-three, board-level/CEO risk.

Quantitative Risk Analysis

The quantitative risk analysis (QRA) team consists of trained analysts with a great bedside manner. You could call them consultants or advisors, but the distinction is that they have quantitative skills. They essentially are decision scientists that can program and communicate clearly with subject matter experts and leaders. This is a highly compensated function, typically with graduate work in statistics and/or a quantitative MBA. While degrees are nice, quantitative skill and business acumen are key. The more readily available statistics and quantitative business experts will need to work side-by-side with security SMEs and leadership. As the reality of cybersecurity as a measurement discipline (as most sciences are) sets in, this role and skill set will be more plentiful.

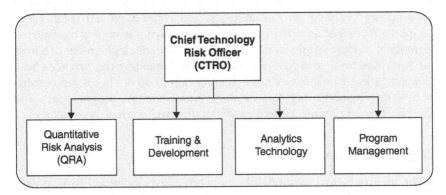

FIGURE 12.1 Cybersecurity Risk Management Function

You will want the right ratio of QRAs to risk assessment engagements. Practically speaking, there are only so many models that can be run and maintained at any given time. Ratios like 10:1 in terms of new models to each QRA may be appropriate. It depends on the complexity of the models. Also, ongoing risk tracking against tolerances is required for completed models. Enterprise technology of course will help in terms of scaling this out. But even with advanced prescriptive analytics there will be ongoing advisory work based on exceedance of risk tolerances. That is, if a particular portfolio of risk needs optimization, perhaps through acquisition of new technology and/ or decommissioning of failing investments, that all takes time. A QRA will be involved in ongoing risk-framing discussions, development of models using statistics and statistics tools (R, Python, etc.), and coordinating with technologists in the organization to design and build real-time risk monitoring systems.

Training and Development

You can certainly use your QRA team to provide quantitative training material and even actual training delivery. But the goal here is to build its DNA at various layers of the broader organization. This is similar to building general security DNA in engineering and IT teams (we assume you do this already). You can only hire so many QRA folks—they are rare, expensive, and prone to flight due to demand. You need to build tools and skills broadly if you are to fight the good fight with the bad guys. You will need a leader for this function and a content and delivery team. Using technology to deliver is key for large, distributed organizations.

Analytics Technology

This will be the most expensive and operationally intensive function. It presupposes big data, stream analytics, and cloud-deployed solutions to support a myriad of analytics outcomes. The analytics team will manage the movement of large swaths of data and the appropriate deployment of telemetry into systems. If you have any hope of implementing the practices from Chapter 11 in an agile manner, this is the group to do it. This group consists of systems engineers, big data database administrators, programmers, and the like. It is an optimized IT organization focused on analytic outcomes.

Program Management

When an activity involves multiple functions across multiple organizations, it's a program. The CSRM function typically will be deployed to a variety of organizations. The QRA team will be the technical face, but tying everything together—from engagement to training and development to technology—is a program management function. No need to go overboard on this one, but don't skimp on program management; you will fail if you do.

We could have gone deep on every single role and function, building out various matrices, job descriptions, Gantt charts, and the like. That is not necessary. All the practices revealed throughout this book provide a glimpse into the core content of a larger cybersecurity risk management function. The roles and responsibilities have some flexibility. You can start lean-targeting one or two projects just using the spreadsheets provided. But if you are serious about fighting the bad guy with analytics, then you need a plan. Start by identifying where you are on the maturity model provided in the beginning of Part III. Then chart a course to build both the skills and organization that lead to prescriptive analytics capability. Having a plan removes a key roadblock to success; as Benjamin Franklin said, "Those who fail to plan, plan to fail!"

While there are many potential barriers to success like failed planning, there is one institutional barrier that can obstruct quantitative analysis: compliance audits. In theory, audits should help ensure the right thing is occurring at the right time and in the right way. To that extent, we think audits are fantastic. What makes compliance audits a challenge is when risk management functions focus on managing to an audit as opposed to managing to actual risks. Perhaps this is why the CEO of Target was shocked when they had their breach; he went on record claiming they were compliant to the PCI (payment card industry) standard. That is compliance versus risk-management mindset and it is a deadly error in the face of our foes.

What if there was an audit function that assessed—actually measured—the effectiveness of risk management approaches? That is, would it determine the actual impact on risk reduction of soft methods versus quantitative methods? And what if scoring algorithms were put to the test? Of course, advanced methods like Monte Carlo simulations, beta distributions, and the like would also need to be tested. Good! Again, we think one of the reasons we lose is because of untested soft methods.

There is, however, a risk that this will backfire. For example, what if methods that were predicated on measuring uncertainty got audited because they were viewed as novel but methods using risk matrix, ordinal scales, and scoring systems got a pass? That would become a negative incentive to adopting quantitative methods. Unfortunately, this is a reality in at least one industry, as described hereafter. We bring it up here as an example of compliance audit gone wild in a nefarious manner that could have a profound negative impact on cybersecurity risk management.

Getting Audit to Audit

Audit plays a key role in ensuring quality of risk models, especially in heavily regulated industries like banking and insurance. If new quantitative models are developed that have any influence at all on financial transactions, then audit is a necessary checkpoint to make sure that models don't have unintended consequences—possibly as a result of simple errors buried in complex formulae. Such scrutiny should be applied to any model proposed for financial transactions and certainly for decisions regarding the exposure of the organization to risks like market uncertainty and cyberattacks.

Auditors might get excited when they see a model that involves more advanced math. The auditors have been there at one point in their careers. It's interesting to finally get to use something for which so much study and time was spent mastering. So they will eagerly dive into a model that has some statistics and maybe a Monte Carlo simulation—as they should. If the method claims to be based on some scientific research they haven't heard of, they should demand to see reference to that research. If the model is complex enough, perhaps the audit ought to be done twice on each calculation by different people. If an error is found, then any modeler whose primary interest is quality should happily fix it.

But even well-intentioned and qualified auditors inadvertently discourage the adoption of better models in decision making. In some cases the more sophisticated model was replacing a very soft, unscientific model. In fact, this is the case in *every* model the authors have developed and introduced. The models we have developed replaced models that were based on the methods we have already made a case against: doing arithmetic with ordinal scales, using words like "medium" as a risk assessment, heat maps, and so on. Yet these methods get no such scrutiny by auditors. If another method were introduced for cybersecurity that merely said we should subjectively assess likelihood and impact, and then only represent those with subjective estimates using ambiguous scales, the auditors are not demanding research showing the measured performance of uncalibrated subjective estimates, or the mathematical foundations of the method, or the issues with using verbal scales as representations of risk.

So what happens when they audit *only* those methods that involve a bit more advanced calculations? The manager who sticks with a simple scoring method they just made up that day may not be scrutinized the same way as one who uses a more advanced method would be simply because it isn't advanced. This creates a disincentive for seeking improvement with more quantitative and scientifically sound methods in risk management and decision making.

For audit to avoid this (surely unintended) disincentive for improving management decision making, they must start auditing the softer methods with the same diligence they would for the methods that allow them to flex some of their old stats education.

How Auditors Can Avoid Killing Better Methods

- Audit ALL models. All decision making is based on a model, whether that model is a manager's intuition, a subjective point system, a deterministic cost/benefit analysis, stochastic models, or a coin flip. Don't make the mistake of auditing only things that are explicitly called models in the organization. If a class of decisions are made by gut feel, then consider the vast research on intuition errors and overconfidence and demand to see the evidence that these challenges somehow don't apply to this particular problem.
- Don't make the mistake of auditing the model strictly within its context. For example, if a manager used a deterministic cost/benefit model in a spreadsheet to evaluate cybersecurity controls, don't just check that the basic financial calculations are correct or ask where the inputs came from. Instead, start with asking whether that modeling approach really applies at all. Ask why they would use deterministic methods on decisions that clearly rely on uncertain inputs.
- Just because the output of a model is ambiguous, don't assume that you can't measure performance. If the model says a risk is "medium," you should ask whether medium-risk events actually occur more often than low-risk and less often than high-risk events. Attention is often focused on quantitative models because their output is unambiguous and can be tracked against outcomes. The very thing that makes auditors more drawn to investigate statistical models more than softer models is actually an advantage of the former.
- Ask for research backing up the relative performance of that method versus alternatives. If the method promotes a colored heat map, look up the work of Tony Cox. If it relies on verbal scales, look up the work of David Budescu and Richard Heuer. If they claim that the softer method proposed somehow avoids the problems identified by these researchers, the auditors should demand evidence of that.
- Even claims about what levels of complexity are feasible in the organization should not be taken at face value. If a simpler scoring method is proposed based on the belief that managers won't understand anything more complex, then demand the research behind this claim (the authors' combined experience seems to contradict this).

One legitimate concern is that this might require too much of audit. We certainly understand they have a lot of important work to do and are often understaffed. But audit could at least investigate a few key methods, especially when they have some pseudo-math. If at least some of the softer models get audited as much as the models with a little more math, organizations would remove the incentive to stick with less scientifically valid methods just to avoid the probes of audit.

What the Cybersecurity Ecosystem Must Do to Support You

Earlier in this book we took a hard look at popular risk analysis methods and found them wanting. They do not add value and, in fact, apparently add error. Some will say that at least such methods help "start the conversation" about risk management, but since lots of methods can do that, why not choose one based on techniques that have shown a measurable improvement in estimates? Nor can anybody continue to support the claim that quantitative methods are impractical, since we've actually applied them in real environments, including Monte Carlos, Bayesian empirical methods, and more advanced combinations of them as discussed in Chapters 8 and 9. And, finally, nothing in the evidence of recent major breaches indicates that the existing methods were actually helping risk management at all.

But we don't actually fault most cybersecurity professionals for adopting ineffectual methods. They were following the recommendations of standards organizations and following methods they've been trained in as part of recognized certification requirements. They are following the needs of regulatory compliance and audit in their organizations. They are using tools developed by any of a myriad of vendors that use the softer methods. So, if we want the professionals to change, then the following must change in the ecosystem of cybersecurity.

1. Standards organizations must end the promotion of risk matrices as a "best practice" and promote evidence-based (scientific) methods in cybersecurity risk management unless and until there is evidence to the contrary. We have shown that the evidence against non–evidence-based methods is overwhelming.
2. To supplement the first point, standards organizations must adopt evidence-based as opposed to testimonial-based and committee-based methods of identifying best practices. Only if standards organizations can show empirical evidence of the effectiveness of their current methods sufficient to overturn the empirical evidence already against them (which seems unlikely given such evidence), then they should reinstate them.

3. An organization could be formed to track and measure the performance of risk assessment methods themselves. This could be something modeled after the NIST National Vulnerability Database—perhaps even part of that organization. (We would argue, after all, that the poor state of risk assessment methods certainly counts as a national vulnerability.) Then standards organizations could adopt methods based on informed, evidence-based analysis of alternative methods.

4. Certification programs that have been teaching risk matrices and ordinal scales must pivot to teaching both proper evidence-based methods and new methods as evidence is gathered (from published research and the efforts just mentioned).

5. Auditors in organizations must begin applying the standards of model validity equally to all methods in order to avoid discouraging some of the best methods. When both softer methods and better quantitative methods are given equal scrutiny (instead of only assessing the latter and defaulting to the former if any problem is found), then we are confident that better methods will eventually be adopted.

6. Regulators must help lead the way. We understand that conservative regulators are necessarily slower to move, but they should at least start the process of recognizing the inadequacies of methods they currently consider "compliant" and encouraging better methods.

7. Vendors, consultants, and insurance companies should seize the business opportunities related to methods identified in this book. The survey mentioned in Chapter 5 indicated a high level of acceptance of quantitative methods among cybersecurity practitioners. The evidence against some of the most popular methods and for more rigorous evidence-based methods grows. Early promoters of methods that can show a measurable improvement will have an advantage. Insurance companies are already beginning to discover that the evidence-based methods are a good bet. Whether and how well an insurance customer uses such methods should eventually be part of the underwriting process.

Can We Avoid the Big One?

The "Big One" we referred to in Chapter 1 is an extensive cyberattack that affects multiple large organizations. It could involve, in concert, interruption of basic services, such as utilities and communications. This, combined with a significant reduction in trust in online and credit card transactions, could actually have an impact on the economy well beyond the costs to a single large company—even the biggest firms hit so far.

The nature of the attack on Target is one indicator of the nature of the risk. They were attacked in a way that exposed a threat common to many firms: that companies and their vendors are connected to each other, and many of those companies and vendors are connected through networks to many more. Even government agencies are connected to these organizations in various ways. All of these organizations may only be one or two degrees of separation away from each other. If it is possible for a vendor to expose a company, and if that vendor has many clients and those clients have many vendors, then we have a kind of total network risk that—while it has not yet been exploited—is entirely possible.

Analyzing the risks of this kind of situation is far too complex to evaluate with existing popular methods or in the heads of any of the leading experts. Proper analysis will require real, quantitative models to compute the impacts of these connections. Organizations with limited resources (which are, of course, all of them) will have to use evidence-based, rational methods to decide how to mitigate such risks. If we begin to accept that, then we may improve our chances of avoiding—or at least recovering more gracefully from—the Big One.

Selected Distributions

Distribution Name: Triangular

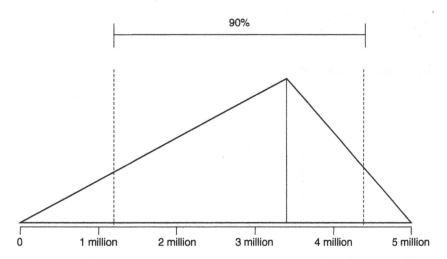

FIGURE A.1 Triangular Distribution

Parameters:

- UB (Upper bound)
- LB (Lower bound)
- Mode—this may be any value between UB and LB.

Note that UB and LB are absolute outer limits—a 100% CI.

For a triangular distribution, the UB and LB represent absolute limits. There is no chance that a value could be generated outside of these bounds. In addition to the UB and LB, this distribution also has a mode that can vary to any value between the UB and LB. This is sometimes useful as a substitute for a lognormal, when you want to set absolute limits on what the values can be but you want to skew the output in a way similar to a lognormal. It is useful in any situation where you know of absolute limits but the most likely value might not be in the middle, like the normal distribution.

- When to Use: When you want control over where the most likely value is compared to the range, and when the range has absolute limits.
- Examples: Number of records lost if you think the most likely number is near the top of the range and yet you have a finite number of records you know cannot be exceeded.
- Excel Formula:

   =IF(Rand()<=Mode,1,0)*((Mode-LB)^2)/((UB-LB)*(Mode-LB))
   +IF(Rand()>Mode,1,0)*(1-((UB-Mode)^2)/((UB-LB)*(UB-Mode)))

- Mean: = (LB+Mode+UB)/3

Distribution Name: Binary

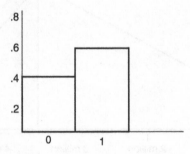

FIGURE A.2 Binary Distribution

Parameters:

- P (Event probability)

Note that P is between 0 and 1. It represents how frequently the simulation will randomly produce an event.

Unlike the other distributions mentioned here, a discrete binary distribution (also known as a Bernoulli distribution) generates just two possible outcomes: success or failure. The probability of success is p and the probability of failure is $q = (1 - p)$. For example, if success means to flip a fair coin heads-up, the probability of success is p = .5, and the probability of failure is q = (1 − .5) = .5.

- When to Use: This is used in either/or situations—something either happens or it doesn't.
- Example: The occurrence of a data breach in a given period of time.
- Excel Formula: =if(rand() < P,1,0)
- Mean: =P

Distribution Name: Normal

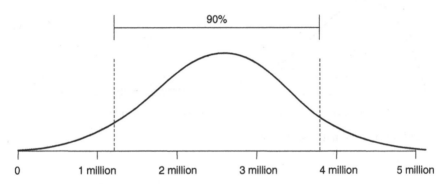

FIGURE A.3 Normal Distribution

Parameters:

- UB (Upper bound)
- LB (Lower bound)

Note that LB and UB in the Excel formula below represent a 90% CI. There is a 5% chance of being above the UB and a 5% chance of being below the LB.

A normal (or Gaussian) distribution is a bell-shaped curve that is symmetrically distributed about the mean.

1. Many natural phenomena follow this distribution but in some applications it will underestimate the probability of extreme events.
2. Empirical rule: Nearly all data points (99.7%) will lie within three standard deviations of the mean.

   - When to Use: When there is equal probability of observing a result above or below the mean.
   - Examples: Test scores, travel time.

■ Excel Formula: =norminv(rand(),(UB + LB)/2,(UB-LB)/3.29)
■ Mean: =((UB + LB)/2)

Distribution Name: Lognormal

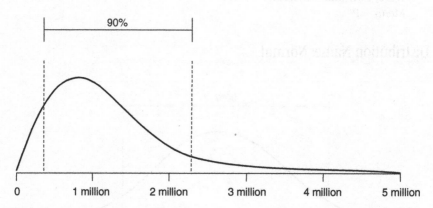

FIGURE A.4 Lognormal Distribution

Parameters:

■ UB (Upper bound)
■ LB (Lower bound)

Note that LB and UB in the Excel formula below represent a 90% CI. There is a 5% chance of being above the UB and a 5% chance of being below the LB.

The lognormal distribution is an often preferred alternative to the normal distribution when a sample can only take positive values. Consider the expected future value of a stock price. In the equation $S_1 = S_0e^{(r)}$, S_1 is the future stock price, S_0 is the present stock price, and r is the expected rate of return. The expected rate of return follows a normal distribution and may very well take a negative value. The future price of a stock, however, is bounded at zero. By taking the exponent of the normally distributed expected rate of return, we will generate a lognormal distribution where a negative rate may have an adverse effect on the future stock price, without ever leading the stock price below the zero bound. It also allows for the possibility of extreme values on the upper end and, therefore, may fit some phenomena better than a normal.

- When to Use: To model positive values that are primarily moderate in scope but have potential for rare extreme events.
- Examples: Losses incurred by a cyberattack, the cost of a project.
- Excel Formula: =lognorm.inv(rand(),(ln(UB) + ln(LB))/2, (ln(UB)-ln(LB))/3.29)
- Mean: = ((ln(UB)+ln(LB))/2)

Distribution Name: Beta

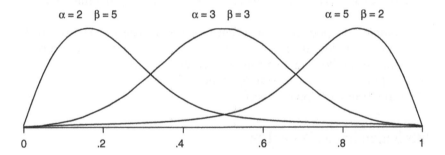

FIGURE A.5 Beta Distribution

Parameters:

- Alpha (1 + Number of hits)
- Beta (1 + Number of misses)

Beta distributions are extremely versatile. They can be used to generate values between 0 and 1 but where some values are more likely than others. This result can also be used in other formulas to generate any range of values you like. They are particularly useful when modeling the frequency of an event, especially when the frequency is estimated based on random samples of a population or historical observations. In this distribution it is not quite as easy as in other distributions to determine the parameters based only on upper and lower bounds. The only solution is iteratively trying different "alpha" and "beta" values until you get the 90% CI you want. If alpha and beta are each greater than 1 and equal to each other, then it will be symmetrical, where values near .5 are the most likely and less likely further away from .5. The larger you make both alpha and beta, the narrower the distribution. If you make alpha larger than beta, the distribution will skew to the left, and if you make beta larger, it skews to the right.

To test alpha and beta, just check the UB and LB of a stated 90% CI by computing the fifth and ninety-fifth percentile values. That is betainv(.05,alpha,beta) and betainv(.95,alpha,beta). You can check that the mean and mode are what you expect by computing the following: mean=alpha/(alpha+beta), and mode (the most likely value) is mode= (alpha-1)/(alpha+beta-2). Or you can just use the spreadsheet at www .howtomeasureanything.com/cybersecurity to test the bounds, means, and modes from a given alpha and beta to get good approximations of what you are estimating.

- When to Use: Any situation that can be characterized as a set of "hits" and "misses." For each hit, increase alpha by 1. For each miss, increase beta by 1.
- Examples: Frequency of an event (such as a data breach) when the frequency is less than 1 per time unit (e.g., year), the proportion of employees following a security procedure correctly.
- Excel Formula: =betainv(rand(),alpha,beta)
- Mean: =(alpha/(alpha + beta))

Distribution Name: Power Law

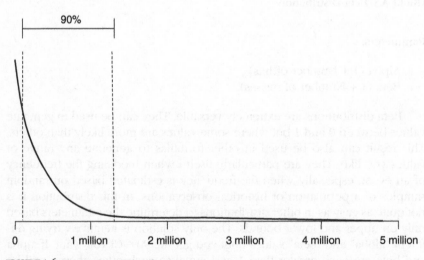

FIGURE A.6 Power Law Distribution

Parameters:

- Alpha (Shape parameter)
- Theta (Location parameter)

The power law is a useful distribution for describing phenomena with extreme, catastrophic possibilities—even more than lognormal. For events such as forest fires, the vast majority of occurrences are limited to an acre or less in scope. On rare occasions, however, a forest fire may spread over hundreds of acres. The "fat tail" of the power law distribution allows us to acknowledge the common small event, while still accounting for more extreme possibilities.

- When to Use: When you want to make sure that catastrophic events, while rare, will be given nontrivial probabilities.
- Examples: Phenomena like earthquakes, power outages, epidemics, and other types of "cascade failures" have this property.
- Excel Formula: =(theta/x)^alpha
- Mean: =(alpha*theta/(alpha-1))

Distribution Name: Truncated Power Law

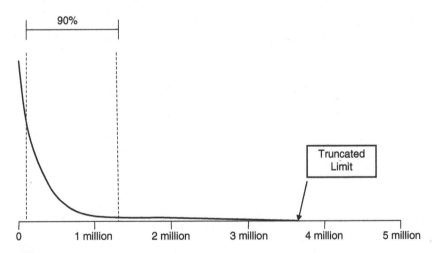

FIGURE A.7 Truncated Power Law Distribution

Parameters:

- Alpha (Shape parameter)
- Theta (Location parameter)
- T (Truncated limit)

The truncated power law distribution mirrors the power law distribution, but with an upper limit that is imposed by the user. While the heavy tail of the power law distribution allows us to account for the rare catastrophic event, there may be a theoretical bound to the size of such an event. If this upper limit is not factored into the model, we may produce a misleading and unnecessarily grim forecast.

- When to Use: The power law distribution should be truncated if an upper bound on the severity of an event is known.
- Example: Losses of records may follow a power law but you know you only have a finite number of records to lose.
- Excel Formula: =(alpha*theta^alpha/(x^(alpha+1)))/(1-(theta/T)^alpha)
- Mean: =(alpha*theta/(alpha-1))

Guest Contributors

You are not alone! The number of people applying statistics to the security problem is increasing. More people are taking what may be considered sparse data and using it to make inferences about large risks. This is not to say "big data" and "data science" are excluded; rather, making actionable inferences using limited empirical data, beliefs, and simulations are increasingly important for informing strategy and even prioritizing tactical decisions. To that end, we have included a number of short papers from various researchers in industry and academia on this topic. Also, stay tuned to www.howtomeasureanything.com/cybersecurity, as we will be including more and more research like this on our book's website.

Appendix B Contents

Aggregating Data Sources for Cyber Insights

Jim Lipkis, VP and GM at VivoSecurity Inc.

Chuck Chan, chief researcher at VivoSecurity Inc.

Thomas Lee, PhD, founder and CEO at VivoSecurity Inc.

Actuarial science provides a wellspring of metrics and insights that are invaluable for managing cybersecurity in a business context. Relevant historical data can be obtained from a wide variety of industry and government sources, and combining data from different sources can lead to unexpected, powerful results. We use an actuarial approach to forecast cyber risk in dollar terms and generate a profile showing concentrations of business risk across various dimensions of the enterprise IT infrastructure.

Cyber risk encompasses three broad factors: the at-risk value of assets (particularly data assets), the expected occurrence of different types of cyber incidents, and the expected financial impact of each incident type relative to specific data assets. All three can be estimated by observing long-term trends in historical data, deriving statistical predictions from the trends, and applying those predictions according to empirically derived characteristics and risk indicators of a specific organization. This section includes three examples: two relating to frequency of breaches, and one to financial impact.

Aggregating data sources is often needed simply for normalization; that is, finding a denominator so as to convert an absolute count into a rate. But with some creativity many useful correlations can be found. For example, here is an unexpected result that sheds light on the frequency of cyber-espionage attacks, and some effective ways of mitigating that risk.

Forecasting—and Reducing—Occurrence of Espionage Attacks

Studies have shown that a high percentage of external espionage attacks enter via phishing,[1] and install malware on the phished user's computer. One technique for countering these attacks is anti-phish decoy training, using fake phishing e-mails.[2] But a decoy program can be expensive and even politically sensitive. Actuarial data led us to an unexpected but even more effective approach.

Crucial data in this case came from Microsoft's published data[3] on malware clean rates on various operating systems. Unsurprisingly, the data show that more recent versions of Windows are substantially more secure against malware attacks, and MacOS and Linux are more secure than Windows. What is perhaps unexpected is the degree to which the OS version can affect the frequency of successful attack.

Figure B.1 shows an analysis of a high-tech company in a highly competitive industry where espionage is a very real business risk. We estimated the probability (expected frequency) of espionage attack at about 12%, as shown by the leftmost bar in the graph. (In other words, given eight similar companies, it should be expected that about one of them will incur a successful espionage attack every year.) This estimate arises from the company's industry, number of employees, and IT infrastructure; the calculation was based on several trends and correlations gleaned from successive years of the Verizon Data Breach Investigations Report,[4] the U.S. Census Bureau, and other sources.

Decoy training reduces the expected frequency of attack substantially, as seen on the next bar to the right: the 12% drops to 2%. But moving further rightward we see an even more dramatic countermeasure: upgrading all of this company's Windows 7 computers to Windows 8 reduces the espionage probability to about 1%, even without decoy training (at time of writing no data was yet available on Windows 10). Combining the OS upgrade with decoy training, or using MacOS in lieu of Windows, yields probability levels far below 1%.

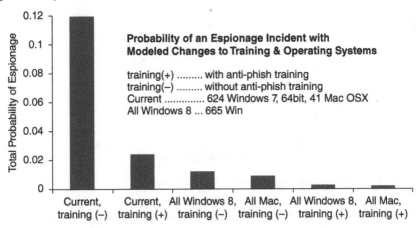

FIGURE B.1 Probability of an Espionage Incident with Modeled Changes to Training and Operating Systems

OS upgrades have a cost as well, and it might make sense to upgrade only computers used by system administrators or others with unusual access to sensitive data. Visibility on incident likelihood allows management to weigh costs and risks and make decisions based on data.

Skyrocketing Breaches?

One often hears that the rate of breaches in the healthcare industry is skyrocketing. Indeed, well over 30 million patient records have been breached in the United States alone since mandatory reporting was instituted in 2009. But the wild-eyed claims of soaring breach rates are not borne out by the data. Breach occurrence has been quite stable over the past five years, when measured in an actuarial context, and can be reasonably projected for future years.

Our research shows a strong correlation between breach rate and number of employees working in an organization such as a healthcare provider. (This is true in other industries as well.) We used the U.S. Department of Health and Human Services database of PHI breaches reported under the 2009 HITECH Act,[5] and broke down the breach occurrence rate for each year by state. Plotting against the healthcare employment data by state in Figure B.2 shows a linear relationship.

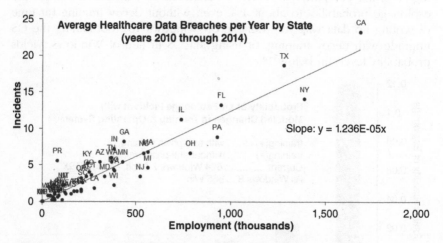

FIGURE B.2 Average Data Breaches per Year by State

Can the slope in Figure B.2 (average breach count per employee) be used to confidently predict expected incident frequency for an organization going forward?

To answer that question, we show the trend over time in Figure B.3. The rate of breaches per employee shot up when reporting first became mandatory in 2009, but has since been quite steady. Only in one year (2013) did the rate increase, and then at a rather modest 31%. This stable trend is perhaps explained by the fact that the most common cause of breaches is accidents, not external attacks. The projected incident frequency can be combined with measurements of the at-risk value of data assets for a credible, dollar-quantified picture of an organization's risk.

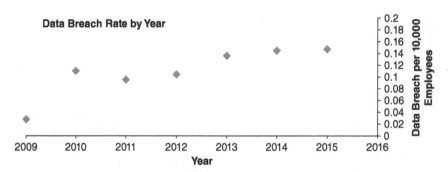

FIGURE B.3 Data Breach Rate by Year as a Function of Number of Employees

Financial Impact of Breaches

We now turn from the expected frequency to the financial impact of cyber breaches. The expense of a breach stems from the at-risk value of the breached assets, and that value may have a number of cost components: notification and remediation; forensic, legal, and liability; and reputation and long-term business impact. Studies of breach cost are available from a variety of sources, such as the Ponemon Institute.[6] We have found, however, that care is required in deploying this data in actuarial forecasting.

Estimating at-risk value of data assets is beyond the scope of this essay, but a simple example shows some of the challenges. Consider a database of custodial data (e.g., customer, employee, or patient data) containing sensitive personal, financial, or health information. It is tempting simply to count records and quote breach cost on a per-record basis. But this assumes that cost per record is constant, which turns out not to be the case.

Figure B.4 shows cost per record plotted against breach size on a log-log scale, and we see that breach cost per record declines logarithmically as the number of records breached increases. This is perhaps unsurprising as there are economies of scale in some of the cost elements. The key here was to bring in data from companies' SEC filings, in particular 10-K reports, which often include extensive detail on both short- and long-term costs of major breaches.[7]

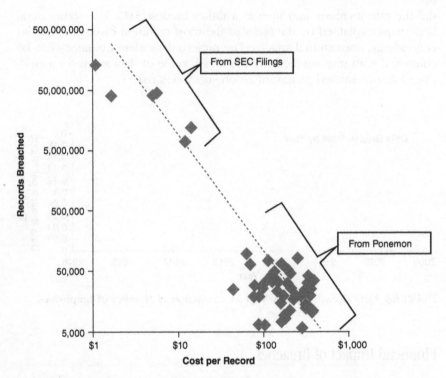

FIGURE B.4 Data on Breached Records: SEC Filings versus Ponemon

In sum, we see actuarial science as fertile ground for credible forecasting that can bring cybersecurity up to the level of sophistication in business risk management long enjoyed in most other areas of risk.

The Flaw of Averages in Cyber Security

Sam Savage, PhD, is the founder of ProbabilityManagement.org, author of *The Flaw of Averages: Why We Underestimate Risk in the Face of Uncertainty*, and consulting professor at Stanford. © Copyright 2015, Sam L. Savage.

The Flaw of Averages is a set of systematic errors that occur when uncertain assumptions are replaced with single "average" numbers. The most serious of these, known as Jensen's Inequality by mathematicians, states roughly that "plans based on average assumptions are wrong on average." The essence of cybersecurity is the effective mitigation of uncertain adverse outcomes. I will describe two variants of the Flaw of Averages in dealing with the uncertainties of a hypothetical botnet threat. I will also show how the emerging discipline of probability management can unambiguously communicate and calculate these uncertainties.

Botnets

A "botnet" is a cyberattack created by malware that penetrates numerous computers, which may then be directed by a command-and-control server to form a network that carries out illegal activity. Eventually this server will be identified as a threat, whereupon future communication with it is blocked. Once the dangerous site is discovered, the communications history of the infected computers can pinpoint the first contact with the offending server and yield valuable statistics.

Suppose you have invested in two layers of network security. There is a 60% chance that a botnet virus will be discovered by the first layer, in which case the time to detection averages 20 days, with a distribution as displayed in the left side of Figure B.5. Note that the average may be thought of as the balance point of the graph, marked by Δ. In the remaining 40% of cases the virus is not discovered until the second layer of your security system, in which case the average detection time is 60 days, with distribution shown on the right of Figure B.5.

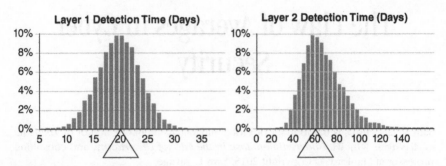

FIGURE B.5 The Distribution of Detection Times for Layers 1 and 2 of a Security System

Window of Vulnerability for a Single Botnet

The average overall detection time of this botnet virus may be computed as the weighted average 60% × 20 days + 40% × 60 days = 36 days. So on average we are vulnerable to a single botnet for 36 days. The discipline of probability management[8] provides additional insights by explicitly representing the entire distribution as a set of historical or simulated realizations called SIPs.[9] Figure B.6 displays the SIPs (in this example, 10,000 simulated outcomes) of both distributions in Figure B.5. Performing calculations with SIPs (SIPmath) can be done in numerous software environments, including the native spreadsheet.

Trial	Days to Detect Layer1	Days to Detect Layer2
1	18.73	54.20
2	25.37	59.97
3	21.31	64.95
⋮	⋮	⋮
⋮	⋮	⋮
9998	14.93	83.68
9999	24.83	78.55
10000	26.23	49.29

FIGURE B.6 SIPs of 10,000 Trials of Layer 1 and Layer 2 Detection Times

Recently Microsoft Excel has become powerful enough to process SIPs of thousands of trials using its Data Table function.[10] Figure B.7 displays such a SIPmath model that combines the two distributions of Figure B.5 to create a distribution of overall time to detection across both security layers.

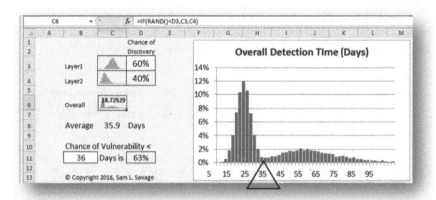

FIGURE B.7 A SIPmath Excel Model to Calculate the Overall Detection Distribution

This workbook takes the two SIPs of Figure B.6 as input, and then performs 10,000 calculations of cell C6 that randomly chooses the Layer 1 distribution 60% of the time and the Layer 2 SIP 40% of the time. The resulting distribution clearly displays the two modes of detection. Press the calculate key (F9 in Windows, ⌘ = on Mac) to perform a new simulation of 10,000 trials. Note that the simulated average is very close to the theoretical value of 36 days, yet 36 is a very unlikely outcome of the distribution. Also note that because the distribution is asymmetric, the chance of vulnerability of less than the average of 36 days is not 50%, but 63%. Experiment with the chance of discovery at Layer 1 in cell D3 and the number of days in B11 to see how the distribution, average, and chance change.

The formula used for calculating the average detection time over both layers was technically correct in that it yielded 36 days, but it provides no clue about the distribution. This is what I call the weak form of the Flaw of Averages. The strong form is considerably worse, in that you don't even get the right *average*. The model of Figure B.7 created a SIP of its own, which we can now use to explore the impact of multiple simultaneous botnet attacks.

Window of Vulnerability for Multiple Botnets

Suppose we put a new system online, which is immediately attacked by multiple viruses that all have the same distribution of detection times. Since each virus is detected in an average of 36 days, you might think that the average vulnerability is again 36 days, as it was for the single virus. But it is not, because your system remains vulnerable until the last of the botnets is detected.

Figure B.8 displays the SIPs of 10 botnet detection times generated by the simulation of Figure B.7. They all have the same numbers, but the order has been scrambled in each to make them statistically independent.

	Detect1	Detect2	Detect3	Detect4	Detect5	Detect6	Detect7	Detect8	Detect9	Detect10
1	76.45	19.33	25.35	15.06	23.54	23.20	20.25	20.96	23.55	45.48
2	25.39	74.46	20.24	16.80	30.64	46.94	20.01	23.28	17.62	22.54
3	21.33	18.77	20.63	19.20	34.76	48.69	18.67	23.99	15.25	22.43
:	:	:	:	:	:	:	:	:	:	:
:	:	:	:	:	:	:	:	:	:	:
9998	14.95	18.69	17.53	25.39	19.91	16.20	22.96	20.25	21.41	16.04
9999	78.57	55.87	67.07	54.93	25.52	14.78	26.78	17.80	36.62	25.50
10000	26.25	18.24	19.18	20.03	20.21	96.24	62.07	16.98	80.89	19.89

FIGURE B.8 The Detection Time SIPs of 10 Independent Botnets

These SIPs are used in the model in Figure B.9, which calculates the distribution of the maximum of the detection times of all botnets in cell C14. Note that you can adjust the number of botnets from between 1 and 10 with the spinner control in column E. Before experimenting with this model, close the model of Figure B.7, as it contains a Rand() formula, which can slow down the calculation.

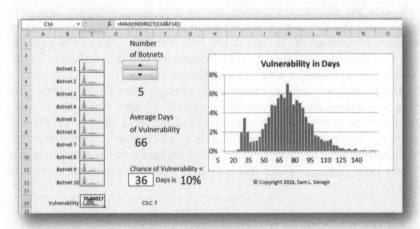

FIGURE B.9 Simulation of Multiple Botnets

Note that the average days of vulnerability increase as the number of simultaneous attacks goes up, and that the chance of coming in at less than

36 days diminishes. This is an example of the strong form of the Flaw of Averages, and for 10 botnets, the average is 78 days, with a 1% chance of being less than 36.

Such modeling could easily be generalized to reflect different variants of viruses attacking at random times instead of all at once. Such insights into the proportion of time when you would expect your system to be vulnerable are vital to making investment decisions involving mitigation strategies.

Password Hacking

Anton Mobley, data scientist at GE Healthcare

Major breaches causing huge financial and brand damage have occurred in recent years. The attackers are varied, including hacktivists, nation-states, and cyber criminals. The targets and data types breached include Target and Home Depot (personal credit information), Anthem/Wellpoint (personal health information), the U.S. Office of Personnel Management, Booz Allen Hamilton and HBGary (military and intelligence information), and Ashley Madison and Adult Friend Finder (private information). Malware and phishing attacks are typically the focus of cybersecurity professionals, but these breaches pose a secondary risk to enterprises due to credential loss. The credential databases from these breaches often find themselves posted on hacker forums, TOR, and torrents.

Using the 2013 Adobe breach as a case study, enterprise exposure can be modeled as a function of enterprise size and password policy. In October 2013[11] Adobe announced that hackers had stolen source code for major Adobe products and customer credentials for over 153 million users. The credential database became very easily accessible. Some amount of users in the data set are likely made up or missing passwords, but the data set was still one of the largest known credential dumps to date.

The database contained e-mail addresses, encrypted passwords, and a cleartext password hint if the user chose to use one. Note that the passwords were not hashed or salted; they were 3DES block-encrypted. This implies that a key loss would compromise the entire database; however, the key is not publicly known as of now. Since no salt was used, the same password encrypts to the same encrypted password. The password hints were stored in cleartext, meaning that an attacker can aggregate on an encrypted password to get all applicable hints for the same password. Frequently in the database, password hints such as "work," "sso," "outlook password," and "lotus notes password" are given, implying password reuse, and pivoting off the encrypted password to the set of applicable hints makes guessing the password trivial. Additionally, the passwords were block-encrypted, meaning that an attacker could breach pieces of passwords and use them to attack other users' credentials in the database.

To model enterprise exposure, we define an enterprise to be exposed if the following criteria are met:

1. The password used by an employee e-mail is the same password used by the employee for a critical type of work function.

2. The password can be easily backed out of the Adobe database by aggregating hints on encrypted passwords.

It follows, then, that the probability of exposure for an enterprise of n employees can be modeled, as the following assuming that employees are independent and that password reuse rate is independent of the employee password being vulnerable.

P(employees exposed >= 1)
= 1 − P(Any employee password is reused AND same password is vulnerable by hint aggregation)^n
= 1 − (1 − P(password is reused)P(Single password is vulnerable to hint aggregation))^n

Security experts have varying opinions on the rate of password reuse between accounts. Some studies put the rate in the 12% to 20% range,[12] but a Princeton study using limited data put the reuse rate at 49%.[13] Using previous results in this type of analysis, a rate of Uniform(0.15,0.25) is used for this model.

Modeling the likelihood that a single password is vulnerable to hint aggregation is a bit more difficult. To be able to do this, an understanding of how users choose passwords must be developed. Since many password leaks have happened in the past, we choose a former leak with minimal password restrictions to model the password selection space. We use the 2009 hack of RockYou, a company that developed plugins and widgets for social media sites and from which 34 million passwords were leaked. The aggregated password set (no user information) was taken from https://wiki.skullsecurity.org/Passwords. The parameter for the rate at which a hint is given that breaks a password is chosen as 0.0001. This parameter is unknown, however; this is a very conservative estimate. Typically only 10 to 20 hints are needed before a password becomes easy to guess. This parameter is also a function of the number of people sharing passwords, but for simplicity the point estimate is used. By conditioning on the number of users that share a password and the RockYou password space as the probability mass function of how people choose passwords, we can model the single employee exposure as the following:

V = event a password is vulnerable to being guessed
X = event that X employees share an encrypted password with the user
N = Adobe User Base in breach: ~153 million
P_{RY} = Density function for each password from the RockYou data breach
h = probability that a password hint is weak enough to allow the password to be guessed correctly

These results are dependent on the RockYou password space PMF. Taking password policy into account by taking the conditional distribution from RockYou that is compliant with the password policy, the initial set of passwords that a user will pull from comes from a much higher entropy distribution.

A simulation of various password policies and number of matches is run using replacement for the number of matches to a password to empirically estimate the cumulative distribution functions under various password policies. The number of vulnerable passwords—that is, passwords that have a weak hint associated with them, based on the number of people sharing the password and the event that the password is reused—is used to calculated the maximum likelihood estimate and 95% CIs for the single employee's rate of compromise.

Combining the reuse rate distribution with the single-employee exposure distribution results in a range of outcomes (given in Figure B.10). The solid lines show the MLE of the probability of exposure and the dotted lines show the lower and upper bounds when using the 95% CI results with the low and high values of the reuse rate distribution.

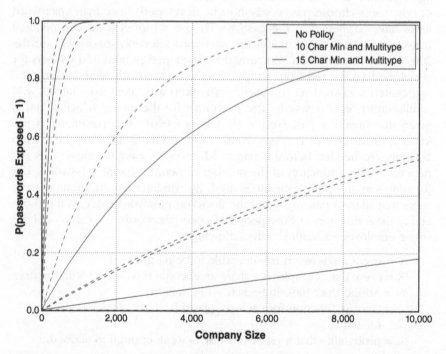

FIGURE B.10 Probability of Compromise by Company Size and Password Policy

This model gives an idea of the risk of compromised credentials for an enterprise given employee accounts and password policies. There are a few points that can and should be corrected to improve the fidelity of the model, including the following two:

1. The password-hint reuse rate is definitely a function of password complexity; that is, people who choose good passwords don't give them away in hints as often, and this isn't corrected for. Additionally, combining hints makes weak hints very valuable, and this isn't accounted for.

2. Forcing a password policy on a user base would likely result in a lower entropy distribution than the RockYou conditional distribution. For example, I imagine an increase in passwords that look like the following if a length/character type policy is implemented: P@ssw0rd123, pr!ncess123, and TrustNo0ne!

Cyber-CI

Douglas A. Samuelson, DSc, president and chief scientist at InfoLogix, Inc.

One especially interesting area in cybersecurity is cyber-counterintelligence: the detection of security threats, particularly insider threats. Since the Snowden revelations, federal agencies have been under an executive order to develop programs to limit insider threats. Only a few agencies to date have come up with meaningful responses.

What one such agency, arguably the leader in the insider threat area, did institute is a computer-based system to identify potential insider threats. This system uses information such as logins, badge-ins, frequency and times of access to certain files and facilities, and possibly related activities such as minor reported security violations, foreign relatives, financial difficulties, and patterns of foreign travel. The general idea is much like credit scoring or medical claims fraud and abuse analysis; the computer can identify patterns of activity that differ from the usual and resemble the patterns of known past culprits.

The key innovation is tuning the recognition of resemblance to past culprits—to use a data mining term, supervised rather than unsupervised search. Computer pattern-analysis methods are very good at turning up unusual patterns of activity, but still quite bad at distinguishing which unusual patterns of activity are meaningful. Close cooperation with field investigators yielded useful insights to identify some of the more frequently occurring "unusual patterns" that were, in fact, of little interest upon further investigation. Modifying the system to downplay these sets of patterns yielded a much more useful set of cases for further human follow-up.

The subjects are cleared personnel, so they have relinquished many of their usual privacy rights as citizens. Still, the agency seeks to avoid excessive intrusion and expedite the exonerations that usually result from investigations of apparent anomalies. The primary goal is prevention, not prosecution.

Many pattern-recognition, association, and rule-based methods are applicable. The most productive uses involve correlating multiple approaches and multiple topics, incorporating feedback from follow-on investigations by humans. This approach highlights assemblies of pieces of information that are most likely innocuous by themselves but may become interesting in combination: for example, unusual behavior toward co-workers *and* financial problems *and* sudden increase in foreign travel. Extensive coding and analysis of behavioral traits, down to the level of biological markers, is possible with these methods and can become part of the analysis, along with more conventional markers.

This agency has built a watch station to provide the capability to observe and correlate many streams of information in one place, at one time. In particular, movements and accesses by persons apparently of interest (from situational data) can be called to the human monitor's attention and examined more closely. Other agencies have expressed strong interest and are likely to copy or share this watch station.

New work in progress at the same agency involves a virtual reality depiction of big data that represents behaviors of interest. The system generates a space in which the human analyst can explore, exploiting humans' still-superior ability to notice unusual patterns.

Captures of actual major security violators are rare and never discussed openly until afterward, often well afterward to avoid compromising prosecution, and then with many details of the detection and investigation omitted. Preventions of violations are less rare, and more desirable, but even more rarely discussed openly. Revelation of sources and methods by which security-related information is developed and used is considered one of the most serious and harmful security violations. Nevertheless, what can be reported is that the agency in question has realized a significant contribution from these methods, as reflected in two of the most reliable measures of merit in any organizational context: They are buying more of it, and their people—including a number of former skeptics—are eager to learn more about how to use it.

How Catastrophe Modeling Can Be Applied to Cyber Risk

Scott Stransky, assistant vice president and principal scientist at AIR Worldwide

Tomas Girnius, PhD, manager and principal scientist at AIR Worldwide

One may wonder how a company proficient in building models to estimate losses from hurricanes and other natural disasters can use their techniques to build a similar model for estimating losses from cyberattacks.

Hurricane Andrew spawned the catastrophe-modeling industry. Although catastrophe models existed prior to that storm in 1992, they were not used by decision makers, nor were they used to their full potential. When the storm struck south Florida, AIR issued modeled loss estimates on the order of $13 billion, a figure that the insurance industry scoffed at for being far too high. As the claims for Andrew started to pile up, 11 insurers went out of business, and the rest of the industry began to see the value in running models. The "Hurricane Andrew of Cyber" has yet to strike the cyber insurance industry, and when it does, those companies using models will be far better off than those using so-called underwriting judgment.

AIR is employing the same stochastic modeling framework (Figure B.11) that it has reliably used for its catastrophe model for nearly 30 years. This is best described by analogy to hurricane modeling. Hurricanes can be visualized and have been widely studied. We begin with historical data on hurricane events, publicly available from the National Hurricane Center and other sources, and determine distributions for various parameters, such as how many storms there will be per year, where along the coastline those storms will hit, how intense they will be, and so forth. We then do a Monte Carlo simulation using all of these distributions to develop our stochastic "catalog" of events. This catalog contains 100,000 simulated hurricane seasons—not predicting 100,000 years into the future, but instead looking at plausible versions of next year's hurricane season. For cyber, we have data from collaborators that will allow us to determine distributions for the number of attacks per year, which industries they are targeting, whether they are impacting larger or smaller companies, and in the case of a data breach, how many records have been stolen. This is in addition to information on the type of data that tends to be impacted, the types of actors doing the attacks, and any ramifications of the attack—for example, whether data is stolen, businesses experience downtime, or are sued. We will use this for our Monte Carlo simulation for cyber events by drawing from these distributions to create a catalog of events.

The next phase of the model is the vulnerability component, in which the catalog, together with information about the risk itself, is used to determine damage. For wind perils, we can use data from wind tunnels, computational fluid dynamics, postdisaster surveys, and engineering studies. For cyber, we are working with data that helps differentiate the risks between various industries, company sizes, company locations, and other features. The final step of the model is to estimate losses, including average annual losses, 1 in 100 losses, 1 in 250 losses—for individual accounts as well as entire portfolios of accounts. To do this, we need historical loss data. We are working with several primary insurers to get such data, in return for cyber-risk consulting studies and early model results. This data allows us to calibrate and validate the loss results that the model produces.

The recent vintage of available cyberattack data—essentially available for only a few years—effectively ensures the "left censoring" referred to by Andrew Jaquith. The extremely large number of cyber events during the past few years ensures that the pool of data available is not impoverished as a result. The large amounts of basic cyber data define the size and shape of the bodies of fitted statistical distributions, very much akin to traditional actuarial methods. That large volume of data assures that the parameters fitted to those distributions are sufficiently robust to allow for sampling from the tails. Here, catastrophe modeling diverges from traditional actuarial practice—it is, indeed, the occasional Monte Carlo sample from the tail of the distribution that results in the extreme scenarios that are the purview of catastrophe modeling. It is only because the body of the distribution has been fitted well that we have confidence in the structure of the tail. This addresses the issue of determining extreme individual events in the catalog.

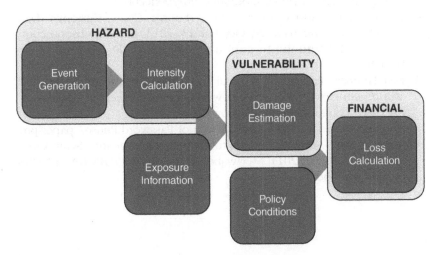

FIGURE B.11 The AIR Worldwide Catastrophe Modeling Framework

Notes

1. *Verizon Data Breach Investigation Report,* 2013, 2014, 2015.
2. Brian M. Bowen et al., "Measuring the Human Factor of Cyber Security," *Homeland Security Affairs* 8, supplement 5 (May 2012): 12.
3. *Microsoft Security Intelligence Report,* 2013, 2014, 2015.
4. *Verizon Data Breach Investigation Report,* 2013, 2014, 2015.
5. HHS published data includes only breaches of more than 500 patient records.
6. For example, see *2015 Cost of Data Breach Study: Global Analysis* by Ponemon Institute and IBM.
7. Other researchers have noted a similar phenomenon, in particular Jay Jacobs, then of the Verizon Data Breach Investigations Report team, in "Analyzing Ponemon Cost of Data Breach" (December 2014), retrieved from http://datadrivensecurity.info/blog/posts/2014/Dec/ponemon/.
8. See Melissa Kirmse and Sam Savage, "Probability Management 2.0," *ORMS Today,* October 2014, http://viewer.zmags.com/publication/ad9e976e#/ad9e976e/32.
9. SIP stands for Stochastic Information Packet. These arrays of potential outcomes may be generated with a wide variety of readily available simulation software, as well as the native electronic spreadsheet. The cross-platform SIPmath standard from nonprofit ProbabilityManagement.org allows SIPs to be shared between applications.
10. Sam L. Savage, "Distribution Processing and the Arithmetic of Uncertainty," *Savage Analytics Magazine,* November/December 2012, http://viewer.zmags.com/publication/90ffcc6b#/90ffcc6b/29.
11. Brian Krebs, "Adobe to Announce Source Code, Customer Data Breach," *Krebs on Security,* October 13, 2013, http://krebsonsecurity.com/2013/10/adobe-to-announce-source-code-customer-data-breach/.
12. Keir Thomas, "Password Use Is All Too Common, Research Shows," *PC World,* February 10, 2011, www.pcworld.com/article/219303/password_use_very_common_research_shows.html.
13. Anupam Das et al., "The Tangled Web of Password Reuse," paper presented at the Network and Distributed System Security Symposium, February 23–26, 2014, www.jbonneau.com/doc/DBCBW14-NDSS-tangled_web.pdf.

Index

Page references in *italics* refer to figures.